T0303193

The Memoirs of
WENDELL W. YOUNG III

THE MEMOIRS OF

WENDELL W. YOUNG III

A Life in Philadelphia Labor and Politics

Edited and with an Introduction by FRANCIS RYAN

TEMPLE UNIVERSITY PRESS
Philadelphia • *Rome* • *Tokyo*

TEMPLE UNIVERSITY PRESS
Philadelphia, Pennsylvania 19122
tupress.temple.edu

Copyright © 2019 by Temple University—Of The Commonwealth System
of Higher Education
All rights reserved
Published 2019

Library of Congress Cataloging-in-Publication Data

Names: Young, Wendell W., III, 1938-2013, author. | Ryan, Francis, 1971-
editor.
Title: The memoirs of Wendell W. Young III : a life in Philadelphia labor and
politics / edited and with an Introduction by Francis Ryan.
Description: Philadelphia : Temple University Press, 2019. | Includes index.
Identifiers: LCCN 2018044537 (print) | LCCN 2018061755 (ebook) | ISBN
9781439918647 (E-book) | ISBN 9781439918623 (cloth : alk. paper)
Subjects: LCSH: Young, Wendell W., III, 1938-2013. | Labor
leaders—Pennsylvania—Philadelphia—Biography. | Labor
movement—Pennsylvania—Philadelphia—History—20th century. | Labor
unions—Pennsylvania—Philadelphia—History—20th century. | Philadelphia
(Pa.)—Politics and government—20th century.
Classification: LCC HD6509 (ebook) | LCC HD6509 .Y58 2019 (print) | DDC
331.88092 [B] —dc23
LC record available at https://lccn.loc.gov/2018044537

Printed in the United States of America

9 8 7 6 5 4 3 2 1

To Kathy

CONTENTS

The Memoirs of
WENDELL W. YOUNG III

INTRODUCTION

I N DECEMBER 1969, *Philadelphia Bulletin* reporter Martin J. Herman
wrote a feature article on Wendell W. Young III, the youngest labor official in the city. Elected top officer of the eleven thousand-member Retail Clerks Union Local 1357 when he was just twenty-four years old,
Young quickly gained a reputation for his independence, daring at times
to publicly criticize the policies of the city's powerful American Federation of Labor and Congress of Industrial Organizations (AFL-CIO) leadership. "I don't think the labor movement generally is fully doing what it
was founded to do. It's getting too professional, too bureaucratic," Young
told the reporter. Organized labor, which represented fifteen million
workers in unions across the nation, had a special role in shaping the
democracy, but, to realize this potential, its leaders must listen to the concerns of members while building coalitions within and beyond the labor
movement. "The power should flow from the members to the officers and
not from the top down. There's a real need for change, for more member
participation in the labor movement."[1] With dynamic grassroots movements emerging at the end of the decade, Wendell believed a historic moment was at hand and promised to align his union in support with these
new social forces across Pennsylvania.

---

1. Martin J. Herman, "Unions Should Be More Democratic, Leader Says," *Philadelphia Bulletin*, December 4, 1969.

More than any other figure of the late twentieth century, Wendell W. Young III was the voice of social justice unionism in the Philadelphia region. As the city's labor beat reporters noted, Young's concept of trade unionism was often in stark contrast to the business model that predominated in the city's labor councils, a tradition that understood labor's true goal as advancing the material conditions of its dues-paying members. While social justice unionism also sought to advance wages, proponents of this philosophy believed labor's institutions must move beyond collective bargaining to play a role in improving the conditions of the working-class majority, whether in a union or not. By 1967, Wendell was an outspoken opponent of the Vietnam War, joining a small cadre in the Labor Leadership Assembly for Peace, a group that sought to educate citizenry about the moral costs of the conflict and its negative impact on working-class families. In these same years, he also built alliances with antipoverty programs and the civil rights movement in Philadelphia and joined in early efforts to bring together environmental and labor activists to push for gas price controls and to promote alternate forms of energy. Into the last years of the twentieth century, Young placed his union behind regional protests opposed to nuclear proliferation, to the struggle against apartheid in South Africa, and to the movement to secure equal citizenship for sexual minorities.

In a city long considered one of the bastions of union power in the United States, the publication of Wendell W. Young III's memoirs is an important moment, the first time an autobiography detailing the behind-the-scenes workings of the trade union movement in Philadelphia has been written. In the first decades of the twenty-first century, an era when organized labor's power has diminished at both the national and the local levels, it is easy to lose sight of the scope of influence it once yielded in the political order. To underestimate organized labor's power in this realm in the mid-twentieth century is a mistake. From the 1930s through to the end of the century, Philadelphia's labor movement was the most consequential political force in what was then the third largest city in the nation, capable of determining which candidates were nominated and elected to office and many of the legislative agendas that followed. No other urban institution matched organized labor's voter education programs, its financial resources, or its Election Day mobilization in wards across the city, where as many as ten thousand volunteers were sometimes dispatched in support of endorsed candidates. Beginning his recollections in the mid-1950s when he joined the Retail Clerks Union as a part-time clerk at Acme Markets, Wendell's account of the trade union movement in the City of Brotherly Love offers insight into this political force at the peak of its power.

Since the earliest days of the American Republic, Philadelphia was a center of labor activism, the site of the nation's first citywide labor council, and the launching ground for early workingmen's parties, urban cooperatives, and some of the most consequential strike actions of the nineteenth century. As the fabled Workshop of the World, Philadelphia's vast network of factories and mills made the city a global polestar of progress and technical innovation, but the insecurities of this emerging capitalist system also brought grinding poverty for many, and the city remained a birthplace for innovations for how to address the problems of the industrial age. Through these years into the early twentieth century, the Quaker City's working classes established trade unions, mostly concentrated in the skilled crafts and building trades, to gain more say in their economic lives. The strength of these institutions reached new levels in the 1930s, when bold organizing campaigns in the city's industrial production plants resulted in the signing up of thousands of politically conscious union members that boosted the trade union movement as an even more consequential force in the city's power structure.

Into the 1950s, strikes were common occurrences in Philadelphia, played out in working-class neighborhoods that surrounded the factories, and the drama that unfolded was covered in depth by labor beat reporters. Regional labor leaders were known public figures, their positions debated and discussed on loading docks, in tap rooms, at dining room tables, and in letters to local newspapers. The collective actions of unionized workers had real impact. Like American workers across the country, wages and conditions for Philadelphia's workingmen and women increased through the postwar period. At their peak in the 1960s, Philadelphia's trade unions represented over 250,000 workers in almost every section of the region's economy—an array that included such diverse occupations as waitresses, factory workers, school teachers, barbers, truck drivers, telephone operators, bartenders, lithographers, garbage haulers, and school crossing guards.

The power of Philadelphia's trade unions stemmed not only from bold, coordinated shop floor militancy but also from strategic engagement in the electoral process. Labor's influence here was part of a broader national narrative, organically connected to the political realignments that had begun across the United States in the 1930s. Channeling the power of the federal government to address the economic calamities of the Great Depression, Franklin D. Roosevelt brought together a new coalition that united the nation's industrial working class with measures that opened increased economic and social opportunities for citizens in the emerging consumer society. Organized labor capitalized on the Roosevelt administration's industrial programs that encouraged union growth and moved its millions of rank-and-file members to rally behind the Democratic Party. In Philadelphia, such groups as the AFL's Labor's Non-Partisan League, the CIO's Political Action Committee, and later the AFL-CIO's Committee on Political Education (COPE) provided financial resources and cadres of poll volunteers that shaped the city's power structure. By the mid-1950s, five of Philadelphia's six congressional districts, and a solid majority of its state and municipal offices, were represented by Democratic lawmakers, all of whom saw organized labor's voter education and mobilization programs as a critical part of their electoral strategies.

In the years after World War II, a new Democratic Party organization formed around William J. Green Jr., the son of a tavern keeper from the city's Kensington and Allegheny section, who, after his election to Congress in 1948, looked to Philadelphia's row house, working-class majority as his party's base. From the start of his labor career, Wendell W. Young III understood the importance of political engagement to labor advancement, and, by the mid-1960s, his deft maneuvering within the city's Democratic Party organization made him a consequential figure. Starting out as a campaign worker for Senator John F. Kennedy's 1960 presidential race, Wendell proved adept at delivering Democratic majorities in his division and by 1965 was elected leader of Philadelphia's 35th ward. With twenty-three thousand registered voters in this pivotal district in the city's Northeastern section, the young labor spokesman was boosted as a key and influential player in one of the most powerful quarters of the Democratic Party in the nation. Coming out of an informal, neighborhood-based culture characterized by face-to-face interactions, Wendell's personal account of this political scene provides insight into how this system functioned and adds a range of mostly unknown personalities to the historical record, enriching our understanding of a lost urban world.

Wendell Young's entry into urban politics paralleled an era of major
social upheavals, pivoting on challenges to the nation's racial order, which
disrupted the Democratic coalition in Philadelphia and elsewhere. His
position in the local political culture allowed him a unique vantage from
which to see how these fractures happened in Philadelphia. Part of this
stems from the peculiar stance he maintained in these shifting worlds.
Wendell was a centaur-like figure within Philadelphia's political scene—
a product of the neighborhood-based order that fused ward and labor
identities—and, simultaneously, an advocate of the new societal norms
encouraged by the New Left, the youth-based challenge pulsing from the
nation's universities that emphasized racial inclusion, expansion of wom-
en's rights, sexual expression, and individual autonomy. As an opponent
of the Vietnam War—a position that made him a pariah among fellow
labor leaders—he bucked the party mainstream by backing antiwar candidate Senator Eugene McCarthy in 1968. In the years that followed,
Young advanced the Democratic Party's most liberal wing, seeking to
maintain the fragile New Deal coalition while acting as executive chairman of George McGovern's 1972 presidential campaign in the City of
Brotherly Love.

Wendell's account of this period coincides with the political rise of
Mayor Frank L. Rizzo, the former police commissioner who led an urban
populist movement among the city's white working class to gain control
of Philadelphia City Hall from 1972 to 1980. From the start, Young was
among Rizzo's staunchest opponents. Seeing Rizzo's law-and-order platform as rooted in racist sentiments, and critical of the alliance between
the mayor and Republican president Richard M. Nixon, Wendell spoke
out against Rizzo and urged labor leaders to do the same. A significant
section did so. In his telling, Wendell recalibrates Philadelphia's political
history to show the role that organized labor's progressive wing played in
shaping a liberal, interracial coalition that arose across the city to fight
Rizzo's programs and political ambitions.

More than has been previously understood, Wendell makes clear that,
in this period, really two labor movements existed in Philadelphia. While
rifts dating back to the 1930s had always divided industrial from craft
unionist along lines of strategy and culture, these tensions intensified in
the 1970s as previously unorganized sections of the working class joined
the city's trade unions. Hospital workers, white-collar government aides,
teachers, educational support staff, and others in the expanding service

economy turned to unions in increasing numbers, altering the dynamics of the local labor movement by bridging workplace and community concerns. With higher percentages of African American, Puerto Rican, and women workers, and with many activists shaped by the civil rights and black freedom struggles and the antiwar and emerging women's and gay rights movements, social justice unionism gained momentum. By the mid-1970s, Wendell was joined by a range of union officials such as Henry Nicholas, president of Philadelphia's National Union of Hospital and Health Care Workers Local 1199c; Coalition of Labor Union Women leaders Pat Halpin and Alice Hoffman; American Federation of State, County and Municipal Employees (AFSCME) District Council 47's Thomas Paine Cronin, Gary Kapanowski, and Judy Hoover; and Machinist Union president Norman H. Loudenslager, who agitated for a labor movement that went beyond the business model. At odds with this more expansive vision of trade unionism remained the city's building trades and trucking union leaders and its AFL-CIO Central Labor Union president Edward F. Toohey, who was labor's chief spokesman in the town for twenty-seven years. In his account, Wendell W. Young III highlights the disputes over what direction the labor movement would take and shows how the lines drawn were consequential to the political alignments that developed in Philadelphia in these years.

Other aspects of Wendell's narrative open original perspectives on the region's history and how national and global economic trends played out here. By the late 1970s, Philadelphia faced the consequence of a major manufacturing fallout; more than one hundred thousand industrial jobs left the city over the course of the decade. Wendell details the consequences of this shift in the retail industry, noting the decline of the city's downtown shopping establishments and the shutdown of supermarket chains, stressing the human dimension that underscored the struggles of department store and food market cashiers and clerks. Importantly, he shows that unionized workers and their institutions were not passive in the face of these downturns but responded to deindustrialization by proposing creative alternatives that included supermarket cooperatives, citizen coalitions against Big Oil, and political campaigns to secure local and federal legislation to meet the needs of the unemployed. Wendell's insight into responses against globalization continues in the later sections of the book, when he lays out the union's response to French hypermarket Carrefour's opening in Northeast Philadelphia, which culminated in a three-year boycott that sustained a diverse community coalition.

Through his half century as a union leader, Wendell W. Young III was a serious student of labor history, and he understood his commitments to human rights as part of a longer narrative that includes working people from across the world and across many generations. Wendell hoped that his memoirs would contribute to how this history is understood, while serving as an inspiration for today's labor and community activists and those to come. I first met Wendell in 1997 when I was organizing labor history workshops at the Comey Institute of Industrial Relations at St. Joseph's University and beginning a project that charted the history of Philadelphia's municipal workers in the twentieth century. As a guest speaker in my class, he provided a rich perspective of the city's working-class heritage and the intrinsic connection between the advancement of workplace rights and politics. No one else I had ever talked to had such a store of local historical knowledge or his gift for telling the stories of the men and women who shaped our times. When he asked me to assist him in putting together his memoirs, I immediately realized the significance of the project. I felt particularly able to take up this task because I was raised in the same Northeast Philadelphia neighborhood he had come from and was familiar with the range of institutions—the churches, schools, political clubs, taverns, and shopping centers his memories are grounded in. More importantly, I had many years' experience working in Philadelphia's unionized food industry, as a warehouseman at Acme Markets produce distribution center in the city's Brewerytown section in the late 1980s and early 1990s, and later as a part-time utility clerk at a Super Fresh Food Market in Wynnewood, Pennsylvania.

Wendell and I started this project in June 2009, and once a week I drove from my home in Bethlehem, Pennsylvania, to meet him at his residence in Lafayette Hill in the Philadelphia suburbs to conduct oral histories. Over the next three and a half years, Wendell's wife, Kathy, and their son Matt welcomed me into their home, as Wendell and I spent the afternoon sitting at the dining room table recording the reflections collected here. During this period, we completed almost sixty hours of interviews, finishing the project in December 2012, just a few weeks before he passed away. After each session, I played back the exchanges at home and transcribed them by hand on legal pads before typing them into a Word document. I followed up with him in subsequent meetings, asking for clarification and additional detail, and fact-checking the historical record he spoke of in local archives and newspapers. While I shaped the document with the kinds of questions I posed, the text in this book is Wendell's own words. Except for some times when I edited the document to correct minor factual errors in the date or place of events, or added some transitional sentences to bridge segments of a chapter, I transcribed Wendell's words verbatim. In the pages that follow, those who knew him will recognize his speech rhythms, his characteristic turns of phrase, and, especially, his sense of humor.

One of the important contributions in the book is the way it allows for a measuring of the changes in the retail industry over time, including the tangible impact that union membership has for the men and women who work in the stores. While his brand of trade unionism always sought to build broad coalitions to effect progressive social change, Wendell backed up his idealism with sizable gains for his dues-paying members. When he took over the leadership of Local 1357 in 1962, supermarket clerks in the region made less than one hundred dollars a week. Starting after the first round of collective bargaining sessions he led in 1965, Young advanced supermarket workers to gain better wages and conditions over the coming generation, the result of tough negotiations and the willingness of rank-and-file members to go on strike. By 1975, clerks' take-home pay had more than doubled, along with a range of other improvements in benefits and security. Following another round of collective bargaining gains a few years later, Wilson Leamy, a clerk at an Acme Market in the Philadelphia suburb of Wayne, Pennsylvania, spoke to a newspaper reporter about the union's impact on his life. At sixty-three years old, Leamy had worked for the company for fifty years, starting his employment in 1932 when he was a teenager and making a dollar a day. In the thick of the Depression, he stayed on despite the low wages, but after the Retail Clerks Union organized the chain, his life changed. "A few years later when I started to make sixteen a week I figured I could afford to get married," he noted. Over the years, the union secured even further advancements for clerks and cashiers who gained financial stability and middle-class lifestyles. The 1978 contract covering twenty thousand employees in three major chains was the best yet, gaining further wage boosts along with prepaid legal services, free medical exams, psychiatric care, improvements in dental, drug, and medical benefits, and pensions. For those who worked in these stores, the retail industry had been completely transformed. Leamy was one of the few who recalled the earlier era when "the only time we got off as far as vacations or anything like that was Wednesday afternoon in July and August. We were open six days a week. I'm telling you, the union has done one heckuva job. They'll get no complaints from me."[2]

Like Wilson Leamy, thousands of men and women in the Delaware Valley worked in the region's supermarkets represented by Wendell's union—some for brief stints and others for the bulk of their lives. Even for those who did not work in the stores, Wendell Young was a household name in the Philadelphia region, a controversial figure about whom people's reactions were usually an indication of their political beliefs. When he died in January 2013, his passing was featured on local television news broadcasts and KYW Newsradio, the city's predominant news station, and it's hard to imagine many other labor leaders whose obituary could generate such notice in mass media in the region. More than two thousand people attended his wake in 2013, some waiting in lines for an hour outside the funeral parlor to express their regards to his family. As I stood in these lines, I had a chance to talk and listen to others there with me, some who were from Philadelphia's labor and political world, others who had worked as cashiers or stocked shelves years before, and those who were current union members at local markets. They shared stories of earlier campaigns and strikes, of memories of their mother or father working at Food Fair or Acme, and, for many, their personal friendship with Wendell; he had been there for them, always a good listener, someone who encouraged them in their personal trials and challenges. I realize from these exchanges that the narrative Wendell and I assembled puts forward only a portion of the man he was, only the contours of his public life. The stories of his friends and family will continue on and shape how he is remembered, and this book will facilitate such exchanges in the future.

The publication of Wendell's memoirs comes at a critical and unnerving period in world history, as resurgent nationalist and reactionary extremists take power in governments across the globe, subjecting workers, immigrants, and the economically vulnerable to virulent political attacks. Wendell speaks clearly to us at this moment. Always an optimist,

---

2. Richard L. Papiernik, "Food Chains Settle with Employees," *Philadelphia Inquirer*, January 23, 1978.

he believed that no matter what the odds may be, there is a path forward and that ordinary people can shape their lives and the kind of just society they seek. As he points out in the final pages of this book, workers are organizing new kinds of movements across the globe at the dawn of the twenty-first century, unwilling to accept the severe social costs of neoliberalism's unfettered market capitalism. Wendell's reflections will hearten those who share his commitment to the social justice unionism that connects workplace to community and human rights issues. Although he does not dwell on this much in later sections of the book, Wendell remained a devout Catholic his entire life, and grounded his labor activism on the Church's social encyclicals that affirm human dignity—this was the unifying thread that connected his public life for over fifty years. How he practiced this faith was never iconoclastic but always generous, and he remained open and friendly to all, seeking to bridge human differences. It was his hope that the narrative he offered here would encourage meaningful dialogue and serve as an inspiration to those around the world who struggle to affirm labor's dignity.

Francis Ryan
New Brunswick, New Jersey

1

ACME CLERK

SOMETIMES, when I was a boy, my grandfather would bring me with him to a back area of his butcher shop and let me watch him work. He had a cutting room with a long metal table, and he'd bring in beef sections and trim them using cobalt steel knives that were about a foot long. The shop specialized in all kinds of meats, which he ordered and cut himself, with help from my father. He used to get pigs and slaughter them and hang them in a big freezer in the back room and every year he'd go down to Maryland to buy turkeys, which he sold to people in the neighborhood around Thanksgiving. He would take me outside and show me how to chop their heads off. This made my grandmother furious, but he'd just laugh about it because it was nothing to him.

I had lots of opportunities to observe my grandfather's work in the butcher trade, since my parents and I lived with him and my grandmother in a two-floor apartment above his meat shop at Park Avenue and Somerset Street in North Philadelphia. This was not too far from Baker Bowl, the old ballpark on Broad Street where the Philadelphia Phillies played then. I was born in that neighborhood on July 7, 1938, at Temple University Hospital, the first of eight children of Wendell W. Young Jr. and Gladys Brenner. Even after my parents bought their own house in another section of the city, I spent a lot of time at my grandparents', running and playing on the side streets that abutted the avenue—Silver Street, Rush Street, Auburn Street—all of which were faced by two-story brick row houses and were so compact you couldn't fit more than one car down them.

My father stayed on helping at the butcher shop until 1940 when my brother Joe was born. I guess my dad figured he needed a better job, so he took one as a policy salesman at a local life insurance agency. That didn't last long, because he got involved in a unionization drive and was fired. After that he went to the Philadelphia Naval Depot in Northeast Philadelphia doing heavy lifting on the supply trucks. He kept the job through World War II and moved the family to the city's Mayfair section, to a row house on Longshore Avenue.

Mayfair was a predominantly Irish and German neighborhood, but you also had Polish, a few Italians, and a sizable Jewish community on the other side of Roosevelt Boulevard, the twelve-lane highway that connected this section to the rest of the city. Our neighborhood was entirely white. I don't recall a single African American family who lived in the area at that time. It was also working class. On the block where I lived, there were firefighters, housepainters, men in the various building trades, bus drivers, machinists and mechanics, police officers, and a few who worked at a nearby municipal sewage treatment plant. Others had clerical jobs in downtown Philadelphia or with insurance firms, and they rode the elevated train every morning to get to their offices. It was not unusual for men to have two or even three jobs so that their wives didn't have to work outside the home. My father only had one job, but my mother was a stay-at-home housewife. He wouldn't think of her working.

THE NEIGHBORHOOD WE LIVED IN was known as Mayfair, but if you asked me where I was from, I probably would have said St. Matt's. This is because my family were congregants of St. Matthew's Parish, which had a big stone church over on Cottman Avenue not far from where we lived. We were devout Catholics and our religion and the parish we belonged to played a big part of our identity. For Catholics, in Philadelphia and across the United States, the parish defined the boundaries of an urban world, the church being the hub around which most social activities were structured. Sunday masses were packed with everyone dressed in their best suit and tie or dress. Next to the church were the parish grade school and the convent and rectory where the priests and sisters lived. The religious who were in charge of these institutions were respected leaders of the community, overseeing a whole range of social, athletic, and recreational programs. Catholics could be very insular, having their own schools and hospitals and a range of other organizations, all funded through money collected each week in church services or through annual charity appeals. To give a sense of the way many Catholics viewed the world, I wasn't allowed to join the local Boy Scouts of America chapter because my father considered it too much of a Protestant organization.

When I was growing up, the head of the Philadelphia archdiocese was Cardinal Dennis Dougherty, a very conservative cleric who for over thirty years was one of the most powerful figures in the city. Dougherty was originally from Pennsylvania's coal country, but, instead of going into the mines like his father, he studied to be a priest and was ordained in 1890. He rose quickly in the church leadership and in 1918, he was named archbishop in Philadelphia before he was elevated to the position of cardinal by Pope Pius XI a few years later. Until his death in 1951, Dougherty oversaw a period of growth, with the construction of dozens of schools, new churches, and other religious institutions built to serve an expanding Catholic population in the region. His views on the world were extremely conservative and antisecular. He was against the integration of Catholics into mainstream American society, refused to cocelebrate ecumenical religious services, was an enemy of the labor movement, and, in the 1930s, called on Catholics to boycott the movie industry until producers made efforts to purge sexual immorality and criminal activities from the screen. His power was considerable, as the archdiocese, which included all of Philadelphia and nine surrounding counties, represented just under a million Catholics.

If Cardinal Dougherty represented a more conservative side of the Catholic Church, many in my family held views that were aligned with what was considered a liberal one. My father had three sisters who joined religious orders that were very progressive, and they were influential in shaping our understandings of the world, and the role of the church in society. My Aunt Florence—whose religious name was Mother Mary Benedict—took vows with the Society of Roman Catholic Medical Missionaries and eventually became head of the American Province of the order. She graduated from the University of Pennsylvania in 1939 and joined the missionary sisters right away. After she earned a medical degree, she joined a hospital administration in East Bengali Province and was stationed in Dacca in the 1950s where she performed thousands of surgeries and worked closely with the Holy Ghost Fathers opening hospitals in India, Pakistan, and Bangladesh. She was a trailblazer in so many ways and through my life remained one of my most important role models.

Along with my Aunt Florence, I had two other aunts who were also Catholic nuns. My Aunt Virginia—Sister Mary David—and my Aunt Jane, who went by the name of Sister Florence Marie, both took vows in the Sisters of the Blessed Sacrament Order. This society was established in 1899 by Catherine Mary Drexel, a woman who was born into one of Philadelphia's most affluent families, to minister to poor African American children and Native Americans. I met her numerous times when I was a little kid when my parents took me to visit my aunts in the order's headquarters up in Cornwells Heights, just outside Northeast Philadelphia. She used to pat me on the head. Sister Mary David eventually ran Xavier University of Louisiana, the only Catholic historically black college in the nation, established by the order in New Orleans. All of my father's sisters were dynamic women who had an important influence on me. They showed me that women could hold leadership positions and take on public responsibilities that made serious impacts on social conditions. Because of their example, I never understood any viewpoint that assumed women were not as capable as men. All of my aunts proved otherwise.

My uncle Henry S. McNulty, on my mother's side, was a priest who was assistant rector at St. Matthew's parish. Because of him, and my aunts, I felt that joining a religious order was something to aspire to. When I was a boy, I used to pretend to say mass in the basement of the house with my brother Joe, who was the second born beside me. We set up a table as a kind of altar, and my brother was the altar boy and I would mumble the words like I was speaking Latin. All the way up until college, I wanted to become a priest and a medical doctor to dedicate my life to working with the impoverished as my Aunt Florence had done.

Because of my aunts' connections with the Medical Mission Sisters, and the Sisters of the Blessed Sacrament, everyone in my family was very conscious of the wrongs of racial prejudice and committed to speaking out against it. My father had zero tolerance for any kind of racism. I always remember an incident that happened between my Uncle Henry and my dad. Sometimes, Henry and his sister Annie would take a bus to visit my family on Sunday afternoons for cookies and ice cream. One time during one of these visits when I was in the fifth grade, for some reason

Uncle Henry started making comments about black people. I don't remember what he was saying, but he actually used the N-word. My father says, "Henry, get the hell out of my house. Nobody uses that word in my house." He wasn't joking. He made them get up and leave, and I think my uncle was a little shocked. Aunt Annie was all upset and crying all over the place. My father explained that he had two sisters who had committed their entire lives to educating minorities and another sister over in India working as a doctor. Later, all of us kids were talking upstairs in one of the bedrooms, saying, "Man, I'll never use that word, ever. He threw Father Henry out of the house." That left an indelible mark on us.

Uncle Henry didn't come back to the house for about three weeks. Then, one Sunday, all of us children were upstairs looking out the window and we see Uncle Henry and Aunt Annie coming down the street. I remember we yelled, "Hey, here comes Father Henry!" My father said that he was no longer welcome in our house and gave us a big lecture again about why. But in came Uncle Henry and he says, "Could I speak to everybody? I want to say in front of all you, my family, that I was 100 percent wrong last time I was here. I am a Catholic priest, and I should not talk like that." He apologized, and that impressed everybody. He and my father shook hands and I remember all of the kids were upstairs talking later, "See, Father Henry admitted he was wrong. Even a priest admits when he's wrong." So that was that; he made up with the family. I actually think that incident changed my uncle, because he became very outspoken for civil rights when he served as pastor of St. Columba's parish in North Philadelphia, one of the largest in the city and with a sizable African American membership. I was very close to him, so much so that I took Henry as my confirmation name.

In 1952, my father took a job as an insurance salesman with Metropolitan Life, which had an office headquartered in the Sears Roebuck Building at Roosevelt Boulevard and Adams Avenue. This was a real step up for him, as he was making more money than he had as a laborer at the Philadelphia Naval Supply Depot, which allowed us to move to a house closer to his office in Philadelphia's Northwood section. This new house was in St. Martin of Tours parish, which had one of the largest congregations in the archdiocese. That same year, I started at Northeast Catholic High School, a high school run by the Oblates of St. Francis de Sales which, at that time, had 2,500 students, all boys. I think the class of 1955 was the largest incoming class "North" ever had. The school was built to hold around a thousand but they packed more than five times as many in there and we used to go through the corridors like cattle. We took pride in how big we were, though, and North was affectionately known as "the Big House"—the largest Catholic school in the nation, we believed, if not the world.

Northeast Catholic High School brought together boys from across Philadelphia's Kensington section—the neighborhoods of Fishtown, Harrowgate, and Port Richmond as well as Bridesburg, Juniata, Northwood, and Frankford—all bastions of Philadelphia's white working class. Out of the class of 1956—which had over one thousand boys, I think we had maybe two black kids. The atmosphere there was not so welcoming for anyone who was not white, and this came even from some of the faculty. When I was a junior, there was a priest named Father Joseph Dunn who started talking about black people in class. He said he knew why, when it came to sports, there were so few black quarterbacks or pitchers. He's telling us it was biological, that black people have small brains and that they can't think right, although some might be good athletes because they can run fast. I raised my hand and challenged him. I said, "Father, you're not right on that because my aunts work with and teach black people and they are very smart, many of them go to college." I wasn't expecting what he did next. He came down and punched me on the right side of the face, giving me a swollen jaw and a big black eye.

I was afraid to tell my parents what happened, because priests were supposed to be right. When I told my mother, she said, "Boy, you better not tell your father. He's going to be upset about that." Later that night, I'm sitting at the dining room table with my whole family and my father sees my beat up face and says, "What happened to you?" I started to cry. I didn't want to tell him; I didn't want to rat on a priest. It was too big a problem for me to handle. After dinner, I went to do the dishes and he comes in, looks me right in the eye and says, "I know there's more to this story than you're telling and you better tell me the truth, because I'm going to find out." I start crying again all over the place and blurted out what Father Dunn had done to me. I could see my father tighten his lips. "Are you kidding me?" he said. I could see him sitting there, the look of rage in his eyes. "Say that again, Wendell. Repeat that story one more time for me," he said. I felt better after I told him the truth.

The next day, I went to school, but Father Dunn didn't show up for class. They had a lay substitute in there. Dunn finally walks in, halfway through the period, all blustered up. He said, "Will Mr. Young come up to the front of the class?" I went up, and he says, "I want to say something in front of all you students. I did something yesterday that was wrong, very wrong. I was telling you about black people, and how they aren't as intelligent as white people, and I was wrong." He went on and on and apologized, just like Father Henry had done. I knew damn well that my father must have come down and taken care of things. A few years later, I was a teacher at the same high school and Father John Tocik, the school's principal, told me what had happened that day. Just as I suspected, my father went down and reamed the hell out of Father Dunn. He demanded that he make an apology not only to me but also to the entire class.

THAT SAME YEAR AS THE incident with Father Dunn, I got my first job as a clerk at an Acme supermarket at Adams and Whitaker Avenues, just a few blocks from where I lived. Since my mother did not drive, my father did the family's weekly grocery shopping, and he had gotten to know the store manager, Al Weiss, pretty well. Al must have mentioned that he was looking to take on a few more part-time clerks, and my dad came home and told me about it. It wasn't unusual for supermarkets to look to Catholic school students to fill their part-time positions because some managers believed that we were less likely to steal. It was September 1954, and I was put on working a few hours in the afternoons and on the weekends.

By the mid-1950s, Acme Markets was Philadelphia's number one supermarket chain with over one hundred stores in the city and surrounding counties. If you included all of the warehousemen, truck drivers, and central office staff along with the store clerks, cashiers, and managers, Acme was one of the largest employers in the region. The company traced its roots back to 1891 when two Irish immigrants, Samuel Robinson and Robert H. Crawford, opened a modest establishment in South Philadelphia. The original store sold bulk items—flour, dry goods, grains in big barrels, molasses, hand-ground coffee, as well as canned vegetables and meats, which were just being introduced at the time. The business was purely cash based and built a reputation for affordable prices and quality customer service. In 1917, they merged with four other grocery stores to form the American Stores Company (ASCO), which soon became the largest chain grocery in the United States with shops in Pennsylvania, southern New Jersey, northern Delaware, and Maryland. ASCO oversaw the production of much of its own merchandise, making over two million loaves of bread a week in a central bakery and owning a series of warehouses from which goods were distributed. By the mid-1930s, ASCO employed over sixteen thousand employees in more than two thousand stores.

Most of ASCO's stores were small corner establishments with a couple of aisles where people shopped with a handcart. Up until that time, most people shopped for groceries at corner stores and proprietor-owned butcher shops, bakeries, and produce stands. Around the city, there were local stores like Frankford-Unity, as well as scores of independent neighborhood groceries, that continued to operate, but, by the early 1950s, supermarkets were becoming more popular. Eventually, the small ASCOs closed and the company transitioned entirely to supermarkets, changing its name to Acme Markets.

These larger stores were more convenient, since they allowed one-stop shopping for not only food items but also an assortment of household goods like light bulbs, soap, laundry detergent, aspirin, greeting cards, and paper cups and towels. Modern home appliances like electric refrigerators made once-a-week shopping trips possible (rather than the everyday stops to the store that had previously been the norm) since most meats, fish, and dairy could now be preserved over longer periods of time. More people had cars now as well, and the new markets were designed with parking lots, which also changed the shopping experience. Bulk purchasing of food and other goods by the stores allowed for cheaper prices and competition among a range of stores. Besides Acme Markets, which was the largest supermarket in the Philadelphia region, a range of other stores like A&P, Penn Fruit, and Food Fair Markets expanded. From the late 1940s on, these stores vied for the patronage of two million shoppers in Philadelphia and the surrounding counties.

Just before I started working there in 1954, the Acme Market at Adams and Whitaker Avenues had just been remodeled with a large parking lot and all the most up-to-date technologies. The store was run by Al Weiss, who like most of Acme's general managers, had worked his way up to the position after starting out years earlier as a clerk. I don't know if Al had a college degree or anything, but he had a basic knowledge of how to run a store. Managers had considerable say over what was stocked on the shelves, negotiating every day with the truck driver

Figure 1.1 Acme Market produce manager, early 1960s. (From the collection of Wendell W. Young III.)

salesmen, who delivered goods from various firms, over the quantity of soft drinks, produce, bread, and other goods they would buy for the store, and at what prices. To make a profit, managers were very frugal with how they ran the stores, since their potential end-of-year bonus equaled 1 percent of whatever the store's annual volume was. (See Figure 1.1.)

About forty employees worked at the Adams Avenue Acme when I first came on in 1954. The store was divided up into departments: produce, dairy, fish, and meat, each with individual supervisors who reported to the general manager. Below these management positions, Acme Markets had two employee classifications—checkers, who ran the cash registers, and clerks, who unloaded the trucks when they arrived a couple days a week and who were in charge of shelving the merchandise. In those days, operating a cash register was a very complicated process. Everything was done manually, from reading the sticker on the sale item, memorizing prices, and weighing produce to punching in and tallying the sum. Most of the employees, both women and men, were eventually trained to work the registers, since the managers needed a flexible workforce in case there was a rush of customers. Along with the cashiers and clerks, all Acme Markets had a maintenance crew, a few men who kept the store serviced, changing light bulbs, mopping the aisles, and doing most of the janitorial work. Each store also had a meat department and deli, which had about twenty butchers who cut beef, pork, and poultry and maintained the refrigerated display.

Strict gender lines marked the jobs in the supermarkets in this period. As a rule, journeymen clerks—the ones who stocked shelves and unloaded the trucks—were men. The only jobs women had in the stores were as cashiers in the checkout lines. Men were trained to do that work too, but they were usually called up to do so only when it was absolutely necessary. Women were forbidden from doing any shelving, unless it was the very light stock in the drug and medication aisle. They weren't supposed to lift anything over thirty pounds. All stores had a room in the back where women could lie down, under the assumption that they would sometimes need to take a rest. All of the meat cutting and maintenance work was considered male as well.

The status women had in the supermarket industry in the 1950s was a reversal of what it had been during the war years. In the early 1940s, it was not unusual for women supervisors to run every aspect of food store operations. Some of the old-timers I worked with mentioned that their stores had women managers overseeing produce and meat departments, as well as women drivers on the delivery routes for some of the local bread and dairy firms. Just as the women who took up industrial production jobs, the women in retail had proven they could take on these kinds of responsibilities and perform as well as any man did. When the war was over, these stores returned to male oversight, and the women managers either left or went back behind the counters. By the mid-1950s, no supermarket advanced women as in-store managers; they wouldn't even think of it. They would promote boys to these positions before they'd give it to a woman.

Because of the gender divisions in the stores, women got paid maybe four or five dollars less a week compared to the men. Full-time men made about sixty-five dollars a week, while the women behind the cash registers took home ten dollars less. This kind of disparity was a serious issue, since most of the women who worked in the stores did so not as a way to occupy their spare time but because of economic necessity. Some of the women were widows, and a few were divorced. Most of the women who had a full-time schedule were married and worked in order to combine paychecks with their husbands since it was hard for families to make it on one paycheck. Many women who worked at Acme Markets had other jobs, too. A few worked across the street at Sears as clerical staff or as part-time sales ladies. I remember others were full-time nurses who took a few hours at the store each week to earn a little extra.

For many of the men and women I worked with, a supermarket job—even if it didn't pay very much—was a better long-term employment strategy than working in the city's industrial sector. You wouldn't get rich doing it, but it was a regular paycheck. Although Philadelphia was still a major manufacturing center in the 1950s, thousands of factory jobs were beginning to slip away. The textile industry, which had always been one of the most important in the region, was decimated after World War II, in part because firms were relocating to the nonunion South. The typical full-time retail worker didn't go to college. For some of the men in the stores, retail was better than construction since it was steady, yearlong employment and it didn't demand any heavy lifting. I always said that nobody chooses to become a retail clerk as a profession; most come into it out of circumstances. If somebody's mother or father died when they were young, it hampered their finances so they couldn't go to college, and sometimes they wound up coming to work in a supermarket. Or they wind up taking a part-time job when they are a teenager and because they like their coworkers they decide to stay on and wind up moving up to deli manager, and next thing you know, it's twenty years later. A lot of the people I worked with at the Adams Avenue Acme were like this.

Besides the men and women who worked the store full-time, every day, were the dozen or so part-timers—usually high school and college students—who were scheduled twenty hours a week or less and often worked as stock boys. This was where I fit in. To the full-time employees, the stock boys were at the bottom of the totem pole, but even though we weren't as respected as the full-timers, the stores couldn't function without us. I usually worked Friday nights and all-day Saturday. In those days it wasn't unusual to work a ten-hour shift—divided up into two parts—a practice known as a split shift. I would be scheduled to come in the morning and would leave in the early afternoon and then return for a few hours in the evening. Almost everyone lived within walking distance of the stores they worked in, so they could come back. Most of us who had these split shifts didn't like it, since it basically took up your whole day and didn't give you enough time to do anything in the few hours you were away from the store. Even full-time cashiers and clerks were sometimes scheduled for these split shifts, and they also disliked having to do it. Most just wanted to put their hours in and go home to be with their kids and family.

Just about everyone hired by Acme Markets knew how to work a cash register, in case the store got really busy and they needed people up front. That was the first thing Al Weiss taught me to do. In addition to this, they trained me to stock the shelves, and eventually I was responsible for the entire frozen foods section. I took a lot of pride in that. If I was walking along and saw something out of place, I always put it back where it should be, and I tried to have all of the items aligned. Sometimes the supervisors would tell me not to make such a project out of it.

Most of our customers walked to the store, bringing their shopping bags home with them in metal carts they wheeled behind them. Most families only had one car in those days and men would drive their wives to the stores and go in and shop with them, or wait out in the parking lot. After I had been there a few months, I knew the regular customers pretty well. There was an Irish lady, Mrs. Flaherty, who would bring her nine kids with her. I always felt sorry for her, and talked Mr. Weiss into selling her day-old bread and cake at a discount, since it was stale anyhow. One guy was always asking for cardboard boxes; I'd close down my stand and go in the back and get him some. Every Christmas, he would come in and give me a five-dollar bill, which in those days was a big deal. A boy named Tommy Spillane, a mentally challenged kid who lived across the boulevard, spent a lot of time hanging out in the store. A lot of supermarkets had someone like Tommy. He didn't work there but would help bringing in the shopping carts from the parking lot, sweep up the front, shovel snow, or get workers some coffee. Tommy would follow me around and on occasion might help me set up the frozen food displays. Sometimes, Mr. Weiss might give him a quarter, but he would never think of hiring someone like him.

ONE DAY, AFTER THE FIRST few weeks I was at Acme Markets, Al Weiss called all of the new guys into the back room and told us to stand behind some stacks of toilet paper boxes. He told us not to come out until he said it was okay. None of us knew what was going on, but we did what he told us. One of the old-timers saw us standing there behind the boxes, and he understood what was happening. He told us that Al was trying to keep us from joining the union. We didn't know what he was talking about. Leo A. McKeever, the business agent of the Retail Clerks Union was in, making the rounds of the store. He was supposed to introduce himself to new members and get them to sign union membership cards. As soon as Mr. McKeever left, Al came back and told us it was okay to come out. "Listen kids," he said, "the reason why I did this is I want to save you guys some money. I don't think you should have to pay those union dues." He told us we could still work there, even though the union didn't know we were on the payroll. We thought he had done us a big favor.

That night, I was sitting around the dinner table with my family and everybody was talking about their day. I started bragging about how nice Mr. Weiss was, how he hid us behind the tissue boxes so we wouldn't have to join the union. "There's a union called the Retail Clerks and you have to pay dues. I'm not sure what it's all about," I said. My Dad was sitting at the head of the table listening to me and he spoke up and said that unions are good for people. He got out the phone book and looked up the Retail Clerks Union office. He got out a pencil and wrote down the address. "Tomorrow, after school is over, you're going to go down to this office here and you're going to join that union," he said. He told me how when he had worked for the insurance firm, he got fired for trying to get a union in. "You go down and you join that union no matter what it costs." After dinner was over, I called up some of the other new guys who had come in with me at Acme and convinced them to go down with me the next day. We met up and took a bus down to the Local 1357 office and joined.

Once I had joined up with the union, I was a little worried that I would get into trouble with Mr. Weiss. I must have mentioned this to my Dad, because the next time he went over to get his order filled, he called Al over to talk to him. You could see Al rolling his eyes. He said, "Okay, Mr. Young, but I was just trying to help the kids out." I remember my Dad saying, "Well Al, this *is* going to help the kids. You are a good manager and the conditions with you are good, but you never know how long you're going to be around, Al." He gave him a big lecture about unions.

My father looked through the literature the union had given me and saw that there were membership meetings once a month. He told me he wanted me to attend. "You don't just join something just to join it, you participate," he said. "You go down there and you get involved because you are a member of the union. I wish I could have been a member of a union, but I got fired." I remember I absolutely didn't want to go and started arguing with him about it—but it was a done deal. Again, I figured that instead of going down to these meetings on my own, I would convince some of the other part-timers to join me. It was around Thanksgiving 1954, and about five of us, all high school kids, went down to our first union general membership meeting at the ballroom of the Bellevue-Stratford Hotel, one of the fanciest in downtown Philadelphia. We got to the meeting, and, of course, there were all these old farts there. We really stood out. Everybody was looking at us funny. I'll never forget, Henry Highland, Local 1357's president came over to us and said, "Kids, what are you doing here?" We told him we were new members and wanted to see what happened at the meetings. "Well kids, welcome to the meeting. You better be good members," he said and started laughing. Little did I know that only a few years later, I'd wind up defeating the guy to become president of the union.

Highland called the meeting to order and the very first thing he did was to have a motion from the floor to increase the union officers' salaries an extra twenty-five dollars a week. In those days, that was a lot of money. As a part-time clerk, I was making just $1.10 an hour, and I thought the union officers were getting plenty already. I didn't speak up, though. When I came home, my dad quizzed me on what went on and I told him about the pay increase. He told me that that was the kind of issue that I had a right to oppose as a member and that I should have spoken out, to let the people know I disagreed. I followed this advice at the next month's meeting when there was a motion to spend several hundred dollars for an office Christmas party. My friends and I again felt this was too much money, and I told them what my father had said, that we had a right to oppose a measure we didn't agree with. None of us stood up to speak against it, but when the vote was put to the membership, all five of the part-time high school students shouted "no!" President Highland looked up surprised and said, "What are you kids doing down there? What are you saying no for? This is something the office is going to do for the executive board." We all sat there and didn't say anything back. "Are you sure you want to vote no?" Highland asked.

"Yes, sir!" we said in unison.

I went home and told my dad about what happened at the meeting and he said it was a good thing that we did that. He said that sometimes you've got to get up and give a speech about why you are doing it. "Don't ever be intimidated by people in power. Everybody puts his or her pants on one leg at a time," he would tell me. I must have heard that speech from him a thousand times.

2

I'M BETTING MY HOUSE
ON KENNEDY

IN SEPTEMBER 1956, I enrolled at St. Joseph's College, one of the region's top Catholic institutions located out on City Line Avenue in Philadelphia's Overbrook section. Besides my Aunt Florence—Mother Mary Benedict—I was the first member of my family to attend college, a fact I never forgot. These years at Hawk Hill, which is what the St. Joe's campus was always known as, were very important in shaping how I came to understand the world and my future life in labor and politics. Here I was introduced to Jesuit traditions of social engagement, principles that encouraged students to see the difficulties of the world as situations they should challenge and ultimately transform and make better. It wasn't surprising that St. Joe's listed among its alumni some of the region's most important politicians and civil servants. During these years, I met some lifelong friends and, for the first time, got involved in the local political scene.

When I started at St. Joseph's College, it was still an all-male institution with about two thousand students, almost entirely from the Philadelphia region. Many of the upperclassmen were Korean War veterans who had enrolled on the GI Bill, and they were older and more experienced. They brought a certain maturity and seriousness to the overall campus scene. I was what was known as a dayhop, one of the many commuter students who went to classes while living at home. In my second year, I bought a used 1948 Plymouth for a hundred bucks and I drove to

Figure 2.1 Wendell W. Young III, graduation portrait, St. Joseph's College, 1960. (From the collection of Wendell W. Young III.)

classes every day. During these years, my father paid half of my tuition, and with the money I made at my part-time job at Acme, I covered the other half, in addition to my gas expenses and car insurance. For these four years, just about every hour was spent either at St. Joseph's or at Acme, going home only to sleep. (See Figure 2.1.)

In my first year as a Hawk, I majored in biology with the intention of becoming a medical doctor and a missionary priest with the Holy Ghost Fathers. This plan didn't last too long because my grades weren't good enough, and I eventually changed to political science, which suited my growing interest in politics. Over my four years at St. Joseph's, I joined just about every activity on campus, including the debating society, the glee club, the law society, and the newspaper. One year, as a member of the theater society, I was cast in a scene from Pyramus and Thisbe out of Ovid's *Metamorphoses* and came in second in a one-act play contest in Washington, DC. I played the woman Thisbe and had the audience rolling with laughter in the aisles, annunciating my lines with a high-pitched voice and fitted out with large breasts. Through the theater and debating society, I overcame whatever stage fright I might have had and learned how to be a decent public speaker. For years after, I knew I could go on a stage and hold myself together.

With all the fun I had in those years, my activities at Hawk Hill had a more serious side too. I was an active member of Sodality, an organization devoted to the Blessed Mother, and each morning before the start of classes, I came to campus to attend mass and receive Holy Communion. As I mentioned, for the first two years in college, I wanted to be a priest, although some of the Jesuits who knew me urged me to think it over very carefully. I met with a priest guidance counselor and he told me that he wanted to be sure that I had more contact with women to be certain I wouldn't change my mind later. It turned out this was a very wise suggestion. Before the start of my junior year, I began to meet women. I went down the shore to Ocean City, New Jersey, the whole summer in 1958, staying with a high school buddy whose parents had a home there. I met a girl named Marilyn Fluehr there, and we started dating. When I came back to Philadelphia, I decided I wasn't really suited for the priesthood, because I liked the ladies too much.

The Society of Jesus's tradition of education espoused at St. Joseph's College encouraged social engagement to grapple with the world's problems. It wasn't enough to learn through books; you had to take that knowledge out into the world, to challenge society, to make it a better place. In that way, my college years set the stage for how I viewed my responsibility as a Catholic layman and, eventually, as a leader in the labor movement. The Jesuits urged us not to accept things the way they were but to ask questions, to challenge things, and to try to make life better for people. This attitude was at the core of the concept of Catholic Action, a lay movement within the church that called upon nonclergy to take a more active role in advocating the church's position in society. Even though I decided I wouldn't be a priest, I could still live a holy life. I was inspired also by the Catholic encyclicals, the various papal letters to the bishops that articulated Church policy, especially *Rerum Novarum*, which called for workers to engage in labor unions as a way to achieve fair conditions and social justice. These ideas were familiar to me because my aunts and my father discussed them, and, as I listened, I was inspired to make these ideals a part of my life and saw my union activism as an outward expression of my faith.

All through my college years, I continued working as a clerk at the Acme Market on Adams Avenue. My work there was the most tangible way I saw myself as acting on these Jesuit principles, which I applied at work and in my understanding of what it meant to be a union member. In my first few years working at the supermarket, the union had very little presence. Leo A. McKeever, our union representative, rarely came around and when he did, it was only to collect dues. Some of the men and women I worked with didn't even know who he was; in fact, I bet that some of them didn't even know they were in a union. There was some good reason to be cynical, but I wasn't, mostly because I thought I could change things if I got involved. Based upon my understanding of Catholic Action, I took a role in the union more and more.

The boldest thing I did was make myself the union shop steward in my store. The steward played an important role in any unionized environment, because he or she was the face of the organization and understood the conditions of the store and each individual member's functions and needs. I read over the contract and made sure that management adhered to the rules, which for years they hadn't done. One of the most glaring breaches was the fact that we didn't get breaks. All employees were supposed to get short breaks, in addition to a half hour for lunch. These breaks weren't too long—fifteen minutes—but they were important in changing up the cycle of the day. It allowed clerks to get out of the store for a bit, get some fresh air, maybe smoke a cigarette or make a phone call, or just catch up with others who worked there with them. Once I was steward, I made sure people got their fifteen minutes; I'd close down the register and tell the employee to go take a break. I made sure this applied to the part-timers, too, since there was nothing in the contract that excluded them. When Leo A. McKeever found out what I was doing, he didn't like it, but he didn't take me on because he knew what I was doing was right.

There was one particular incident that got me known around all the Acme Markets in Northeast Philadelphia. The first big confrontation I had with store management was over the way Acme Markets made its employees give so-called voluntary contributions to the United Way. I wasn't against giving to charity, but I resented the fact that my family was already contributing to Catholic Charities, and I thought the men and women in the stores should have a choice over where they put their money. I organized a boycott, which almost everyone in the store supported, even though I was so young. During the first week of the boycott, one of the district supervisors came around and said to me, "What's the matter with you, kid? You're not helping us out here."

I said, "You don't have anything for Catholics. It's all Protestant stuff."

He said, "There's a lot of non-Catholics working here too. Why don't you let them do it?"

"Because we're having a boycott," I said. "You're playing favorites. Why should we all give what you say? You're forcing everybody to give because Paul Cupp, Acme Market's president, is also general chairman of the United Way. He's forcing quotas on all the stores to make himself a big shot."

When store supervisors handed out the envelopes to collect money a few days later, I went around to all of my coworkers and asked if their contribution was voluntary. If it wasn't, I ripped up the envelope. No one in our store gave anything more than they wanted to. I think there were maybe five or six donations. Poor Al Weiss had the lowest contribution in the district. He actually started to cry over it, that's how sensitive he was. That story got around and got me known all over Acme Markets in Philadelphia.

It was unheard of that a nineteen-year-old kid would so brazenly take on store management rules. My boldness in challenging this kind of authority came also from my interest in politics. I believed that in a democratic society, ordinary people had the right to speak back to authority figures. If you didn't like the conditions that you saw, you had the ability and the responsibility to try to change it, and to join with others to try to do so. I liked reading history and knew that if you wanted to make big changes, the American political system gave the means to do that.

UP UNTIL THE MID-TWENTIETH CENTURY, Philadelphia was one of the most Republican cities in the United States, with the Grand Old Party controlling City Hall virtually unopposed since the days of Abraham Lincoln. The Republican Party played an important role in everyday life in working-class neighborhoods across the city. If you looked at a political map of Philadelphia, the city was divided up into sixty-six wards, each one a distinct zone controlled by individual leaders who maintained their authority by their ability to provide services to constituents and in turn get out the vote for approved Republican candidates. Each ward had a leader who sat on the citywide Central Republican Committee, which determined policy, selected candidates, and distributed patronage jobs to loyal party workers.

Every ward was further segmented into smaller sections known as divisions, usually no more than a few square blocks. Two committeemen were elected from these divisions and were the human face of the party, providing services and aid to their constituents and mobilizing voters to get to the polls and support the approved party candidates on Election Day. Almost all of these neighborhood committeemen had city jobs with some municipal bureau, and they served as intermediaries for voters with City Hall, securing a range of services: getting copies of birth certificates or marriage licenses, speeding up the process of getting zoning approved for construction projects, and removing abandoned cars or fixing parking tickets, to name but a few. In the early days of the twentieth century, if you were unemployed, they got you some coal to hold you over, clothing and food, maybe pay a rent check or help with funeral expenses. The city of Philadelphia's government was the largest employer in the region with over thirty thousand jobs across a wide range of departments and bureaus. Committeemen controlled these positions and distributed them to their political loyalists as patronage. Because of the kind of economic power they had, and their ability to maneuver in the municipal bureaucracy, they had a lot of respect in the neighborhoods where they lived.

The economic collapse of the 1930s weakened the Republican Party's traditional role of providing these jobs and neighborhood-based services. By the time I was born, a rival Democratic Party organization had emerged to challenge them in Philadelphia. John B. Kelly, the new Democratic Party chairman, was a loyalist of President Franklin D. Roosevelt who won by two hundred thousand votes in wards across the city in 1936. That same year, all of Philadelphia's congressional seats were in Democratic control as well. Thousands benefited from unemployment relief or jobs with the Works Progress Administration or in federal agencies like the U.S. Mint or the new postal distribution hub at 30th and Market Streets. Organized labor, which was gaining more power through militant strikes in industries across the city, was also emerging as a political power base and mobilized thousands of members behind the revitalized Democratic Party.

Despite the popularity of Franklin D. Roosevelt, the Grand Old Party stayed alive in Philadelphia and somehow maintained control of City Hall and its massive patronage system through the 1930s and 1940s. The Republicans held onto their local power because people often split their votes—going Democrat in national races while staying with the Republicans in municipal elections, in part because they had family members who worked for the city, and casting ballots against the party might threaten their jobs. In the years just after World War II, this political order shifted when the local Republican organization was finally overthrown after a series of major scandals. Philadelphia's Democratic Party launched a reform movement that instituted a new Home Rule Charter that modernized city government. Riding this reform sentiment, Joseph S. Clark Jr. was elected mayor in 1951, the first Democrat to hold the office since the end of the Civil War. In 1955, Mayor Clark stepped down to run for senate, and Richardson Dilworth, the former district attorney, was elected in a landslide.

Philadelphia's Democratic Party, even after the elections of Joseph S. Clark Jr. and Richardson Dilworth, still didn't have much of a presence in some sections of Northeast Philadelphia where a majority of registered voters remained Republican. I think this was because this section developed differently than the more densely packed industrial neighborhoods, and it was really more an independent suburban tract. Because of this, in the late 1950s, there were some divisions in my ward that lacked active Democratic committeemen. This vacuum allowed me to get involved at an official level at an early age, and I stepped in to serve as a 35th ward committeeman even though I wasn't twenty-one and couldn't even vote yet.

The 35th ward had once contained almost all of the section of Philadelphia known as the Great Northeast, from Frankford Creek all the way up to the Montgomery County Line. This was a vast area that, right up until the end of World War II, still had a lot of farmland, woods, and open fields. New housing developments sprung up in the immediate postwar period, bringing thousands of residents to these neighborhoods. In response to the new residential patterns, the ward was divided up into five new wards in the mid-1950s, but, even cut down from its previous size, the 35th ward still covered a pretty wide territory. When I got involved, the Democratic Party leader in this section was a young man named John M. McDevitt Jr., a single guy who lived in a row house near St. Martin of Tours church with his mother and a sister who had Down's syndrome. I think he'd gotten involved in politics during the 1940s, and through his social and civic activities with the parish he delivered his division in the Democratic column handily. In an area with a Republican majority, he had a lot of ambition and took over as ward leader at a pretty young age. With backing from Congressman Bill Green and the other ward leaders around the city, he was elected to Philadelphia City Council in 1955.

Even though we lived in a predominantly Republican area, most of the members of my family were staunch Democrats even before the Depression. By the time I was at St. Joseph's College, I was interested enough in politics to get involved with student government, and, through my activities there, I met some of my closest friends. I ran for class president my first year but was defeated by William J. Green III, the son of the congressman. Bill and I became close friends and bonded over our shared political beliefs. Through student government, I also met John Flanagan, who, like me, worked part-time at an Acme supermarket and was also involved with Retail Clerks Local 1357. John was an outstanding public speaker and served as chairman of the college's debating society, which won a national championship, and, in our senior year, John was elected class president.

By 1959, I was very involved with the College Democrats at St. Joseph's College. Young Bill Green and I were working to get Democrats elected in Philadelphia, and we organized an on-campus debate that hosted the various candidates who were running for mayor in 1959: Mayor Richardson Dilworth was up for reelection and on the other side Harold Stassen was the eventual Republican nominee. When we were planning for this debate, I met Bill at his house. His old man, Congressman William J. Green Jr., was home from Washington, DC, and he began to instruct us about politics. Something old man Green said to us that night stayed with me for years after. He explained how close he was to the Philadelphia labor movement. I don't think he knew I was involved with the Retail Clerks Union, but he turned to his son and said, "In the future, when you're dealing with these labor guys, you talk to them, you go along with their programs, you try to accommodate them if you can—but you never bring them in and tell them everything. They are good Democrats and they control a lot of votes. You court labor leaders, but you never marry them." I never forgot that comment; it stayed in my mind for the rest of my life and colored my relationship with young Bill Green, who in the years to come was elected congressman and, eventually, mayor of Philadelphia.

Besides the College Democrats, I was also a leader of the campus chapter of the National Federation of Catholic College Students (NFCCS).

Figure 2.2 Philadelphia Executive Committee of the National Federation of Catholic College Students (NFCCS), 1959. Wendell W. Young III is seated on the bottom row on the right. (From the collection of Wendell W. Young III.)

The group was founded in 1937, and by the end of the 1950s had almost two hundred chapters and one hundred thousand members at colleges across the nation. The NFCCS sought to unify lay students to promote Catholic values and social engagement, and its popularity on campuses revealed the trends toward higher education and the movement of Catholics into the mainstream of American society. Philadelphia had an NFCCS regional council with two representatives from every school who served on the executive board, and, by my senior year in 1959–1960, I was elected the number two officer. This connected me to a national network of young activists and gained me experience that would be useful for years to come. We were very active in those years, organizing relief drives and sponsoring educational forums that promoted collaboration across campuses. In November 1956, we brought together a thousand college students in the region to pray for the victims of the Soviet invasion of Hungary. (See Figure 2.2.)

Philadelphia's regional council of the NFCCS also dialogued about how college students were treated by school administrators. In a fundamental way, we believed students should have more say in college governance. Most of us had contacts and friends at other local colleges—like Temple University, the University of Pennsylvania, Swarthmore, and Haverford College—and we believed they had more involvement in shaping school policies. We wondered why things seemed so much more top down at our own institution. By my senior year, I talked about introducing a new model of campus governance based on collective bargaining between students and administrators. The model for this went back to the fifteenth century at the University of Padua in Spain where student unions got together to discuss conditions, declaring they wouldn't pay tuition unless they got recognition. Many students at St. Joseph's supported this concept but were too afraid to demand it.

Through both the NFCCS and student government, we had motions to enact certain changes on campus. Usually, these were summarily revoked by the priests who ran the school without any kind of debate or explanation. St. Joe's wasn't unusual in this, as most of the Catholic colleges were conservative and expected students to behave a certain way. The political climate at St. Joseph's was decidedly conservative, and many of the student body were disengaged, a fact that didn't help our initiatives. One of the things that grated me most was the fact that the college maintained a list of books that students were forbidden to read. These titles were on the Index of Forbidden Books that the Catholic Church had officially condemned. Something like five thousand titles were on this list, which included René Descartes's *Meditations*, John Milton's *Paradise Lost*, Voltaire's *Candide*, and works by philosophers Immanuel Kant, Jean-Jacques Rousseau, Benedict de Spinoza, Simone de Beauvoir, and John-Paul Sartre. Supposedly, these books were locked up in some room in the library. I thought this was ridiculous, but the college administration wouldn't even discuss the matter.

Despite this climate, I gained a reputation for speaking out against these kinds of arbitrary policies. One time, I drew a cartoon in the college newspaper that showed a big boot crushing down on "Joe College" to criticize the lack of respect the administration had for students. I got called into the dean's office and was reprimanded. My uncle Charlie Carvin, who was a successful industrialist and philanthropist, served on the college's Board of Trustees, and, if this hadn't been the case, I think I might have been expelled. I wasn't alone in my resistance to these kinds of policies against the authoritarian nature of civic life. There was a rising student consciousness on college campuses around the country at the start of the 1960s. Toward the end of my years in college, I read about an organization called the Student's League for Industrial Democracy, which proposed that youths take an active role in all aspects of modern society and work toward the realization of a full social democracy. In my final semester in 1960, this organization became the Students for a Democratic Society (SDS), and its founders drafted the Port Huron Statement, calling for civil rights, disarmament, and youth engagement in challenging mass consumer society, becoming one of the important documents of the student movement of the 1960s. When I read about it, I had an idea to initiate a chapter at St. Joseph's College, but when I wrote a letter to the priest moderator in charge of student activities to see about starting one, he rejected it without even talking to me about it.

Even though student government didn't make much impact in changing the way things were done at St. Joseph's College, our call for more say in college governance reflected in part the broader changes going on in the Catholic Church in the United States in the years after World War II. In the 1950s, Catholics were entering the American mainstream, and there was a new attitude that embraced secularization. The Vatican encouraged this change, especially after Pope John XXIII called the Second Vatican Council, which initiated major reforms in the church between 1962–1965, encouraging lay people to take a more active role in all aspects of the religion. Masses, which had always been celebrated in Latin, were now said in English. Priests now faced the congregation from the altar during mass, lay members were encouraged to participate in the service, and more music was incorporated into mass. I was encouraged by this new attitude. Even though I had changed my mind about becoming a priest, I still wanted to be active in the church, and the changes that were coming about during these years gave me a sense that I could have a mission as a lay person.

I graduated next to last in the St. Joseph's College class of 1960. When my name was called at commencement, I walked up onto the stage to get my diploma; when it was handed to me, I kissed it and threw it up in the air. The place went crazy with cheers and laughter. Everybody knew what I was doing because I challenged the rules they had for the students, and it was my final act of protest. My uncle Charlie Carvin was there, of course, and I could hear him laughing out in the audience like a son of a bitch.

IN OCTOBER 1960, MARILYN FLUEHR and I were married and moved into an apartment complex right around the corner from where my parents lived in Philadelphia's Northwood section. Soon after, our first son Wendell was born followed by another son, Brian, a year later. I was still working a few hours a week at the Acme. I liked it there and intended to stay, but with the family growing I knew I needed to get a second job to help us get by. I got the idea that I would become a teacher, since I always liked being with young people. I saw a notice for high school teachers in the *Catholic Standard and Times*. I wrote a letter down to the Philadelphia archdiocese and eventually got an interview with Monsignor Hughes who headed the Board of Education. At the end of the interview, he asked if I would like to teach social studies at my old alma mater, North Catholic, and I was pretty enthusiastic about it; I taught history and civics classes, and a special topics course called National Problems—which gave an overview of the prominent issues of the day. All in all, I taught five classes, each with about fifty students. I was just out of college myself, and, as some of my colleagues liked to point out, I looked even younger than some of my students. The Catholic school system didn't pay very much, so even as I taught full-time, I also kept my part-time job at Acme, working nights and weekends.

With my two jobs and family responsibilities, I also somehow managed to get more involved in Philadelphia politics. The year 1960 was a presidential election year, and, after almost a decade of Republican rule, a lot of Democrats felt that there was a solid chance at taking the White House. With the success of so many liberal candidates around the country in the 1958 congressional elections, it seemed possible that the Democratic Party could chart a broad, liberal agenda in the coming decade. Even so, my involvement in the 1960 presidential campaign was not shaped by hopes for any specific policy agenda but rather my personal like of Senator John F. Kennedy. From the moment he declared his candidacy, I was a staunch JFK supporter. I probably wouldn't have been as motivated to help him except for the fact that he was Catholic. I was such a knee-jerk Catholic I didn't even care what his program was about—I just wanted him to get to the White House to show that we could succeed, just like any other group. I wasn't alone in that sentiment. In fact, the first organizing meetings for the Kennedy campaign in the neighborhood came through some people I knew from St. Martin of Tours Church, who called meetings in a row house over in the Summerdale section in the spring of 1960.

Our program was to get other Catholics behind Kennedy in the primary election against Hubert H. Humphrey. I knew we would have a hard time electing Kennedy, even in such a predominantly Catholic neighborhood. Although it had been decimated in other sections of the city, the Republican Party remained pretty strong in the 35th ward. Austin Meehan, the county sheriff, controlled the entire political world in Northeast Philadelphia and since the late 1930s had been the most powerful Republican leader in the city. By the mid-1950s, his son Billy took over the party leadership, and he had a lot of sway over patronage appointments with state jobs. In 1960, the Republican 35th ward leader was John Kane, the chairman of the Board of Commissioners of Philadelphia and Austin Meehan's son-in-law. With the ward having a majority of registered Republicans, Kane believed that he could push Nixon to victory, even with the groundswell for Kennedy. In my division, the Republican committeeman serving under Kane was a guy named Eddie Becker, who would eventually become pretty powerful in Philadelphia politics and go on to become a federal judge. He was very hardworking and used to come around to my family's house and every other house in the neighborhood, giving us literature and reminding us to vote the Republican ticket. My parents never did go for his candidates, although they liked him personally and would invite him in for coffee and cookies.

After the first meeting of Kennedy supporters, Joe Daley, the Democratic committeeman in the 26th division of the 35th ward, told me I could go around and get people registered. This was a really important function; if voters weren't registered in the spring, they wouldn't be able to vote in either the primary or the general election in November. From watching how Eddie Becker worked the division, I knew I had to go around, knock on doors, and talk to voters in their homes. They had to know me. That's what a good committeeman did. To help with this, I came up with an idea to create a 35th ward "Kennedy for President Committee," which would be open to any voter who contributed a minimal fee of two dollars toward the campaign fund. To give it a sense of being official, I printed up cardboard membership cards with a local printer who did some jobs for the Retail Clerks Union and had about a thousand made at my own expense. I figured if I went around and sold memberships at that price, then people would be personally invested in Kennedy's campaign. (See Figure 2.3.)

Figure 2.3 Senator John F. Kennedy addressing the crowd in Center City Philadelphia, October 31, 1960. (Special Collections Research Center, Temple University, Philadelphia, Pa. Photograph by Joseph McGuinn.)

I went door-to-door in my division and they sold like hot cakes, many people buying a membership for their kids as well. With some volunteers from Local 1357 helping me, in just a few weeks I got hundreds of new Democratic registrations. Some of the people in the ward had never had a Democratic committeeperson knock on their door before. Eddie Becker, my Republican counterpart in the division, came to me and said, "Listen kid, you're making my job harder. What are you trying to do to me?" That's how I knew the registration drive was really having some impact.

Joe Daley couldn't believe how successful the registration drive was. He took me over to the 35th ward meeting and had me explain what I had done. The ward leader Jack McDevitt thought it was fantastic and offered to refund me for the money I had paid for the cards. He told me to print up another couple thousand for use throughout the ward and asked if I would help coordinate similar drives in other divisions. This is how I got to know a lot of people, and eventually it positioned me to become ward leader a few years later. I also learned how to work as a politician. One of the other ward committeemen I got to know in 1960 was Lou Sigel, who ran a pharmacy. Lou was Jewish, and he told me he was 100 percent for Kennedy because he believed that if a Catholic could make it to the White House, a Jew could make it, too. Lou used his pharmacy to get people to register to vote. If someone didn't have enough money to cover a prescription, he'd say, "I'll tell you what. If you register Democrat, don't worry about the money you owe me—just register." I think Lou had more Democrats in his division than anyone else.

Many of the Kennedy volunteers who joined me on the doorbell campaign were pretty young, mostly college students and some who were still in high school. We plastered Kennedy bumper stickers all over the place. If you walked through that neighborhood in the fall of 1960, every single pole, every bridge overpass, and the backs of hundreds of street signs had a red, white, and blue sticker with Kennedy's name. A couple times, we put stickers in places we shouldn't have. The worst was when we went into a Jewish cemetery and plastered some of the tombstones that faced the street. I bragged about this to my father the next morning, and he got furious. He said, "That's not going to get you votes. That's going to get people mad at you, and at Kennedy. You get your friends over there this afternoon and you get that stuff off." I found out the hard way that taking bumper stickers off tombstones is almost impossible. I went down to the hardware store, got some wallpaper razors, and filled some buckets with warm, soapy water and went back over there. It took us hours to scrape those stickers off. My dad was so angry with me. He walked over to the cemetery later that night to make sure that I had gotten every trace of those stickers off.

During the campaign, I was living at the Northwood Apartments near the intersection of Roosevelt Boulevard and Summerdale Avenue. Frank Barbera, the building superintendent at the apartments, also happened to be the Republican committeeman for the 35th ward's 26th division. I told him I was going to put a picture of Kennedy in my second-floor apartment window. With his grudging permission, I put a floodlight on the lawn to highlight the poster at night. It was pretty big, three by five feet or so, and red, white, and blue with a photo of Kennedy, emblazoned with the words "Leadership for the 60s." I got it from the campaign headquarters downtown and I fixed it up, weathered it, and put it on cardboard. Frank Barbera was very nice about it, but a month or so later, during the thick of the campaign, he came to see me and he asked me to take it down. He said it was making him the laughingstock of the local Republican Party. At strategy meetings, all the other Republicans would joke that he couldn't even control his own apartment building.

He never let on, but I think Mr. Kane, the Republican leader in the 35th ward, knew that he was facing a serious challenge this time around. Although Philadelphians voted for Democratic candidates for local and national offices all through this period, many of them had never bothered to officially change their party registration, and the GOP still showed a strong base. This had changed by the 1960 campaign, when a surge in Democratic Party registrations across the city occurred. Of course, this change had been coming since the 1930s. Mayor Richardson Dilworth was elected in a landslide in 1955, but he never took this success for granted and pressed for registration drives in the neighborhoods to move voters into the Democratic Party column. By this time, I think he had already decided he wanted to run for governor and knew that he would have to get a massive vote count in Philadelphia if he stood any chance of winning. The fact that John F. Kennedy was the Democratic Party candidate for president also caused this political turn. Besides the registration push from the mayor, the president of Philadelphia City Council, James H. J. Tate, was an Irish Catholic, and worked hard in his neighborhood to register Democrats for Kennedy. Across the city Catholics organized, and this was an important factor in this political turnaround.

More than any other force in the city, organized labor, which had many Irish Catholic leaders, came out strongly for John F. Kennedy in 1960. Earlier that year, the city's AFL and CIO had finally merged, and political action was high on its agenda. The two sections of the labor movement consolidated their political operations to form the Committee on Political Education (COPE) to mobilize the 250,000 union members across the city to vote for prolabor candidates. In 1960, COPE was headed by Edward F. Toohey, a member of the Plasterers Union who learned about Philadelphia politics from his father, who was also an active member of the union and would take his son with him to meetings and to the polls on election days. Largely because of the groundwork laid by organized labor, by the end of the 1950s, Philadelphia was a majority Democratic town.

In the months leading up to November 1960, I got to know a lot of the old-timers who'd been active in Democratic Party politics going back to the days before President Franklin D. Roosevelt. One guy that stands out in my memory is Herb McGlinchey, a onetime congressman from the old 35th ward, who was then serving as a state senator in the district. He was a classic old-school neighborhood politician who knew the row house voters in his area really well. Herb was white haired and balding, and, anytime I ever saw him, he had a cigar in his mouth, which he smoked down all the way to the end until it got squishy. His teeth were darkened by years of that awful habit.

On Election Day, Herb came over to visit all of the different areas in his senatorial district, including my polling place. There had been this black guy going through the neighborhood with a megaphone on the back of a pickup truck urging everyone to get out to vote for Richard Nixon. McGlinchey came around laughing and smoking his cigar. "Hey kid, how do you like that Nixon shit? Isn't that the greatest? Boy, am I fucking those guys," he said to me with a grin. I didn't know what he was getting at. He mentioned the man on the truck and said, "That's my man. I'm paying him!" He was laughing. He was really proud that he had this guy going all over the Northeast pushing for Nixon. It had to do with the white racial prejudice that marked that section of the city. McGlinchey understood that sending an African American man around for Nixon would turn off many voters. I thought it was a stupid thing to do, but he thought it was the greatest thing, coming over to brag about it. He used to say to me that I was the future of the Democratic Party and that I should stick with him, that he'd teach me all the ropes. But I thought about what he had done and knew that I wouldn't have done that in a million years.

There are lots of memories I have of this election in the autumn of 1960. By far, the most exciting moment of the campaign was seeing John F. Kennedy when he came to Philadelphia. There was a big rally up near the Roosevelt Mall in Northeast Philadelphia where, as part of the Young Democrats for Kennedy group, I got to sit on the stage when he gave his speech. I was also invited down to Convention Hall for a Democratic Party dinner fund-raiser for Kennedy, who appeared there with Congressman William J. Green Jr., Congressman William A. Barrett, and Mayor James H. J. Tate. I sat in the front row right behind the stage with a sign that said, "I'm Betting My House on Kennedy." After the speech,

I leaned over and the senator signed it for me, and I smiled and wished him luck. I'll never forget making eye contact with him as he shook my hand, his gray-green eyes looking right at me, his smile so warm.

ALL THROUGH OCTOBER 1960, I was a Kennedy volunteer knocking on doors, handing out campaign flyers, talking to voters, and selling more "Kennedy for President Committee" memberships. I did anything I could do for the campaign. Although so few Democratic candidates ever took the ward, we knew we had a real shot this time. On November 8, the areas we canvassed came out big time and those of us who had worked the campaign knew we had played a part in the win. Early that night, a bunch of us went to the ward headquarters, an office in a strip mall over on Rising Sun Avenue behind the Exide Battery Works. As the results were called in, we couldn't believe we'd won the ward as solidly as we did. As I had believed would happen, all the Catholics voted for him, even if they weren't registered with the party. Across the city, Kennedy obliterated Nixon, winning by over 320,000 votes, more than even Franklin D. Roosevelt got in 1936. Pennsylvania came out for Kennedy, too. Nationally, it was a close win, but we knew that Kennedy had taken the White House, and that was all that mattered. I was so excited that I don't think I slept at all that night.

3

MEET THE CHALLENGE

WHEN I WAS CAMPAIGNING for John F. Kennedy in 1960, I realized how much power the Philadelphia labor movement had. The unions and their leadership were able to place their issues at the center of the public debate, and they affected tangible gains by mobilizing thousands of voters for their cause. The decisive role labor played in the city's politics was undeniable, and as the new decade opened, few doubted that its influence would continue to grow. Across the United States, my own union, the Retail Clerks International Association (RCIA)—more commonly known as the Retail Clerks Union—would soon reach almost half a million members, and some predicted it could be the largest labor organization in the United States by 1970. Still, considering the weight labor had, I felt at the time that Philadelphia's Retail Clerks Union didn't yet wield the kind of influence I knew it could, and I wanted to change that. To do that, I was convinced that the leadership that had run the organization for a generation needed to be replaced, and in 1961 and 1962, I joined an effort to put together a reform movement to do that.

Before I explain how I worked to change the Retail Clerks Union in Philadelphia, I should tell a little more of its early history in the city. Like many unions, the RCIA really took form during the Depression years. In the 1930s, working people joined labor unions by the thousands in an attempt to secure basic job protection, pensions, wage increases—and, perhaps most important, a say over the conditions they faced on the job. Industries as diverse as steel and food production, garments, transport, and the construction trades saw a surge in organization after 1932. Retail supermarkets joined the ranks of the unionized workforce in these days as well, one of the major developments of the period. To some, the fact that supermarket clerks and cashiers were organizing indicated how deep the unionization impulse was in this era. Before the 1930s, few in the labor movement believed that retail clerks, who were poorly paid and seemingly without any power, could come together to fight for better conditions. By 1937, drives launched by the Retail Clerks Union took in more than five thousand workers under the union banner, the bulk of the membership at Food Fair, Acme Markets, and A&P. In these early days of its history, Philadelphia's local of the RCIA was one of the most active in the United States, calling or threatening strikes and organizing in supermarkets and department stores across the region.

The first push for unionization in Philadelphia's food industries came from the truck drivers and meat cutters. Drivers had a lot of power because Philadelphia was a major distribution and warehouse center servicing surrounding Pennsylvania counties and southern New Jersey. They were heavily organized with the International Brotherhood of Teamsters, one of the most militant labor organizations in the city. In 1935, truck drivers of American Stores warehouses walked out in protest of wage reductions and increases in hours. From these bold actions, the Teamsters set up a powerful joint council, and eventually represented two hundred thousand members in Philadelphia and the surrounding area. Similarly, meat cutters formed an organizing committee in Philadelphia in 1933, and by the end of the decade had signed up most of the region's trade with the Amalgamated Meat Cutters and Butcher Workmen Union, securing better pay and job security.

The strength of the organized truck drivers and butchers in Philadelphia encouraged food clerks that they too could gain power in the stores. The first beachhead in membership came when a group of clerks and managers signed union cards and held meetings to spread the word across the ASCO chain. Support for the union began to build, and in April 1936 almost eight hundred clerks walked off the job, claiming discrimination against union members in the stores. Over a thousand supermarket workers joined in the course of the year and in September 1937, ASCO and RCIA signed a closed-shop pact marking the birth of

Figure 3.1 Philadelphia Retail Clerks Union members picketing outside Penn Fruit Market, 52nd and Market Street, January 12, 1938. (*Philadelphia Record* Photograph Collection, The Historical Society of Pennsylvania.)

Retail Clerks Managers Protective Association, Local 1357, the first large-scale contract in a major chain store. Soon after, A&P and Food Fair also recognized the union as the bargaining agent in their supermarkets. Philadelphia's regional council of the union represented about six thousand workers in food stores from Allentown into Reading, Trenton down to Atlantic City, New Jersey, and as far south as Delaware and Maryland. (See Figure 3.1.)

In many ways, the 1950s represented for supermarket workers what the 1930s had for industrial unions. With the expansion of supermarkets around the country bolstered by the suburban housing boom and population surge, this period was one of tremendous growth for the Retail Clerks Union. The union was founded back in the 1880s, but, in its first few decades, it brought in very few members and exercised little impact on conditions in the industry. In the 1930s, the RCIA experienced a boost, paralleling the successful unionization drives in the industrial sector, and this trend continued into the next decade under the leadership of James A. Suffridge, who took over the union national presidency in 1944. Suffridge had been a supermarket clerk in San Francisco and after organizing his store and building a movement in California, he gained a reputation as a hard negotiator who was not afraid to use militant tactics like picketing stores and calling strikes. He was committed to organizing the new supermarkets and department stores in the big cities and suburbs, and by the mid-1950s when I joined, the union had close to 250,000 members nationally—a number that would boost to almost a half million just a decade later.

The men who founded the Retail Clerks Union in Philadelphia during the Great Depression were still in charge in the early 1960s. Local 1357's president was Henry Highland, a tall muscular guy, whom I believe had started out as a meat cutter at an A&P. One thing I remember about him was the size of his hands. They were huge. All meat cutters have monster hands—I guess from slugging that beef around. Even though he was a meat cutter, somehow he was in the clerks' union; I don't think he really understood the jobs most of the members had. He was completely bald and very rough mannered. Instead of talking, he tended to yell at his audience. He used to get run off the stage when we were having difficult contract meetings in the late 1950s. He didn't know how to handle it. Even at my young age I could tell he wasn't that smart, but he had the loyalty of some of the old-timers, and so he stayed in office.

Things were starting to change by the late 1950s, though. By that time, a dissident movement was growing within Local 1357. There was a lot of criticism of the way Henry Highland ran the union, and many felt he was out of touch with the members. The officers didn't really communicate with the members. Our union's business agent, Leo A. McKeever—the man who was supposed to be the face of the union in the stores—rarely came around. Some of the stores didn't even have an in-store steward, a union representative that workers could go to with problems. They might as well have not had a union at all. Understandably, some members were

pretty cynical. Another point was how Highland oversaw contract negotiations. Clerks' salaries were low, far lower than truck drivers' who made
the deliveries and the meat cutters' in the deli departments who worked
in the stores with them. Under the old guard leadership, the Retail Clerks
Union wasn't much of a fighting organization.

Even though I was a young part-timer, I got pretty involved with this
emerging reform movement that aimed to make a change in the union's
leadership. An increasing number of the union's members were part-
timers, mostly under the age of twenty-five, and these guys made up the
most vocal section of the reformers. By that time I was going to all the
meetings and a lot of people knew me and encouraged me to run for office, but I was still in college and I thought I wasn't ready. Instead, John
Lennon, who had been one of the original organizers of the union back
in the 1930s, became the opposition leader. You had to see John Lennon.
He was only in his early fifties, but he looked a lot older, and had almost no teeth in his mouth. He started with Acme Markets as a clerk
back in 1930 but eventually became a produce manager and a night crew
chief over at one of the stores on Germantown Avenue. John challenged
Henry Highland for the presidency in 1959, and, even though he had no
organized slate running with him, he lost by only fifty-six votes. After
this narrow loss, a bunch of us tried to keep the reform movement going,
and would meet at Lennon's house for breakfast sometimes, making
plans for how we would challenge Highland's leadership in the days
to come.

Both Acme Market officials and the union's old guard monitored my
involvement with the opposition movement, since they knew I posed a
threat to them as I was so outspoken in how I believed the union needed
to be more active. Both were hoping that I would quit once I finished college, but I had no intention of doing so. In a not-so-subtle way, Acme tried
to push me out in the summer of 1961, when for some unexplained reason, my work schedule was downed to about five hours a week. Usually,
in the summer months, when full-time employees took vacations, store
managers would offer part-timers increased hours, but, this year, they
pushed me aside. My son Wendell was just a baby, and we had another on
the way, so I was really strapped for money. I filed a grievance with the
union, but Highland and his staff didn't do anything about it. In the face
of their stalling, I tapped my political connections to get some traction.
My ward leader Jack McDevitt arranged to have a lawyer write a letter to

Acme Markets on my behalf, demanding I get my full schedule back—and that did the trick. I got my normal hours.

But Acme wasn't done yet. When I was put back on schedule, I was transferred back and forth from store to store, in another effort to make my situation difficult and to get me to quit. Luckily, I still had my 1948 Plymouth, so I could handle it. In the long term, the hassle of these transfers worked out to my advantage. I was working in different Acme Markets all over Northeast Philadelphia, and I met literally hundreds of retail clerks, many of whom wound up supporting me when I ran for union office the following year.

The story about how that happened began in early 1962 when the union's business agent Leo A. McKeever got sick and could no longer service the stores he was assigned to. Local 1357's executive board, for some unknown reason, decided that McKeever's position would be split into two separate business agent jobs. My friend John Flanagan, who I knew from the St. Joseph's College debate team and who also worked part-time at a local Acme Market, had never thought much of the way McKeever did his job. We had discussed replacing him previously, but now we decided to run for the two open positions on a reform platform. Most of us thought President Henry Highland's strongest loyalists, Jimmy Brown and Ronnie Rosmini, would oppose us, but for whatever reason, they didn't. John and I campaigned around the city, reaching out especially to the young part-timers who now made up such a large portion of the union's membership. On March 19, 1962, John and I won decisively, defeating two men from the shops whose names I don't recall, by a margin of about eight to one.

Being one of the Retail Clerks Union's business agents was a full-time commitment, so I had some difficult choices to make. I was still teaching at North Catholic High School, and to work on the union staff meant that I would have to leave my students midyear. This really tore me up. I spoke to the boys in my classes about it, and they all urged me to take the union job—a fair number of them were working after school as part-time clerks in the supermarkets, and they wanted me to represent them. After a lot of thought, I decided to go for it, and, in March 1962, I joined John Flanagan as a business agent.

Henry Highland was not too pleased to have us on the union staff. He tried to get rid of us in the first week we were there, shipping us up to Wilkes-Barre, Pennsylvania, to get involved in an organizing campaign in a supermarket chain and to service some of the other stores that the union represented. It was obvious that Highland was trying to keep us out of the loop in Philadelphia. A funny thing happened when we got up there: we walk into the store with some of the business agents from the Wilkes-Barre and Scranton area, and damn it if John and I didn't know half the clerks in the store. Most were students from the University of Scranton who we knew from debating team competitions. Word of our elections had reached them and they were glad to see us. We lasted two or three days there before we got shipped back to Philadelphia, because management didn't want us in their stores, I guess suspecting that we would stir up problems for them as well.

The job of a union business agent is to meet with members, to hear if they had any problems, to intercede with management to fix any issues that come up, and, if needed, to institute formal grievances. I took this work very seriously. I knew I was the face of the union to hundreds of members. As I met our members in the stores, I kept a record of who might be a good shop steward and who might be good to have on our reform team in the union. I kept a book where I outlined the history of every store, who was a member and for how long, what department they worked in, the nature of any problems that existed, and soon I had the demographics of every store.

I had worked in the stores now for almost a decade and had a very good understanding of what issues people had on the job. There were times when certain store managers acted like petty tyrants. People could be fired for almost anything. Different rules seemed to apply according to the temperament of specific managers in individual stores. You could be fired for being just a little bit late. Favoritism was common. If a particular manager liked a pretty girl, she could get away with a lot more than a young kid who may be working his ass off in college. If you were a little higher on the payroll, a manager might find a way to get rid of you for the smallest infraction. Remember, general managers' annual bonuses were based on profit margins, so it was in their interest to keep expenses as low as possible, and this included wages. Other times, you could be reprimanded for not stocking shelves fast enough. If a person was overweight, they might be told they weren't working hard enough. If a person's personality in any way grated on a supervisor, they could be let go, on the flimsiest excuse. Some infractions guaranteed termination no matter who you were: if you got caught stealing or you damaged goods or equipment. Say you left a whole crate of ice cream cartons out on a pallet and didn't put it away, it might be a loss of a couple hundred dollars. The union might get a worker a second chance, but if the manager didn't like you anyway, you were done.

Because retail workers only made a couple dollars an hour, how they were scheduled from day to day was an important matter for most of them, since it determined their weekly take-home pay. If there wasn't enough work in the store, managers would send clerks home, and this was a major gripe, since it cut back on wages. One of the main reasons people were losing hours was because the truck drivers who made deliveries to the stores were stocking shelves themselves, instead of letting clerks do it. The soda companies and bakeries had driver salesmen who were allotted twenty-five inches on the shelf and would try to get a couple extra. Buyers and company jobbers negotiated shelf space with general managers, and these drivers got a commission on the amount of merchandise that they brought to stores: if they could get a manager to buy more cases of cola, they got a cut of the sale. So they would come in, and if they were allowed to stock the shelves themselves, they would do it to the maximum, even if it meant infringing on a competitor's allotted space. This kind of stuff was wrong because they were cheating their competitors, but to me, more importantly, because they were taking work away from my members.

Once I became business agent, I decided to fight it and began throwing driver salesmen who were doing clerk's work out of our stores. This pitted two sets of unions against each other: the truck drivers, who were Teamsters, and the Retail Clerks. Philadelphia's Teamsters had a reputation for being really tough, and many of my members thought I was nuts for standing up to them. Some of the drivers would really curse me out when I confronted them about stocking bread on the shelves and word soon got back to the city's top Teamsters' officials. One day, John B. Backhus, the leader of the Teamsters who represented the food delivery driver salesmen in the city, called me down to his regional office at 10th and Chew Street. You've got to imagine what this meeting was like: I'm twenty-three and he's sixty and had been in the labor movement since the 1920s. He starts giving me a big lecture.

"I'll tell you something. You better watch your ass, kid," he blurts out. "You're taking our work."

I said, "I am? How?"

"Teamsters stock them shelves," he said. "We've been doing it since before you was born."

I was insistent. "The retail clerks do the work in the stores," I told him.

I already knew what this meeting was about and I thought ahead and brought a full loaf of bread with me. To make my point, I started poking my finger through the cellophane, mashing the loaf to pieces. I said emphatically: "I won't let you put that bread on the shelf," pushing my finger into the bread, poking holes in it, with each word.

Mr. Backhus looked at me. He was finally getting my point. "I'm telling you," I said—pointing to the now broken bread—"I won't allow it. It's our work." We would put our fingers right through the cellophane, make it unsellable so that the bakery would have to buy back the bread, and cost the driver the commission. I'd tell the union stewards to do that. The Teamsters started to get the message. In fact, all of a sudden, the Retail Clerks Union started getting a little more respect from those trucker guys because they knew now they couldn't mess with us, that we'd stand up for ourselves. The members in the supermarkets loved that because the tough Teamsters were finally giving in, because we were fighting back and protecting our jobs.

IF THE TEAMSTERS DIDN'T LIKE what I was doing in enforcing the store rules, Acme Market's management liked it even less. For years, the union was complacent and here I was, a twenty-three-year-old coming in and demanding they abide by the rules of the contract. I caught a lot of flak for it. One day I was over at an Acme Market at 10th and Erie, and one of the store managers, a guy who looked like a Prussian general, hears that I'm in the store checking on the bread. I forget his name, but he stormed across the front of the store. I never saw a guy walk so fast. He comes right to me and says, "Mr. Young, we meet again! Who are you to come in this store and throw those salesmen out?"

I said, "I'm the union business agent, that's who I am."

He ordered some guys over who literally picked me up and forced me out of the store. There was a public phone booth on the side of the store and I called up Bill Callahan, Acme's personnel director. Bill had gotten to know me pretty well by now, because managers across the city were calling him to report how I'd been challenging things by insisting on the enforcement of the contract. He picked up the phone and whined, "What's wrong now, Wendell?"

"I just got thrown out of the 10th and Erie Acme by a tall white-haired Prussian. Your manager has just thrown me out bodily."

"Well, Wendell, he's a pretty tough guy; I might not be able to do too much."

I said, "I'll tell you what I want, Bill. If he doesn't take me to the front of the store and apologize to me in front of those clerks for what he just did, I'm pulling this store and maybe all of the stores in the whole area out on strike, and I'll call the newspapers and tell them why." It was all over the papers that John Flanagan and I had won office, and I knew that the city's labor beat reporters would take up this story if I brought it to them. "If you don't, it will cause a very embarrassing situation, and you're going to lose customers."

Callahan said, "You can't do that Wendell; we have a contract."

I said, "You're breaking the contract right now, and you're telling me I can't break the contract? Guess what? Watch me."

I told him to call the store manager and that I'd be waiting out by the phone booth. In a few minutes, one of the assistant managers comes out and says, "Wendell, would you please come inside. The manager wants to meet with you."

I go in to meet this tough manager in private in the back of the store in the break room. His face was all red. He mumbled, "Listen you son of a bitch. I've been instructed by the main office to apologize to you."

I said, "Wait a minute, I want you to apologize out there, not in here."

He says, "Give me a break, would you kid."

"You didn't give me a break when you threw me out, insulting me like that. I want you to stand out there near those cash registers and call the clerks' attention and say that you apologize and that you were wrong for what you did. You would make a clerk do that, if they made a made a mistake in front of a customer, which you've done."

We walked out to the front of the store and he calls out, "Excuse me. I didn't realize who Mr. Young is. He is kind of young looking." He gave that half-assed excuse, and apologized, but I accepted it and that was that. That's the kind of stuff I went through when I started out as a business agent.

No one had taken this kind of action in the Acme Market chain before I started doing it. It put a target on my back. Maybe I was just young and naive, but it took a lot of guts to put myself in that kind of position. When I think back on what moved me to be so bold as a young union representative, my courage was rooted in my idealistic commitment to the spirit of social Catholicism. I believed strongly that the church's teachings had to be brought out through action to shape the modern world. It was about making the ideals I had have impact in real life. This was what challenging problems looked like in the real world. You don't back away from conflict, even if it makes people in charge uncomfortable. A lot of the problems I felt were happening had to do with the fact that those in power in the stores operated the way they did simply because they said that was the way it was going to be, without any discussion. I didn't like that kind of authoritarianism and fought against it any time I saw it. The reform spirit in the Catholic Church after the Second Vatican Council supported this view, one that demanded democratic engagement. If it was supposed to happen in the Church, I believed it needed to happen in the shops, too.

This understanding of my role as union agent in the stores led me to evaluate a range of practices in the retail industry that for years had been the norm. As in other industries in Philadelphia, African American workers in the retail establishments worked in the lowest-paying and least desirable types of jobs. There was one black guy in every Food Fair Market, and as a rule he worked in the maintenance crew. When I would visit the stores, I would seek these men out and ask them if they were members of the union; they would always say no, they were not eligible because they were superintendents of maintenance, which, they were told, made them part of management. I asked them how much they made. They took home way less than anybody else in the store—say the minimum wage was a buck and a quarter, they were making like sixty cents an hour, if that. They were working all kinds of hours, as many a fifty a week, because they were told they were supervisors. It boiled me that the Retail Clerks Union officers were aware of this situation and had signed off on it. In fact, Henry Highland's brother Roy was Food Fair's vice president in charge of maintenance, and he had a blind eye when it came to enforcing the contract. I decided to make a stand: over the course of a week, I went around and signed all these maintenance guys up and brought them into the union since they weren't really management, and the contract specified all workers in the stores below supervisor rank were eligible to be members.

When word got to Henry Highland that I had signed these men up, he went berserk. He called me into his office and yelled at me. I knew I was in trouble, but I took the issue up at the next general membership meeting, demanding that we go to arbitration to have the case settled by an impartial, outside expert who was familiar with labor law. I thought we had a good case and was sure we could win it and get the Food Fair maintenance guys in as union members. The union's staff lawyer argued the case before an arbitrator from the University of Pennsylvania—very reputable, supposedly. I didn't realize it, but I was being set up. When I gained a little more experience a few years later, I understood that the case had been thrown. Highland had gone to the arbitrator before the case and the lawyer gave a sham arbitration, took his fees, and went through the motions, but the outcome had been predetermined. We lost the case and all those maintenance guys who signed up to join the union got fired. They didn't want any more problems so they did away with all the maintenance crews.

When I saw the arbitration case going south, I was sick to my stomach. Once the case was lost, I got all the discharged maintenance guys together at a meeting downtown. I promised every one of them that I was going to be running against the man who controlled the union—the one who had screwed them over—and I told them that I would get them a job, no matter what I had to do. It took me like two and half years to get every one of those men back to work, but I did—at one of the other companies the union represented. This was one of the incidents that convinced me to challenge Henry Highland in 1962.

STORIES ABOUT HOW I WAS CHALLENGING the status quo in the stores got around. John Backhus and other Teamsters chiefs probably called Henry Highland to complain about me, as I'm sure Acme Market's managers did as well. It was a tough thing for Highland and the union old guard to swallow. They didn't like me rocking the boat. Word eventually got to the Retail Clerks Union's top brass about how I was doing things in Philadelphia, and this raised some red flags for them as well. The RCIA was a very top down, bureaucratic organization, and since the 1940s almost all of the power came directly from the president, James A. Suffridge, who ran the union out of the international office in Washington, DC. He did this by controlling things at a regional level, and I soon learned how autocratic this system could be. During the early 1960s, there were a number of regional directors, the most powerful being James T. Housewright, the union's organizing director who had come out of Indianapolis RCIA Local 725. In 1964, Housewright was put in charge of RCIA District Council 11, which took in Philadelphia, Trenton, Camden, Atlantic City, Allentown, Reading, Harrisburg, Maryland, Delaware, and parts of Washington, DC. This was an important position, and showed how Housewright was Suffridge's right-hand man. As soon as he started operations in Council 11, Henry Highland apprised him of the reform movement I was leading in Local 1357. From that time on, he saw it as his mission to put me in short pants.

The RCIA's efforts to block my growing power base in the union in Philadelphia in many ways shaped the dynamics of the 1962 supermarket contract talks. About a month after John Flanagan and I were elected business agents, we joined the union's contract negotiating committee for the three major supermarkets—Acme, A&P, and Food Fair—all of which were covered by one contract, with various differences, across the region. We were in negotiation into the summer, in long sessions that seemed to last night and day. Contract talks that happened three years previous had been strained, so much so that the membership came close to voting to go out on strike. Anticipating a replay of that, the companies brought their top guys in from around the country to play hardball. A&P sent a guy named Robert F. Longacre, the chief negotiator out of the Graybar Building, the company's main office in New York City. A&P—the Great Atlantic and Pacific Tea Company—was at that time the biggest food company in the world, with over seven thousand stores from the West Coast all the way to New England. On the Retail Clerks side of the table was Henry Highland; Camden's Joseph J. McComb, president of Local 1360 and the top RCIA leader in the region; and John T. Haletsky, who oversaw Local 1393 in Reading, Pennsylvania.

The core issue in the 1962 talks was weekly take-home pay. The top rate for retail clerks in the United States was something like eighty-five dollars a week, and Joe McComb wanted our region to be the first in the nation to hit the one-hundred-dollar mark. In the early 1960s, contract negotiations in supermarkets dealt with pennies an hour—not even nickels or dimes—so this was a pretty big proposal. To get it, the union's old guard was willing to accept what the company would ask in return. During talks, it was clear that the companies were willing to grant the one hundred dollars a week, but in return they wanted a five-year contract, which in those days was unheard of. People who worked in the supermarkets wanted one- or two-year contracts at the most because with contracts that expired quickly, they could negotiate for more advances, more often. That was the standard for collective bargaining in the retail industry.

When I look back on this round of collective bargaining talks, I am pretty sure that both the Retail Clerks Union big shots and the supermarket negotiators wanted to scare John Flanagan and me. They put a real show on for us. Toward the end of the negotiations, A&P's Robert Longacre made a blustery speech to try to dampen any strike talk. "We are the Great Atlantic and Pacific Tea Company!" he yelled, "and when Mother A&P wakes up, everybody shakes. You are going to wake us up here and we are going to fight you like you never saw before. We will destroy this union." I was new to this process, and I admit I was a little intimidated by his tough talk. If it was ten years later, after I had been through a lot of contract talks, I would have told him to go fuck himself; but in those days I didn't use that word. All the older union guys, men who had been through this process over the years, they just sat there quiet. The union should have shot right back at them, but nobody said anything. It was all done for the young militants in the room, because Jim Housewright and Joe McComb were trying to scare us, too—they didn't want a strike on their hands either.

Finally, the union representatives start to talk, going around the table and weighing in with their views. Housewright and McComb went first, and both said that they hoped we would accept the deal that was offered. When it was my turn, I said, "Our members aren't going to go for this. You come to our membership meeting and make a speech in favor of this settlement, they'll run you off the stage." I told them they were going to have to shorten it up, something less than the five-year deal they wanted. With that out in the open, we finally bargained down from five years to thirty-three months. The terms we left with constituted a thirteen-dollar-an-hour pay boost—which meant ninety-five dollars a week for full-time clerks and cashiers. So we didn't get everything we asked for either, but pretty close. Part-timers would get thirty-two-and-a-half cents more an hour, a concession that I thought would be well received. We also gained a paid holiday and lowered the time it took before one could get three weeks' vacation from ten years on the job to eight.

The next stage of the contract negotiation process was taking the proposal to the general membership—the men and women who worked in the stores across the region—for their approval. I knew that the negotiating committee could point to some significant gains, but, from the mood of the membership, I was certain that we would have a difficult time selling this deal. When you called together all the members of the Retail Clerks Union across the region—all the clerks and cashiers from Acme, Food Fair, and A&P—the meetings were huge, as many as five thousand people. Our general membership ratification meeting was scheduled on June 13, 1962, at the Philadelphia Athletic Club, which had a big auditorium down on Broad Street near the old *Philadelphia Inquirer* building. From the outset, I was feeling uneasy about how the offer would be received. Driving down to the meeting, John Flanagan was in the front passenger seat and I was in the back. John already had a few beers in him and began boasting that he could convince the members to accept the terms. I said, "John, be careful, this isn't going to be an easy sell for us, it's not what the people want." Going into that meeting, I knew it could very easily get out of hand.

Late that night, eighteen hundred members were there in the auditorium, and there was a buzz of excitement and anticipation. Newspaper reporters knew it was a big story, and they were all over the place. The meeting is called to order and Henry Highland gets up and starts talking. He didn't last ten minutes before members wanted to run him off the stage. He'd told them a basic outline of the thirty-three-month contract and members started booing and hissing him. A couple of chairs were thrown. I looked out and could tell some of the members were probably drunk. John Flanagan—who I knew for sure was drunk—got up, banged the gavel, and yelled for order. The members only yelled back at him—so he yelled even more. The meeting was falling apart.

I don't know what possessed me, but I grabbed John by the back of his pants and pulled him away from the microphone and took over the meeting myself. I told everyone in the hall that when they sat down and stopped screaming, I'd tell the story of what happened in negotiations, from the beginning to the end. We would then vote to either accept the deal or to go on strike. Everyone finally calmed down and I started reading through the whole contract, point by point. As I did this, I also told them the behind the scenes of what happened at the negotiation table, and let them know about my own sense of frustration at points. Nobody had ever heard this kind of background to the process. It took about three and a half hours until I was finished, past midnight, but most of the members were still there and ready to cast their votes.

Finally, we took the vote at 12:15 A.M., the members forming lines to cast their ballot in boxes on the stage. It was agreed to in the rules of the election committee that all the locals would take their ballot boxes with them and bring them back to the mediation service downtown the next morning where they would be tallied. I got volunteers to stay with Local 1357's ballot box—which had all of the votes cast by the union's members in the Philadelphia area—all night to make sure nobody messed with it. If I didn't, I knew there would be allegations that someone stuffed the ballots. We taped up the box and all the volunteers wrote their initials all over it and we transported it to the union's Broad Street office. I brewed some coffee and everyone stayed until morning, and at the appointed hour we took the ballots down to the mediation service. When I got there I noticed something disturbing. When I saw the Trenton ballots coming in, every ballot was marked the same way, all in support of the contract offer, all in the same blue ink; I knew they'd been tampered with. Knowing how their relationship was over the years, I think Joe McComb had instructed Maurice Doyle, president of Trenton's RCIA Local 1371, to do the dirty work. McComb knew the members were against the offered contract proposal, but he didn't want to risk a strike, and he made sure the votes reflected his position. The contract was accepted by just over a hundred votes; so if you factor in those votes that I believe were tampered with, it did not really reflect the will of the members. Many at the meeting were challenging the ballots left and right, but it was no use, it was a done deal. (See Figure 3.2.)

THE RESULT OF THE 1962 CONTRACT ratification convinced me even more that I needed to challenge Henry Highland for leadership of Local 1357. In the weeks to come, the reform movement went into high gear to support this campaign. John Lennon was a force in this coalition, but most of the direction came this time from John Flanagan, who had announced he was running for president, and me, on the ballot for the union's secretary-treasurer position. During this campaign, John was the spokesman, and I was the organizer who set up the meetings and made the phone calls to get our membership out. There were some people in the

Figure 3.2 Retail Clerks Union members gather at the Philadelphia Athletic Club, Broad and Wood Street, to vote on the contract offer, June 14, 1962. (Special Collections Research Center, Temple University, Philadelphia, Pa. Photograph by Russell C. Hamilton.)

labor movement who discounted us because we were so young, but our age was actually a plus—especially with the hundreds of part-timers who made up the bulk of the general membership. There was a spirit of youth and change in the air during the Kennedy years, and it inspired our efforts and shaped our campaign. Our platform was pretty simple: to service the members, to get an eight-hour day for part-timers, to end split shifts that required workers to return to the stores in the evenings, and to initiate health and welfare benefits at the next round of contract talks. Of course, better wages were also part of our platform. Everyone in the stores knew that the Teamsters' drivers and the meat cutters had better deals than we did, and we promised to improve wages to be on par with them.

Because I knew that we needed to publicize our campaign, I came up with a name for our opposition ticket—Meet the Challenge. This reflected the kind of attitude toward life I had been taught by the Jesuits at St. Joseph's College, one that embraced the need to challenge the problems of life, not just accept conditions as they are. It also embodied the spirit of Vatican II, which was transforming the Catholic Church by encouraging lay members to step up and meet the difficult issues of the twentieth century. Just like the Catholic Church, the labor movement needed reform and change, it needed to open up the windows and let the fresh air in. For our campaign literature and posters, I chose blue and white, the colors associated with the Blessed Mother. We set out getting our information to all the stores, meeting with members, and answering questions, and as we went out and shook hands with the workers at Acme, A&P, and Food Fair across the city, I knew we had a good chance at winning.

The election was held on November 19, 1962, with our members voting in five designated polling places around the city. When the ballots were tallied, the Meet the Challenge slate creamed Highland and his team by a ridiculous margin, something like three to one. Our election was covered in all the Philadelphia newspapers the next morning, most of the reports highlighting the fact that John Flanagan and I were only twenty-four years old and fresh out of college. It was one of the major turning points in my life, and a successful culmination to the reform movement that had been brewing in Local 1357 for years. There was a big celebration the night we won; but I remember when I went home after, I felt so nervous that I literally got sick to my stomach. But I knew I couldn't turn back now. I had just accepted a huge responsibility and taken on a set of problems I didn't know how to solve. I looked at myself in the bathroom mirror and whispered, "What the hell did you just do?"

4

THE KID

ALTHOUGH THE MEET THE CHALLENGE SLATE won the election in November 1962, we did not formally take over day-to-day operations as the union's officers until the day after New Year's. The month in between was a time of transition, as John Flanagan and I worked with the union's old guard to ensure a smooth turnover. Some unexpected things developed in these early weeks of the year. Sometime in March, John received an Army draft notice, and although he could have probably received a deferment, he decided against it. Soon after, he was inducted into military service and was no longer involved with the union. From then on, I was on my own to head the union and, as I came to see, would have an uphill battle to establish myself as Philadelphia's youngest labor leader. I was so young looking that some of the people who came to Local 1357's office actually mistook me for an intern.

I was well aware of how my youth and inexperience was a liability as I took leadership of the city's largest union. I knew that the management in the stores would try to test me because they figured I was so new to the game that I'd be weak and easily intimidated. Sure enough, a few weeks after I was in office, I got a call from Jack Hellmack, Food Fair Market's personnel director, who told me about some changes they were instituting. In an arbitrary move, he had decided to transfer some of the store's employees, including several of the union's in-store representatives. Sam Brotsky, one of our most effective and popular stewards who worked in the Upper Darby store, was being sent to Feasterville. In the early 1960s, very few people who worked in retail in the city had their own cars; many took public transit to get to work. For Sam to get to Feasterville out in Delaware County, he would have to take three different buses, something he just couldn't do. Five other stewards besides Sam were being transferred, for no reason other than the fact that the company wanted to transfer them. It was an attempt to antagonize and test the new union leadership.

Everybody was really upset about it. I told my staff we'd have to fight hard—even if it meant calling a strike. If Food Fair got away with this, we'd be ruined, since they'd tell all the other companies that we were weak. I scheduled a general membership meeting at the Benjamin Franklin Hotel in downtown Philadelphia the following week to have a strike call. I didn't have much time to spread word about the meeting, so I decided I needed to go to the members directly. I came up with an unusual tactic. I drove out to St. Joe's, went to the Athletic Department, and borrowed a big megaphone. Later that night I drove out to the Food Fair at 54th and City Line Avenue, walked right to the front of the store, and yelled into the megaphone that the union had scheduled a strike call meeting for the following week and that all members should be there. I did this with the customers all there in the aisles and checkouts, to the shock of the managers. Before that week was out, I'd driven to every one of the forty-nine Food Fair stores in the region, getting the word out about the meeting.

The following Monday, a week after the original phone call, I get another one from Jack Hellmack. He says, "Wendell, we've thought this over. I know you've been around pushing this meeting and we want you to call it off." He said he was willing to keep things as they were, and not make the personnel transfers. I told him I would have to go ahead with the meeting anyway, because I've got to tell the people what he had just told me. I also asked him if Food Fair's industrial relations head Arv Johnson would be attending, and he told me that he would not. I said, "Well, I'll have a chair for him on the stage anyway. He's still welcome to come." I also made it clear to him that if he was double-crossing me, the union would strike. Later that week, we held the meeting and it was packed with men and women from the supermarkets from around the region. We had our five stewards who had been scheduled for transfers up on the stage and an empty chair for Arv Johnson. I put forward a resolution that the members would support the union by going on strike if Food Fair went back on its promise not to initiate the arbitrary transfers. It passed unanimously. Everybody was yelling and clapping like crazy. It was one of the best things that ever happened, it really put the new leadership on the right track with the membership.

The showdown with Food Fair taught me that I needed to be confident and bold in how I handled situations as a young labor leader. This was an important lesson to learn, as the opening months of 1963 were tumultuous in the history of the Philadelphia labor movement. A series of protests were organized by a section of African American workers who were tired of how they were treated by both unions and management. For years, black people were relegated to the lowest-paid positions in every industry, and, even into the 1960s, whole sections of the city's industrial and construction sector were entirely white. Foremost among Philadelphia's black union activists leading this challenge was James H. Jones, a representative of the Philadelphia branch of the United Steel Workers. In 1957, he founded a branch of the Negro Trade Union Leadership Council (NTULC), which was organized by A. Philip Randolph to fight for black advancements in the trade union movement. The NTULC demanded more inclusive policies in the building construction industry, which remained the city's largest bastion of white union membership. Various civil rights groups made job access to apprenticeships a priority from the 1940s on, but little progress was made. This really became a hot issue after the Kennedy administration initiated major federal building projects in urban centers, opening more jobs for all kinds of construction workers. Sixty million dollars channeled into Philadelphia sparked a building construction boom that set the stage for a major fight to desegregate this industry. In 1963, the Philadelphia branch of the Congress on Racial Equality started to protest construction sites to bring attention to the lack of opportunities for black workmen. A week later, these pickets swelled as hundreds more people from the National Association for the Advancement of Colored People (NAACP) joined the effort.

By June 1963, there were hundreds of protestors at the job sites each morning, effectively halting the construction projects. Bands of protestors also showed up outside Mayor James H. J. Tate's house, and in his office suite in City Hall, a move that really annoyed the mayor. While this protest was launched, the struggles for civil rights in the South gained attention around the world, as images of youths being knocked over by fire hoses in Birmingham, Alabama, were televised, reinforcing a sense of a national struggle in both the North and the South.

The push to desegregate the city's construction industry had some supporters within the labor movement besides Jimmy Jones and the NTULC. The most outspoken was Joseph Schwartz, head of Knit Goods Workers Local 190 and secretary of the AFL-CIO Human Rights Committee. Joe was born in Russia and began working in textile mills after coming to the United States in the early twentieth century. By the time he was a teenager, he was a committed Socialist and an organizer with the International Ladies Garment Workers Union (ILGWU). In the 1940s, he was what would be called a hard-core liberal, staunchly anticommunist, and chairman of Americans for Democratic Action (ADA) political committee. In response to the protests in spring 1963, he called on Mayor Tate to hold hearings to determine the condition of the construction industry in the city. These hearings revealed the practice that restricted trade apprenticeships to those who had either a father or an uncle in the union. This alone ensured that the building trades would remain white. Not a single black apprentice was enlisted in the city's plumbing or sheet metal organizations, and the same situation was found with the electricians', roofers', and bricklayers' unions. Joe Schwartz testified along with Jimmy Jones at these hearings and denounced the building trades' customs, demanding that all union construction sites in the city be shut down.

After all of the testimony was heard, Philadelphia's Human Relations Commission put out a scathing report accusing the construction unions of blatant racial discrimination. James O'Neill, president of Philadelphia's Building and Construction Trades Council, argued back that no black people were in the apprentice programs because none had applied. He was adamant that he wasn't racist and defended the way that the building trades provided jobs to the sons or nephews of current members. He said the various trades bring in family members first and keep others out not because of prejudice but because they took care of their own families first. For years, most of organized labor's leadership across the region had no issue with what was called the father-son custom in the building industry, but things would soon change. In June 1963, President Kennedy issued Executive Order 11114 establishing new hiring rules on federal construction sites that guaranteed access to all regardless of race, principles that became the blueprint for national affirmative action programs.

By the end of that summer, an integration plan for Philadelphia's building trades was announced, opening up more positions for young black tradesmen.

I FOLLOWED ALL THAT WAS HAPPENING in this construction industry dispute in early 1963 and believed that black workers should be given more of a chance to work and advance in building trades jobs. Construction wasn't my jurisdiction though and these battles weren't something I got involved with. I was too new on the scene, and I wouldn't have been able to make much of a difference. Instead, I thought about ways I could work to make changes in my own industry. Although there were more black workers represented in the retail trade than in construction, there were clear patterns of discrimination here as well. A handful of African American clerks worked for Acme Markets, primarily in West Philadelphia and Germantown where the black customer base was more substantial, but other areas had almost no black employees stocking goods or handling produce. I had already been thinking of how to address this situation when I was approached by the 400 Ministers, a group of African American pastors committed to advancing economic opportunities in the black community. I signed on to their program, which called on citizens who believed in racial equality not to patronize businesses that refused to advance black workers to management positions, and I put the Retail Clerks Union in Philadelphia behind their efforts.

The most outspoken leader of the 400 Ministers was Rev. Leon H. Sullivan, pastor of North Philadelphia's Zion Baptist Church. Since the early 1950s, he had been involved helping at-risk youths and in fighting the causes of juvenile delinquency, which he believed stemmed from a lack of economic opportunities. He sought to correct this lack of opportunity by providing job training and working with employment agencies. He worked closely with Philadelphia's NAACP president Cecil B. Moore, organizing selective patronage campaigns that mobilized black consumers to only support businesses that hired black workers. Simultaneously, he led the 400 Ministers to press local businesses to hire more black people. Some initial success was achieved with gas refineries and bakeries, including Tastykake, Philadelphia's famous pie and cupcake maker. Supermarkets were a primary focus for him because of the sizable number of jobs in the stores across the region. Although some advancement had been made with Acme Markets, other firms had only white cashiers, clerks, and managers. This was especially true at A&P because the company was basically all Irish Catholics, and they tended to look out for one another.

When the 400 Ministers reached out to the top brass at A&P, the company said they supported the program in principle but were limited in what they could do because of regulations imposed by the union contract. They promised to hire more black people, but since the union had specific rules about seniority and promotions, they couldn't jump over more qualified white people who were ahead of them on the promotion list. It was an excuse for inaction, and the pastors knew it. This is why they came to talk to me.

I remember Rev. Sullivan and a handful of others came down to see me at the Retail Clerks Union office on Broad Street. They told me that John Daly, A&P's personnel director, had told them that my union was the main stumbling block to the kinds of promotions they were seeking. I asked the ministers what they were asking the company to do, and they said they wanted ten manager positions—either in the produce, dairy, or meat departments or in the front end overseeing the cashiers. I told them they could have ten as far as I was concerned. I knew that my executive board and many of the members would give me a hard time, but that's the way it was going to be.

To let the ministers know that I was serious, I got on the phone with Mr. Daly while they were still sitting with me there in my office. When he got on, I said, "John, I'm sitting here with the reverends. The union has agreed to go ahead with ten promotions in department heads within the next thirty days. Whenever there are vacancies we agree to have any black people in the stores who are qualified to get these promotions. If they are not qualified, we agree to work with you to get them there." Daly started cursing me over the phone. He said he'd never heard of such kinds of actions in the retail industry. I told him, "I'm going along with the reverends, if you don't want to do it, it's on you. Whatever they call for, I support them." Just from that phone call, ten managerial posts opened.

From this, word got around in the black community that if you wanted something done in the retail industry to give me a call. I was an advocate for their cause due largely to my upbringing in a family that was deeply committed to racial justice. It was really engrained in me that any form of racial discrimination was morally wrong. By the early 1960s, the growing civil rights struggle was all over the news: the television images of the Montgomery bus boycott, the sit-ins organized by students with the Student Non-Violent Coordinating Committee, and the Freedom Riders. As the prominent national spokesperson against racial injustice, Martin Luther King Jr. articulated the values of this movement, calling on civil disobedience to change America. I supported the struggle as a Catholic committed to social justice. Although most of the coverage in the media these years was of the South, the abuses in Philadelphia were just as real, and I believed white people needed to get involved in whatever way we could to get some changes. I knew I could play a role—that I had to play a role—now that I was the leader of one of Philadelphia's largest unions.

Following my work with the 400 Ministers, I remained close to Rev. Leon Sullivan. He had been active with A. Philip Randolph and Bayard Rustin in the March on Washington movement, which Randolph had first proposed back in 1941 to bring thousands of African Americans and supporters to Washington to demand jobs in factories. In 1963, the 400 Ministers called me up and asked if I would join them in Washington, DC, for a major rally in support of civil rights. I got a couple people from my staff to go, but a lot of the guys in the local were not on the same page with me on civil rights. Most of them said no. In Philadelphia, you didn't have too many labor leaders working on civil rights. There were lots from other places but not Philly; you couldn't get too much participation from them.

On August 28, 1963, I went with my family, including my sons Wendell and Brian, who were still babies really, down to Washington, DC, taking a train to the capital. Philadelphia's 30th Street Station was packed with people from all backgrounds that day, all headed down to the gathering. Once we arrived at the mall near the Lincoln Memorial, I was really impressed by the number of national labor leaders I saw there, including United Auto Workers (UAW) president Walter Reuther and civil rights and labor movement activist A. Philip Randolph. There were UAW signs everywhere, calling for jobs and an end to discrimination. I felt something big was happening. It was a movement that was going to bring about significant changes in the country, the number of people gathered there was a show of moral force that amazed me. I was very proud that my family had for a long time been right in the thick of things, working to make America a true democracy. To see Dr. Martin Luther King Jr.

command all those people in Washington that day made an indelible mark on my soul. There was tremendous hope that laws would change and that President Kennedy would be an ally to push this historic movement. I was very proud of him when he finally did come out and support voting rights.

IN THE SUMMER OF 1963, I was still a new face in the local labor movement, but I went to every AFL-CIO meeting I could, speaking out on issues in an effort to get myself known. Many of the old leadership were skeptical of me and gave me the cold shoulder. They didn't want me in any kind of leadership position, thinking I was untested. So the few allies I made in this first year were important to me. My most valued mentor early on was Joseph Burke, the business manager of Local 19, International Association of Sheet Metal Workers. Joe had been president of the powerful Philadelphia Building and Construction Trades Council in the 1940s and had been one of the architects of the labor movement that emerged here during the Depression years. He lived not far from me, and I used to see him sometimes when I went to mass at St. Martin of Tours.

I remember one Sunday as I was leaving church, he called me over and introduced himself. He said he was with the Sheet Metal Workers Union, and I remember when he told me that, I had no idea what a sheet metal worker did. From then on, when he saw me at union meetings, he was sure to bring me over and include me in any of the discussions he was in. One time, he sat down with me and advised me on how I could become a better labor leader. "In your position, over the next couple of years, just listen. Don't talk too much," he said. "When you listen, you learn. Philadelphia is steeped in the history of labor and if you listen to some of the older guys, you are going to learn a lot." I took that advice to heart.

It was important for me to have Joseph Burke in my corner. This was especially so because a lot of the other labor leaders in Philadelphia did not take an immediate liking to me. They thought I was an upstart without any experience in the labor movement. I was the youngest labor leader in the city, no question about it. Some of the older union leaders used to call me "kid," and it wasn't as a term of endearment. Their suspicion of me was partly generational. I had not come out of the 1930s and 1940s, had not been there when the movement came together, and had not taken part in those early fights. I wasn't in the building trades, which were the most powerful section of the movement in Philadelphia and, even worse, I had a college degree, which was unusual in the labor movement at that time. Some thought it meant I was soft. To a lot of the guys in the Philadelphia labor scene, I was a gadfly. Add to that the fact that I came out of an organization that represented retail shop clerks, who they didn't respect, and this included hundreds of women cashiers and young part-timers. Joseph Burke was an important ally to have as I made my way around this scene in the early 1960s.

Even though I wasn't accepted by many of the old guard leaders from Philadelphia's labor movement, I still held considerable influence since I represented one of the largest unions in the city. Philadelphia's food industries represented an important base of union power, and this also underscored the kind of pull I had. In 1958, the AFL-CIO Food Council of Philadelphia and Vicinity was formed, bringing together forty thousand workers across the various food sectors to facilitate cooperation in organizing campaigns, contract negotiations, and job actions, and to boost political power to maintain standards in the industry. The Retail Clerks Union was an important part of this council, along with the Bakery and Confectionary Workers, the Meat Cutters, and all the Teamsters locals that serviced the dairy, beverage, food, and bread companies across the region. When I first came into office, Al Sabin, head of Teamsters Joint Council 53, was council president, serving alongside Secretary-Treasurer Fred Rauser from Meat Cutters Local 195 and Executive Vice President Frank Keane, who represented about ten thousand Teamsters who worked in the warehouses servicing the supermarket chains across the region. Once a month, we would meet at the Schwartzwald Inn, a German bar and restaurant over in the city's Olney section, to discuss the progress of current campaigns and to work together. This is how I got to know most of the leaders from these organizations and to understand the regional food trade more broadly. By 1967, I was elected as Philadelphia's AFL-CIO Food Council's secretary-treasurer, and I helped steer this organization to become one of the most progressive labor voices in the city.

In 1960 when the AFL and CIO merged in Philadelphia, the old AFL unions were the more dominant section, representing about 65 percent of the unionized workers in the region, mostly in construction and skilled craft trades. There were historic divisions between these two organizations, with jurisdictional disputes in transport, construction, and other industries leaving a bitter legacy. Most of the differences were political. Generally speaking, the CIO was more left wing, favoring militant direct action tactics, and had stronger commitments to racial equality. When I first came on the scene, Philadelphia's CIO's central body—the Industrial Union Council—was headed by Harry Block, the longtime leader of International Union of Electrical Workers (IUE) District 1, which represented about thirty thousand workers at production plants such as General Electric, Westinghouse, Philco, General Motors, and RCA Victor in Camden, New Jersey. Other strong sections of the industrial unionism were the Steel Workers District 7, which had thirty-five thousand members in the greater Philadelphia region, and Transit Workers Union Local 234, representing the roughly five thousand bus, trolley, and train drivers and mechanics who oversaw the city's transit system. Even though the CIO was not as large as their AFL counterpart, the 120,000-member Philadelphia Industrial Union Council's commitment to direct action and social justice unionism made it a player in the urban political order.

The historic divisions between the AFL and industrial unions were out in the open the first year I came on as Retail Clerks Union president. Even though a lot of the older labor guys didn't like me, they couldn't ignore me. The Retail Clerks Union was one of the largest in the city, and, because of this, Henry Highland had served as one of the executive vice presidents on the Philadelphia AFL-CIO Central Committee, the group of top union officials that decided the direction that the region's labor movement would take. This was an important position since it gave officials a say in any of the policy decisions that organized labor made and a seat at the table to express their organization's needs. When I took over Highland's post, I assumed that I would sit on this board, too, but I was wrong. There was a lot of opposition to me. They told me I was too young and advised me to wait a few years. I refused to back down and started campaigning for the spot. All of the old CIO unions—the various locals of the textile unions, the Steel and Auto Workers, the IUE, and the Transit Workers Union—all came out for my candidacy right away. None of the AFL unions backed me. One exception to this was Ray Hemmert, president of the International Association of Fire Fighters Local 22, who always charted an independent course and gave me his vote. Ray's support, combined with that of the CIO, got me over the top, and the old AFL guys couldn't believe it.

In some important ways, my belief in the social role unions should play in transforming society aligned me more closely with the traditions of industrial unionism. Of all the important labor leaders in the United States, I felt most connection to the United Auto Workers president, Walter Reuther, whom I had seen at the March on Washington in 1963. Like him, I believed that a program for racial justice was a major part of what the modern labor movement did.

November 22, 1963, the day of the president's assassination in Dallas, came as a total shock. I was in my office meeting with John T. Haletsky, the president of Retail Clerks Union Local 1393 from Reading, Pennsylvania, and Bill McGrath, an official from the RCIA at 5933 N. Broad Street, when we got the news; one of my secretaries heard it on the radio and came in to tell us. We went down to Holy Child Catholic Church at Broad Street and Duncannon Avenue, to pray and stayed there for over an hour. We came back, closed down the office, and sat there for a long time discussing Kennedy. I went home and watched everything on television, in shock and in tears. I was still living at the Northwood Apartments, and, later that night, Frank Barbera, the ward Republican committeeman, came over to offer his respects. I remember he couldn't stop crying. He was so upset. Local 1357 had our general membership meeting the week after, and I'll never forget that during the moment of silence we had, so many people were crying. It was pretty tough not to cry.

O N THE DAY OF PRESIDENT KENNEDY'S assassination, the meeting I had scheduled with John T. Haletsky and Bill McGrath was set to discuss some ongoing problems we were having with Food Fair Markets. After their first attempt to test my leadership in early 1963, Food Fair management continued to press the union. In mid-1963, they started opening up new stores, but instead of calling them Food Fair, which would have made them subject to our union contract, they would give them different names—Food City, Quality Foods, or other such things. They were very stealthy about it, covering up their trailers with canvas so that no one, including the union, would realize that it was a Food Fair operation. I sent letters and called the company about this contract violation, but they ignored me.

I knew they were testing me, and I knew I'd have to show a little re-solve. I called a meeting to have a strike vote, and our rank and file at Food Fair backed the motion, deciding on a one-day shutdown, the first time a strike had been called in the local in almost twenty-five years. The day of the walkout, the company sent me all kinds of telegrams warning me that I was in violation of the contract provisions, but I reasoned, if I let them get away with this violation, the RCIA in Philadelphia would be destroyed. The members supported it all the way and the stores under Food City sent a letter that they would abide by the contract.

Even with this agreement, problems persisted. In 1963, Food Fair Markets acquired a mercantile company called J. M. Fields, which had operations around the Eastern Seaboard. When they took over these de-partment stores, Food Fair ignored the agreement they had with the union that all of their operations would be covered by existing contract clauses—and starting pay for employees at J. M. Fields was a paltry $1.15 an hour—ten cents below the standard that had been established in the area. By now, the Retail Clerks International Association in Washington, DC, was aware of the situation and sent Food Fair a letter reminding them that under the contract's terms the union had jurisdiction to repre-sent employees at all stores they opened. They made it clear that a strike would result if the situation wasn't rectified. In early February, the Retail Clerks Union pulled out all of its members in Food Fair's eighty-five stores across New Jersey. On February 18, 1964, Philadelphia joined the walkout and soon after, Baltimore and other sections of the union joined in a kind of rolling job action, a tactic where the impact of the work stop-page could be leveled strategically across a wide region. (See Figure 4.1.)

Food Fair declared they would remain open despite the walkout and they began to bring in strikebreakers. I remember they even had Food Fair president Lou Stein's wife working behind a checkout booth. Some of the stores did stay open, but for the majority it was impossible, because they didn't have enough managers to train all the scabs. That's how I knew we were a powerful union; they just couldn't replace us.

The 1964 Food Fair strike, which lasted a total of thirty-two days, was one of the toughest I waged in all my years in the labor movement. As the strike entered its second week, I knew it would be a prolonged one, and I wanted to raise the pressure up a little. I figured some psychological war-fare was in order. I had a friend named Eddie Keller, who was a bird

Figure 4.1 Pickets outside Food Fair Market, 25th and Snyder, February 18, 1964. Twenty-six-year-old Joseph O'Neill, the store's shop steward, leads. (Special Collections Research Center, Temple University, Philadelphia, Pa.)

keeper down at the Philadelphia Zoo. Eddie was a young guy and headed an independent zoo workers' union and I called him up to ask if he could help me out with an idea I had. I went down to meet him and got some containers filled with the types of insects they used to feed some of the animals, things like ants, spiders, and roaches. One night, I went down to the Food Fair at 54th and City Line Avenue and let a big box of roaches loose in the front of the store, right near the checkout booths. These monsters went flying around looking for cover as customers screamed and banged into one other, trying to get out of the store. It was a morale builder for the strikers. In a couple other stores, we razored sugar bags and opened up containers filled with ants and let them go. In another store, we brought boxes of mice and let them out in the meat department. These measures were by far the most destructive ones I ever took, as far as direct provocation. They were successful, because Food Fair wound up closing all of their stores for the duration of the strike.

I knew as the strike continued that Food Fair might respond with a little intimidation. Strikes could be violent affairs, there was enough proof of that from the various war stories I'd heard from union veterans who came out of the struggles of the 1930s. Of course, I knew I'd be a primary target if management wanted to send a message and that I had better be careful. At the time, my family lived in a house on Castor Avenue in the city's Northwood section, and I took precautions. I parked my car in the garage because I didn't want to have my tires slashed or any of the engine wires or the brake hose cut. My wife liked oriental rugs, and we had one in the front living room. I rolled it up and put the furniture off to the side, because I knew one old tactic was to smash an open can of paint through the front parlor window. In the media, and in popular perception during these years, the unions were often blamed for violence, but the other side would try to intimidate just as much.

There were times during these early Food Fair fights that I really felt I was in over my head. One of the few persons I felt I could reach out to for advice was Father Dennis J. Comey, SJ, a Jesuit Catholic priest who ran St. Joseph College's labor-management program. I became especially close to him. Comey was a veteran of Philadelphia's labor scene going back to the 1930s and had the respect of both labor and management officials around the country. His workers' education program had an impact on the type of labor movement that developed in Philadelphia. Many of the labor leaders were Catholic, and the church's position was to help guide the workers away from communism toward democratic trade unionism. Since 1943, the Jesuits took the lead around the world in this task, and, in the Philadelphia region, Father Comey's Institute taught hundreds of new labor officials the basics of industrial relations as well as parliamentary procedure, contract dispute resolution, economic theory, business ethics, and practical skills like public speaking and how to run a union newspaper. Father Comey had a very big following especially from the building trades and among the city's longshoremen. He got me to take a couple of courses. I never finished the program, but he was one of my main advisers in my early years as a labor leader. During the Food Fair strike, I called him many times, and he helped me, made suggestions, and was a sounding board.

It was now the second week of the walkout, and our members were holding out, and Meat Cutters and most of the Teamsters' drivers wouldn't cross our lines. I knew that they could use some additional resources, and I requested strike benefits from the union's international treasury in Washington, DC, to provide strikers with a little money each week to help them through. Some of the top officials of the Retail Clerks Union took this request as a sign that we were losing. Unbeknownst to me, they began working behind the scenes to get a settlement. Around week three, some of the other regional RCIA leaders, John Brennan, Joe McComb, Bill Shlenner, and I were called to Washington, DC, to meet with some international union chiefs. When we were driving down together, Joe McComb, who'd been around the horn, says to us not to get too excited about what these guys would say. He was prepping us for what he knew was going to be bad news.

When we arrived at the international offices, RCIA secretary-treasurer Murray Plopper, one of the executive assistants to the union's president James A. Suffridge, announced that an agreement with Food Fair Markets had been reached. The store had conceded on the recognition issue—that J. M. Field's employees would make wages the same as those in other stores we represented—and promised to notify the union when new stores were planned. This was a clear victory for the union. The problem was this: they agreed to take back all the workers who had been out on strike, except the ones they believed had been the most militant, the ones they considered troublemakers. They had a list of those they claimed had caused damage to store property, and not only would they not take them back; they planned to prosecute them. Almost all of the strikers on this list were from Philadelphia.

I blew a socket when I heard this. I couldn't take this settlement back to my membership. By firing the union's staunchest rank-and-file members, the men and women who had been the most assertive on the picket lines, they were sending a message and trying to destroy our union. Plopper said I would have to accept these terms; he didn't think I had much of a choice. He said I was losing the strike, since I had asked for ten thousand dollars in strike benefits the previous week. I told him I would never settle on these terms. I wouldn't go back until everybody on strike was brought back, no exceptions. It was in these heated exchanges with Murray Plopper that I cursed for the first time. I started using the F-word in negotiating sessions, something I had never done before. I found that they would take me more seriously if I dropped that word. I walked out of the meeting and promised I would never take the terms they were offering.

The lack of support from RCIA's national officers for Local 1357's militancy really convinced me they were lousy, causing an even deeper rift between myself and the leadership in Washington, DC. The strike lasted another two weeks and Murray Plopper eventually came to Philadelphia to meet with me, and, by this time, he had changed his tune. It was clear that Food Fair was getting demolished. To finish the strike, they agreed to put everyone back before the end of the week and to get rid of all the strikebreakers. I gave a little, too: they gave me a list of six people who they claimed had engaged in destruction of store property. Instead of prosecuting them, they said they would fire them. I didn't mind them getting fired because I could get them jobs somewhere else, with one of the A&Ps or Acme Markets we represented in the city.

In the weeks that followed, there was an inquiry about some of the vandalism that occurred during the strike. We had a woman by the name of Frieda Gudenkunst, a shop steward, an older Jewish lady who had been arrested for destroying store property. Apparently she had cut an air hose to a Food Fair truck, making it inoperable. I went to court to defend her. I said that Mrs. Gudenkunst is a wonderful lady and that there was no way she could have cut an air hose. The company's lawyer then produced a film projector and showed footage of Mrs. G on the back of a truck, cutting the wires with a big knife. My mouth was down at my feet. I was actually speechless. There was no denying it, people like Frieda were so upset with the company that some got carried away with what they did. It showed me how militant women could be. They were worth as much on the picket line as any man. Some in the building trades used to dismiss the Retail Clerks as "the skirts union," because we represented so many women in the stores. In my view, having so many women made us stronger. My aunts always showed me the score. I just didn't buy into that macho stuff.

These were the kinds of ideals I was standing for in these first years as leader of the Retail Clerks Union in Philadelphia. I believed that RCIA

Local 1357 needed to be a democratic organization, one that encouraged the full participation of our members in every facet of the union's activities. By the end of 1964, I had expanded the Active Ballot Club, which was the union's political action unit, started a club for retirees, and improved the union's monthly newspaper. I also hired Noah White, who was a bookkeeper in a Food Fair and an active member, to join the union staff as education director, to meet with clerks to explain the collective bargaining agreements and the purpose of the union in the stores. He also organized training workshops for stewards, to get them up to speed on the kinds of problems they might encounter and to foster better connections between our representatives from stores across the region.

Sometimes, I would organize group outings for the union stewards to see the Philadelphia Phillies play down at Connie Mack Stadium. As a Phillies fan, 1964 was an exciting year, because the team—which was usually in the division basement—had been in first place since the start of the season and seemed a shoo-in to take the pennant. On September 21, 1964, Local 1357 had a group that went down to the see the Phillies play the Cincinnati Reds. There were about fifteen of us sitting along the third base line when the Reds' Chico Ruiz stole home on Phillies pitcher Art Mahaffey, who was asleep at the switch. Everybody was screaming. The Reds won the game 1–0, and the Phillies went on to drop their next ten games straight, falling out of the pennant race. For years after, we used to joke that we were the ones who jinxed them.

5

THE LOYAL SIXTEEN

ONE THING I HAD IN COMMON with most of the other labor leaders in Philadelphia in these early days was an understanding of the ways formal politics had a hand in shaping the kinds of gains we could make for our members. As a ward leader, I connected labor action with political action, at both the national and the local levels. This way of thinking positioned me well in 1967, which proved to be a pivotal year in urban politics, and for my own position within the Philadelphia power structure. In that year, the Philadelphia Democratic Party was divided over its mayoral candidate, as Francis Smith, the party chairman, refused to support Mayor Tate for reelection. Like most of organized labor, I stayed with the mayor, and this decision would launch me into a more influential position for years to come.

At the time of President Lyndon Johnson's landslide victory in 1964, the U.S. labor movement was at the high point of its power. The AFL-CIO was the strongest backer of Johnson's domestic and foreign policy programs, and George Meany, Walter Reuther, and other national labor leaders had access to the White House and pull over economic affairs as key advisers to the president. Philadelphia was one of the strongest bastions of labor power in the nation, with over 250,000 union members across the region, and ties to the dominant Democratic Party organization that allowed us undeniable political clout. In many ways these years were also

Figure 5.1 Philadelphia labor leaders meet with vice presidential candidate Hubert H. Humphrey, October 1964. Wendell W. Young III is third from the right. To his immediate right is Democratic senatorial candidate Genevieve Blatt, Hubert H. Humphrey, and AFL-CIO Committee on Political Education director Edward F. Toohey. (From the collection of Wendell W. Young III.)

the apex of union power in the City of Brotherly Love, though ironically both the labor movement and the city's Democratic Party machine were marked by serious schisms in this period. Since I played an important leadership role in both the city's labor and political worlds, I observed some of the most dramatic moments and events of this era up close and behind the scenes. (See Figure 5.1.)

Like other cities around the country, there were serious tensions between the craft and the industrial unions in Philadelphia, a mutual mistrust that went back to the 1930s. Although the national AFL-CIO merged in 1955, it took a full five years before the rival factions united into one organization in the City of Brotherly Love, and only after the national union president George Meany threatened them. Initial problems emerged in 1960 over who should be in the top union leadership. The CIO unions did not like the fact that Norman Blumberg, who was out of the AFL Painters Union, was named president of the new AFL-CIO Central

Labor Union, the citywide organization that was the mouthpiece for the region's labor movement. This was a sore spot in the labor movement, but the CIO went along with it because they assumed that one of their guys would gain the top office at the next election. With this in mind, a crisis developed in January 1965 when Norman Blumberg died, and the labor movement split over who should succeed him. The building trades and most of the other AFL unions were adamant that Edward F. Toohey, director of labor's COPE, take over the post. The CIO unions pushed for Joseph T. Kelley, the Central Labor Union's second in command, and head of the seventy-five thousand-member Philadelphia Council of Industrial Organizations and the IUE Local 113. As I mentioned, these CIO unions believed that Kelley would automatically move up into the position, as this was normally the case in union leadership rotation. Even though the Retail Clerks Union was out of the AFL, I agreed with most of the industrial unions that Joe should get the post. I was close to him because he had supported me in my bid to get on the AFL-CIO executive board, and, based on his past experiences, I thought he was more qualified than Toohey. Joe had a more solid track record in the labor struggles of the past, starting out as an organizer for the left-leaning United Electrical Workers (UE) at the Electric Storage Battery (Exide) factory out in Southwest Philadelphia in the late 1930s. Since the company had resisted unionization since the end of World War I, they fought hard against the workers organizing campaign and the confrontations on the streets and in the production plants were often violent. Joe Kelley was in the thick of those battles, and it took a lot of guts.

Of course, my support for Joe put me at odds with the other AFL leaders. I remember when I was at Norman Blumberg's funeral, and I was standing in line next to Bill McEntee, the president of the eleven thousand-member AFSCME District Council 33, which represented the city's blue-collar municipal workers. He leans over to me and says in his gruff voice, "Hey kid, I want you to know something. All the AFL guys are supporting Ed Toohey, and you're going along with us." He told me there was a meeting later that day so that they could get their act together and stop the CIO from taking the presidency. It took a lot of guts, but I told him I thought Joe Kelley was more qualified, that I liked him, and that I planned to support him—I didn't care if he came out of the CIO or not. McEntee was incredulous. "Hey kid, you be at that meeting and you do what we tell you to do." That's exactly what he said to me.

I didn't go to Bill McEntee's meeting. Instead, I called up Joe Kelley that afternoon and told him I would support him and help him out with the campaign. Of course, he was glad to hear it. The next day, I went over to his house in the city's Germantown section, met his wife and family, and stayed for lunch. I believed that Joe was the better candidate because he had a background in leading strikes and job actions and, like Walter Reuther, believed in social justice unionism and connecting the needs of organized labor with the civil rights movement. This was a key issue that was dividing the two rival groups, exacerbated by the protests of the construction industry two years earlier. For his part, Ed Toohey had no background in the kinds of shop floor militancy that marked Philadelphia's industrial union histories and was concerned primarily about political mobilization. He'd never been on strike or organized members. That fact that I put the Retail Clerks Union behind Joe Kelley was a big deal because we were one of the largest unions in the city and had a lot of sway with the other unions in the food industry: the bakery workers, meat cutters, and even the delivery drivers. I talked up how good Joe would be for the labor movement among the leaders of these unions, and many of them agreed to go for him. It was a divisive campaign. At the meeting for nominations, there was so much jeering and yelling from the floor that the proceedings were stopped with repeated calls for order, you could hardly hear anything. It brought out the divisions between the industrial unions and the building trades and municipal workers that had been brewing for years.

To make a long story short, Joseph T. Kelley put up a good fight, but he lost. The election was a disaster. On the evening of February 10, 1965, all the labor union delegates met at the Philadelphia Athletic Club at Broad and Wood Street, and as the paper ballots were being counted, fistfights broke out. A lot of Kelley's backers, including myself, believed the AFL guys rigged the vote. It was so bad that some of Joe's supporters rushed the stage, carried off the ballot box, and wouldn't give it back. In response to a formal complaint from Kelley, the national AFL-CIO president George Meany investigated the proceedings, and after a few months the election results were sanctioned. When this was announced, the bulk of the CIO unions refused to recognize Toohey, bolted the Central Labor Union, the umbrella organization that represented the city's labor movement and set up an independent council that unsuccessfully petitioned the national AFL-CIO for a separate charter. This request was denied, and in the meantime efforts at reconciliation between the two sections got nowhere. It took a couple of years before the industrial union returned, and it showed me how divided organized labor in Philadelphia was all through these years.

My support for Joseph T. Kelley in early 1965 brought me further contempt from the old AFL chieftains who already disliked me. I didn't dwell on this because my major responsibility was to my five thousand members in the supermarkets, whose contracts were about to expire. The Retail Clerks Union was in heated negotiations with the three major chains in the region, and Local 1360 president Joe McComb and I were pushing for wage boosts, to make good on what we had not been able to do in the previous round of talks. In these hard negotiations, we got a major breakthrough securing full-time clerks a five-dollar-a-week raise, matched by a similar increase the following year. This boosted weekly take-home pay from $95 a week to $105 over the course of the twenty-eight-month agreement. When I announced these terms at a meeting of three thousand the night of April 7, 1965, at the Hotel Philadelphia, our members were ecstatic, interrupting me with applause as I laid out the new contract. I told them the other deals—a new pension plan, increases in health benefits and job security for the stewards, and including part-timers in all of these advancements. They ratified the vote overwhelmingly.

All of the details of the new settlement were covered in the newspapers the following morning, but some of the most important points of progress were under the radar. Since 1953 when I started as a part-time clerk, I had noticed how the supermarket industry had unwritten racial codes that structured access to employment across the city. If black people were employed at all, they were assigned to maintenance crews, the lowest category of workers in the stores. There were some exceptions to this, but, generally speaking, this was the way things were in most stores. I had witnessed this discrimination in the Acme Market at Adams Avenue when I started there in 1954. Soon after I came on, Al Weiss hired a part-time guy, an African American man named Smitty who also worked as a nurse up at Byberry State Mental Hospital in Northeast Philadelphia. Smitty's only job at the store was sweeping floors, and he got paid the lowest wage in the store. I used to say to Al, "Why don't you give him a job stocking shelves or checking at a register?"

"Well, you know blacks. They steal," Al said.

"Al, he's a darn nurse! He's a good man, a respectable man. He won't steal. Let him stock the shelves then," I said.

He looked at me and said, "I'm not going to pay him that kind of money."

I remembered that exchange with Al Weiss when contract negotiations opened in 1965. I changed the conditions by a simple shift in contract classifications. I demanded one rate of pay for all clerks: all employees would be classified as clerks—no separate categories for cashiers, custodians, or maintenance personnel. We agreed to this overhaul with one rate of pay, for the three major chains in the region. The result was immediate. After the contract was signed, I went back to visit my old store at Adams Avenue and I saw Smitty working behind a register at checkout booth number one. I said, "Smitty, you're working the checkout booth!" He looked at me and smiled and said, "Man, I made it!" I asked Al Weiss what made him put Smitty behind the register. He looked at me and said, "You think I'm gonna pay that kind of money to him just to sweep the floor?" The kind of breakthrough I saw there at the Adams Avenue Acme was happening at all the three major supermarket chains across the Philadelphia region. We'd integrated the stores just by standardizing the pay rates.

The 1965 supermarket contract broke down barriers in the retail industry in others ways as well. For years, women had been the bedrock of supermarket cashiers around the city, but they still were not treated fairly. They were doing the most critical and complicated job in the store, and they were grossly underpaid. Full-time women working the registers made ten dollars less a week than men doing the same work. With the hierarchy of job classifications that had existed in the stores since the 1920s, women were lumped in as "checkers," with men listed as journeymen clerks at a higher pay scale. The men stocked the shelves and unloaded the trucks, but they also worked the registers. Even with that, I always thought working a checkout booth was harder work, since it involved so much knowledge of the store inventory and because it was where the actual exchange of cash took place. Eventually, with the changes in classifications, women got on an even pay scale and began to move up to better positions through promotions. By the mid-1970s, women were advancing to supervisor positions in many of the stores across the region.

ALL OF THE ISSUES I was dealing with as leader of the Retail Clerks Union were, in so many ways, directly shaped by the dynamics of the local political order. The union had always understood that improvements in working conditions would be aided by the political support of candidates we supported. I knew that the most important officer in the city was the mayor, and labor had a friend in Mayor James H. J. Tate. I had been a delegate to the 1964 Democratic convention in Atlantic City and got to know Jim Tate pretty well during that time. He knew I was a 35th ward committeeman, and word must have reached him about how effective I was in mobilizing the ward during the 1960 Kennedy campaign. He knew that I could be an important player in his campaign if he was to be reelected in 1967, and he built ties to me.

James Hugh Joseph Tate was a neighborhood guy from the city's Hunting Park section, just to the north of Temple University's campus. Like most Democrats of his generation, Tate got involved in politics during the 1930s, knocking on doors to get out the vote for Franklin D. Roosevelt and other New Deal Democrats. You had to be tough to do that. Political divisions were real. The Democrats were still the minority party in most sections of the city then, and activists in the neighborhoods often faced intimidation. There are lots of stories of campaigners being beaten up by gangs hired by the Republican ward bosses. If you dared to go against these local chieftains, one of their underlings might smash a paint can through your front parlor window at night or you might have your car tires slashed. Tate proved himself able in this world, and rose through the 48th ward committee as he put himself through Temple University Law School at night. He was elected to the Pennsylvania State legislature in 1940 serving three terms before his election to Philadelphia City Council in 1951. Soon after, Tate was named president of that body, and when Mayor Richardson Dilworth stepped down to begin his unsuccessful gubernatorial campaign in 1962, Tate assumed the office of the mayor.

Jim Tate was quite literally what they used to call a Philadelphia row house Democrat. Through his years in City Hall, he continued to live in a modest, two-story brick row house in Hunting Park, with the one exception that there was a police detail outside the house twenty-four hours a day. Mayor Tate's main constituency were the city's thousands of working-class voters. One thing we all knew was that he was 100 percent prolabor. If labor wanted x and y, he would agree to that and add z to it.

Organized labor was Tate's most solid base when he ran for mayor in 1963, and with our support he defeated Republican James T. McDermott handily. He had close personal friendships with many of the city's labor leaders, especially Bill McEntee and James O'Neill. Tate would listen to both of them on policy matters, and follow their calls on appointments to zoning boards and other powerful committees.

A few weeks after President Kennedy was assassinated, Philadelphia's political world took another hit when Democratic chairman and 5th district congressional representative William J. Green Jr. died unexpectedly. I was very close to Bill Green III, and his father's death was a personal loss to me, as it was to many others. He was only fifty-three years old, and his passing left the city's political order in disarray. Right away, former congressman Francis Smith was appointed the new Democratic city chairman, but there was a big question about who might run for the unexpired congressional seat. Bill and I had a lot of talks in the days after his father died. After he graduated from St. Joseph's College in 1960, he enrolled at Villanova Law School and bought a house down the street from me in the Northwood section. Around Christmas 1964, he came to my house one day and said that he wanted to run for his father's congressional seat, which, if he won, at age twenty-five, would make him one of the youngest congressmen ever. Bill was well liked, but his nomination wasn't a foregone conclusion. If he were to run for Congress, he would have to get the support of party chairman Frank Smith, and we talked about how to get the right people to bang away at him to convince him to get on board.

I stepped in as Bill Green's campaign treasurer and started introducing him to labor leaders around the city, often visiting them at their homes. I told Bill it's the only way you're going to get their votes. You've got to go see these people; you can't do it over the phone. That's how you change a ward around: you got to go visit people and sit in their living rooms, tell them how nice their pictures look, ask about their children and their elderly parents, and talk about Little League baseball games—really get to know them. I told Bill what organized labor's issues were, and he supported them very well. He said he'd be as good to the unions as his father had been and that everything they needed, he would fight for. In April 1964, Bill won his father's old seat in a special election, beating Republican Edward H. Rovner, a business agent with the local Waiters Union.

Figure 5.2 Congressman William J. Green III and Wendell W. Young III, 1965. (From the collection of Wendell W. Young III.)

By taking his father's old congressional seat, Bill Green now became one of the rising stars in the Philadelphia political scene. In the year that followed, I would also take more of a role as a leader of the Democratic Party in Northeast Philadelphia. Right after Kennedy's election in 1960, 35th ward leader Jack McDevitt announced that he was leaving politics to become a Catholic priest, and before he stepped down, he asked me to take over the ward for him. I told him I wasn't ready to do it, that I was too young. A woman named Maria White came in instead, and for a brief time was one of the city's only woman ward leaders. Soon after, she moved away to the suburbs, and Tom Kuter took over for a time, but he ran afoul of some of the committeemen and many wouldn't support him. When he decided not to run again, I was nominated to the position, and this time I agreed to do it. All of the 35th ward committeemen knew me from the 1960 campaign, and I had many friends and supporters. I was learning how a ward was supposed to run, so being ward leader seemed like a good fit. (See Figure 5.2.)

Now that I was on the Democratic City Committee, the powerful board of all the city's sixty-six Democratic ward leaders, I had more recognition and sway in local politics, and I combined it with my role as a labor leader. After his election, I made sure to take Bill around to monthly union meetings of the ILGWU, the Maritime Trades, and the Building Trades, any meeting we could, just to introduce him to as many labor people as possible. For many of these unions, it was the first time a congressman had ever come to their office, and it impressed them. Bill was well received in the labor movement and worked very well with them. The national AFL-CIO kept an index for every elected representative, listing their voting record on prolabor positions, and Bill had an absolutely perfect score—100 percent for labor. This was during the early days of President Johnson's Great Society programs, and Bill was right on board with these as well, making him one of the most liberal members of Congress.

Although Bill Green represented a new, younger generation of Democrats, his support for organized labor reflected the same program that bound unions to the Democratic Party since the New Deal. The cohort of Philadelphia's party chieftains from this era was led by Congressman William A. Barrett from South Philadelphia's Point Breeze neighborhood. Barrett was the most powerful man in Philadelphia. Nobody, not even old man Bill Green ever told him what to do. He'd been around longer than most, and some of us referred to him as The Professor, because he knew so much. Bill Barrett dropped out of school after his father died and worked as a laborer and boilermaker at a gas refinery. He knew what hard work was and the role that unions played in helping working people. The city's other congressmen, Joshua Eilberg and James A. Byrne, along with Senator Joseph S. Clark, all saw organized labor as their most significant power base, and they voted for labor's legislative agenda without question. Because Mayor Jim Tate sincerely believed in organized labor's cause, under his watch, unions held considerable power.

Having Philadelphia's legislators on labor's side was a very important part of union power in this period. Labor's influence was growing because of this alliance. One of the big developments happening around the country in the mid-1960s was the growing power of teachers' unions. Teachers had formed unions in Philadelphia in the early 1920s, but they had never been officially recognized by the school board and had very little clout. As a result, teachers made low wages and had virtually no say in their working conditions. They would make suggestions on budget spending, explaining how the profession was hurt by the low pay rates, but no one ever listened to them. The teaching profession was changing in the postwar years, and as more funding went to building schools, and the baby boomers started school, teachers demanded more respect. In the early 1960s, New York City's chapter of the American Federation of Teachers (AFT) called an illegal but successful strike, one that set a precedent for teachers to take similar action around the nation. The AFT, which had only a small section of members in Philadelphia, was gaining a reputation as a militant organization, and it built an outreach campaign among teachers to gain support. In February 1965, Philadelphia's 10,500 public school teachers voted for representation from the AFT Local 3 and by the end of the year, secured their first contract granting higher wages, a decrease in class size, and a say in basic working conditions.

Although I was no longer in the classroom as a high school teacher, I played a role in how teacher unionism developed in Philadelphia. As bad as the public school teachers had it, Catholic schoolteachers had it even worse. Philadelphia's archdiocesan school system expanded across the region in the 1950s, and by the early 1960s, there were twenty-eight diocesan high schools, educating fifty thousand students and employing seven hundred lay teachers. Priests, Christian Brothers, and nuns, none of whom received any pay, had traditionally been the teachers in the high schools. This was still the case in the mid-1960s, but conditions were rapidly changing. Just as student enrollment spiked, vocations in the Catholic orders fell, and there was a corresponding rise in the number of lay teachers. Pay was terrible, about one-third what a public school teacher made. Even as a part-time clerk at Acme Markets, I made a few hundred dollars more a year than I did as a full-time social studies teacher at Northeast Catholic High School. Women teachers' starting salaries were two hundred dollars a year less than their male counterparts, even if they had the same classroom experience and education level. Both male and female teachers were pressured into taking on extra duties, such as serving as an assistant coach or chaperoning weekend dances, all without compensation. This made it very difficult for those who had families of their own.

Many Catholic school lay teachers came from union families in Philadelphia's industrial sector and talked about forming their own union after seeing the gains public school teachers had made. This wouldn't be easy. The bishops and priest administrators who ran the Catholic school system, especially Philadelphia's Archbishop John Krol, were adamantly against any union in their institutions and saw any effort to do so as an attack against the church itself. This was hypocritical, I thought, since it was very clear that the church's own policies, expressed in the social encyclicals, especially *Rerum Novarum*, actively encouraged the formation of trade associations, and this included the church's own workers, too.

Teachers started forming committees to discuss ways to improve their conditions and out of this a new organization was formed—the Association of Catholic Teachers (ACT). By 1966, a membership drive was in high gear, coordinated by John Reilly, a history teacher at Archbishop Kendrick High School, and Rita Schwartz, from St. Hubert's High School for Girls up in Northeast Philadelphia. John knew I had been a teacher and called me up to see if I could help them out. The first thing I advised them to do was to get formal support from the Philadelphia labor movement. I took John and Rita with me to an executive board meeting of the AFL-CIO Central Labor Council and put forward a resolution to support their new organization. I thought this would be an easy sell, but, to my surprise, it met a lot of resistance. We had a big debate, and the funny thing was, all of the Jewish and Protestant labor leaders were for the teachers, while Catholic leaders, especially Ed Toohey and Bill McEntee, argued against it. The resolution eventually passed because I lined up most of the unions in the food council, especially the Teamsters and Meat Cutters, which, along with the strong support of the Philadelphia Federation of Teachers, got it over.

At the end of the meeting, Ed Toohey appointed me to a committee to meet with the archbishop to see if they could work out a deal that would lead to recognition and collective bargaining. The ACT was trying to get some traction but Archbishop Krol wouldn't budge. In January 1967, ACT organized pickets outside his residence—a lavish gated mansion out near St. Joseph's College, as well as outside the archdiocesan headquarters building near the Parkway in Center City. I went to some ACT meetings and rallies and got up and spoke as a former teacher. One time, I criticized the archbishop because he rode around in a fancy limousine, wore elaborate clothes, and lived in a fancy house while Catholic teachers got substandard wages. This was reported in one of the papers, and Krol called me in and confronted me about it. "Your eminence, it's true," I said. "You live in a very fancy house, but the teachers hardly have anything." He said something about needing to look at things in relative aspects. I remember saying to him, "You mean you believe in the theory of relativity now?" He never liked me very much.

Little progress was made from these protest rallies, and, into the spring, many ACT members were backing a strike to gain recognition. On April 17, 1967, the ACT planned a work stoppage and shut down most of the high schools across the region—the first strike by Catholic school-teachers in the history of the church. Newspapers were all over this story, causing a major embarrassment for the archdiocese. The walkout lasted only half an hour, and superintendent Monsignor Hughes made concessions to open a new round of talks. With the aid of Father Francis X. Quinn, a priest from the Comey Institute, a union representation election was a few weeks later in which the teachers chose the ACT as their collective bargaining agent, opening the process for their first contract negotiations. As part of that first agreement, the teachers got pay raises, free lunches in the schools, pay parity between men and women, and the initiation of a fund to help teachers with tuition for graduate school. A year later, the ACT affiliated with the Philadelphia AFT, chartered as Local 1776. When the archdiocese formally recognized the union as the official bargaining agent the following year, Philadelphia became the first unionized Catholic high school system in the nation.

THE STRUGGLES OF THE ACT represented just one of many labor issues that were in the news in Philadelphia during these years. It was critical to have a prolabor mayor like Jim Tate. Toward the end of his first term, however, there were some serious questions about whether he could get reelected. As much as many of us liked him, he could be abrasive and rubbed many people the wrong way. He wasn't the best of candidates, really one of the lousiest public speakers you'd ever want to hear. He put people to sleep in under two minutes, spoke with absolutely no emotion, and had a tendency to go on for too long. One time, at a graduation ceremony of Father Judge High School at the Philadelphia Convention Center, he spoke for almost an hour!

Many of the party leadership did not like Jim Tate personally and wanted him out of City Hall. The reform element of the party was critical of him, seeing him as a return to the kind of machine politics that had been removed under Clark and Dilworth the previous decade. Frank Smith also nursed a grudge against him because Tate had openly opposed his becoming Democratic Party city chairman after Congressman Bill Green Jr. died in 1963. Jim Tate wanted to be the big boss in the city, to call all the shots, but Smith let it be known he wasn't taking orders from him. Their personal clash led to outright political warfare in 1967 when Tate was coming up for reelection. Instead of backing the mayor, Frank Smith announced support for City Controller Alexander Hemphill, who identified with the party's reform wing. Through the early 1960s, Hemphill made a name for himself by launching investigations of inefficiencies in various municipal departments, including the court system and, especially, the Streets Department, where he claimed sanitation crews were drinking in local taverns when they should have been out working. He had a lot of support from around the city and was recognized as a rising star with a promising political future.

I think by late 1966, Jim Tate was resigned to the fact that he wasn't going to get the nomination. Sometime that summer, he met with Jimmy O'Neill, head of the Building and Construction Trades Council, and had a few beers at his home down the Jersey Shore. He let him know that he wasn't going to run for reelection. Jimmy wouldn't hear of it. He was absolutely emphatic that the mayor had to run again. He told him labor would give him the support he needed, even if Smith wouldn't. All of the other labor leaders felt the same way. AFSCME's Bill McEntee simply despised Alexander Hemphill, since he had led the investigations on city workers, calling them all lazy drunks. It was a class thing, too, I suppose. All the city's labor leaders liked Tate not just because he was a proven labor man but also because he had never forgotten where he'd come from. He still lived in Hunting Park, the same working-class neighborhood he'd grown up in. I always liked that about him. Hemphill, on the other hand, was a blue blood from the city's posh Chestnut Hill section, which made him a real elite.

Frank Smith put the word out to all the city's ward leaders that we were to back Alexander Hemphill against Tate in the May primary. Knowing the way the ward system worked, it would have been very unusual for a district leader to go against such a recommendation by the party chief. Smith had a lot of power over job appointments and other aspects of how the Democratic machine operated. Smith was calling in ward leaders and threatening them if they didn't stand with him. Most ward leaders had buckled under the pressure he was bringing. I wasn't in the same kind of bind as some of the ward leaders, since I was running the union and didn't owe my job to the party chieftain, but he could still make my life very difficult and end any hopes I had of continuing as a party leader. But I was also part of the city's labor movement, and all of the unions were backing Tate, and this had an equal sway over my views. As the election season was getting under way, I was sitting on the fence.

One day, before a big meeting of the city's top labor chieftains, Jimmy O'Neill got me alone in a room and asked me who I was going for. I knew where he stood on the matter, but I told him I didn't know if I could support Tate, since I didn't think he could win. Jimmy says to me, "You're a ward leader and you don't think he can win? Guys like you got to make him win." I told him I'd think it over. Then Bill McEntee asked if he could talk to me outside. "Listen kid, I know you have reservations, but be that as it may, I'm telling you, Tate is the guy," he told me. "I have to rely on the Mayor. I need a guy who's going to be sympathetic to the union's cause. You think Alexander Hemphill gives a shit about the workers? You're a real worker, kid. I like your heart. Stick with me on this." More than anyone, Bill McEntee was the guy who convinced me on Tate. I said, "Ok, Mr. McEntee, I'll go with Tate. It's going to be hard, but I'll go with him." Bill said, "You're going to see how good he is."

I went back into the meeting with Bill McEntee and told all the other guys that I was in with them. They had scheduled this gathering to make an announcement of all the unions in favor of Mayor Tate's reelection, and with the Retail Clerks Union on board, it was unanimous. Now we had to convince other key Philadelphia elected officials to go for Tate as well. A week or so later, the Philadelphia AFL-CIO Executive Committee had another meeting up at Cottage Green, a club owned by Congressman James F. Byrne up in Northeast Philly where all the Democrats used to meet. I got up there and I saw Josh Eilberg, the Democratic congressman from Northeast Philadelphia, and he was talking to some of the labor guys. Following Frank Smith's lead, Eilberg had recently come out for Hemphill and the union leaders were trying to get him to change his mind. I remember at one point, they had Josh surrounded, some of the most powerful labor leaders in the city talking to him, putting some pressure on. Josh was sweating so badly he was like a football player at an August practice. I went over, closer to where this confrontation was happening, and Josh actually stank. Jimmy O'Neill had him by his tie, and Bill McEntee's got him by the shirt. They're looking him right in the eyes. Josh was as white as a sheet but holding his ground, saying he had to stay with Frank Smith and the party regulars. Jimmy O'Neill was screaming back at him at the top of his lungs, "You're going to be for Tate, or you'll never see the light of day as a congressman again!"

When Mayor Tate found out that I was for him, all of a sudden I became his buddy. Right away, he had put me on the City Policy Committee, a powerful group of about ninety top Democrats chaired by Congressman Bill Barrett. This was the body that determined who political candidates would be, and, this year, that would be a battle zone because of the feud within the party. On March 11, 1967, this important board met at the Bellevue-Stratford Hotel to decide on who would be slated. Barrett was in charge of the reelection committee for Tate and was adamant that others on the City Policy Committee support the mayor. Frank Smith was there, of course, and he put forward Hemphill's name, and most of the committee members followed suit. There were only a handful of us who voted for Tate—Jack Kelly Jr., state senator Joseph J. Scanlon, Congressman Bill Barrett, Congressman James A. Byrne, and a few others. It was extremely rare that such a vote wasn't unanimous, especially for an incumbent mayor, and Bill Barrett was furious. The party was divided, and it was out in the open.

The drama over this nomination wasn't over, since the recommendation of the policy committee had to be sanctified by the city's sixty-six ward leaders. Congressman Barrett, already knowing that the majority of ward leaders were committed to Hemphill, got up and nominated Jim Tate anyway. Of course, Tate's at this closed door meeting, too, because he's the leader of the 43rd ward, and he was watching very closely how everyone voted. Out of sixty-six votes, Tate only got sixteen, mine being one of them. I'll never forget Bill Barrett up there admonishing the ward leaders for not supporting the incumbent mayor, a man who had stood by them for years. He was turning red in the face as he spoke.

What happened next, I'll never forget. Jim Tate got up and asked Barrett if he could address the ward leaders himself. For the first time in my life, I heard Jim give a forceful, inspiring speech, full of emotion, not a word that wasn't perfect. He said, "You guys will rue the day that you opposed me. I will be around long after you"—and he pointed at some of the guys in the room and called out their names—"and I will *never* forget what happened here today." So many of the guys in that room were Irish Catholics, just like Jim, and he reminded them that he was the first one of them to have been elected mayor of Philadelphia and that they should have stood by him. Earlier that day, Ed Toohey had appealed directly to every single ward leader to support the mayor, and Tate told everyone at the meeting that he had organized labor on his side, too. "I'm going to be elected Mayor again and you will rue what you did here today to me. I've been a good Democrat all my life. You're putting in this blue-blood Hemphill from Chestnut Hill. The people won't vote for a Chestnut Hiller, the people from Philadelphia are working class, they're going to stick with me, believe me!"

From then on, they called the ward leaders who stuck by Mayor Tate the Loyal Sixteen. During Jim's speech I was so proud of the fact that I

Figure 5.3 Philadelphia mayor James H. J. Tate and Wendell W. Young III, 1967. (From the collection of Wendell W. Young III.)

was on his side, even though he only got sixteen votes out of sixty-six. From that day forward, every speech I heard him give was wonderful. I couldn't believe the transformation. It's like a boxer in the ring getting punched in the mouth, struggling through, and coming back and winning by a knockout in the final round. He would turn this race into a crusade, and organized labor's rank and file would be the troops. (See Figure 5.3.)

NOW THAT I WAS ONE of the Loyal Sixteen, my status was boosted in the party—or, at least the portion that Jim Tate controlled. Considering that he was still the mayor, this wasn't a minor thing. In addition to being on the policy committee, Jim Tate called me down to his office at City Hall and said, "Listen Wendell, I know your family. I know your dad and your grandpop are very active in some of the German societies, the Bavarian Clubs up there in the Northeast. A lot of people think Northeast Philly is all Irish and Jews, but there's more Germans up there than all the Irish and Jews put together." He was right about that, too. As part of his effort to reach out to the German American voters in those neighborhoods, Jim asked me to set up meetings and to talk to the various social clubs, since they knew my name. Of course, I was also very active in the largest parish in the city, St. Martin of Tours, and I told him I would get out the word for him there as well.

All of the labor unions across Philadelphia were mobilized for Tate in a way I'd never seen before. Bill McEntee's AFSCME District Council 33, with its seventeen thousand members, took the lead. Tate had reached out to them and supported across-the-board pay raises in 1966, an early pension program, and the union's organizing drive of about eight hundred school crossing guards. They pumped lots of money into AFL-CIO COPE funds. Besides the city workers, the Building Trades and the Teamsters all had committees for him and raised thousands of dollars.

Even with all of the individual unions endorsing Tate, there was something new about how Tate's campaign was coordinated. Labor's efforts were tied together by a centralized plan most of us called the Matt Reese operation. This is because a man named Matt Reese, an election consultant, was hired to oversee the Tate campaign in the neighborhoods, and he introduced some new ideas that shaped the way things were done for years to come. Matt was quite a character. He was really heavyset, one of the biggest men I'd ever seen up to this point, weighing in at over three hundred pounds. He was from the coal districts of West Virginia and had a very heavy Appalachian accent that was hard for many of us to understand. It was funny hearing him out on the streets of South Philadelphia, directing volunteers with his drawl, as he dragged on his cigarette.

Matt Reese got involved in Democratic Party politics in 1960, when he successfully organized the vote in West Virginia for John F. Kennedy during the hotly contested primary against Hubert H. Humphrey. After that, Kennedy brought him to work for the Democratic National Committee in Washington, DC, where he stayed for a couple years. With all of the connections he was making around the country, Matt started his own political consulting firm. His system involved phone banking, residency and voting lists, and Election Day mobilization. Philadelphia ward leaders had always conducted campaigns in their districts with a firsthand knowledge of their constituents in the neighborhoods and by reaching out to them personally to get out to vote for their ticket. This kind of localized strategy was becoming harder to do, since ward leaders could no longer rely on patronage workers in their district to knock on doors to mobilize the vote. Reese formalized a process by which each voter was tracked and contacted. About fifty women were hired to make phone calls to poll about where people were leaning in their voting and to ask people to become block captains for Mayor Tate. In the weeks before the election, eighty thousand people were called and hundreds of volunteers enlisted. To be sure people got out on Election Day, squadrons of cars picked up people and took them to the polls to vote.

During the street campaign leading up to May 16, I was very involved, joining in on the weekly planning sessions on Friday afternoon. All the organizers were assigned to certain wards and given the contacts of specific labor unions to coordinate voter outreach. If you were from South Philadelphia, we would assign the longshoremen or some union with a lot of Italians to work with the ward leaders down there. Each week they'd come in and the ward leaders would say how many new registrations they had signed up and how many voters pledged to Tate. They would tell us how many people they had canvassed, how many doors they had knocked on, what kind of feedback they were getting, and anything else that was happening. The labor leaders would say how many workers they could provide to work the polls on Election Day. Matt Reese did all the background work, all the studies that showed where all the Italians lived,

Figure 5.4 Members of the 35th ward Democratic committee with Mayor Tate during the primary campaign, 1967. (From the collection of Wendell W. Young III.)

where there were concentrations of Jewish voters, and we made sure everyone was covered. With the building trades and transport unions thousands of white ethnic voters were reached, and AFSCME, which represented many African Americans in the Streets Department and other municipal divisions, had strong operations in North and West Philadelphia, sections of South Philadelphia, and Germantown. (See Figure 5.4.)

It was a real gutsy grind-it-out campaign. On Election Day, the whole machine was in operation, volunteers driving people to the polls, posting Tate campaign signs, knocking on every door in the areas they had canvassed previously, all of it paid for with funds raised by Philadelphia labor's COPE. The bottom line, with all this activity, is Tate beat Hemphill in the primary on May 16. Hemphill absolutely got creamed. Tate won it hands down and all the ward leaders who went with Smith were in shock, immediately regretting that they'd broken with the mayor and were now facing the consequences.

With all this internal division, it was still not a foregone conclusion that Jim Tate would be elected in November. Beating Hemphill was only the first hurdle. Philadelphia, like the nation as a whole, was deeply divided, and the house of the old Democratic coalition was coming apart, brick by brick. Throughout the 1960s, the city had experienced a surge in crime, and many voters wanted stronger policing and supported law-and-order policies. The Republican Party was beginning to master this tough rhetoric, and it stood a good chance of winning when Arlen Specter, a young lawyer who'd just been elected district attorney, was their nominee. In what was probably a decisive move, Mayor Tate announced that if reelected, he would reappoint Frank L. Rizzo as police commissioner. This was clearly an attempt to appeal to both the law-and-order sentiments of the city's white ethnic working class, since Rizzo appealed very strongly to the white ethnic vote around the city, and his tough-on-crime stance. In the general election, labor once again went into the streets to mobilize its members, and this played a role. Tate squeaked in by winning by about eleven thousand votes, the closest margin of victory for a mayoral race in the city's history.

Eventually Frank Smith stepped down as Democratic chairman and, with Mayor Tate's nod, was replaced by Congressman Bill Green. Representative Josh Eilberg never buckled into the pressure to back Tate in the primary that year even after labor pushed him to, and I thought that, politically speaking, was the end of him. But about a month or so after the mayor's reelection, I saw Eilberg at a labor-sponsored Christmas party somewhere up in Northeast Philly. Jimmy O'Neill—who had threatened never to support Eilberg again if he didn't back Tate—was up at the podium introducing him, "Here's our man, a true friend of organized labor, Josh Eilberg!" I'm sitting there thinking what the freak is going on? It just blew my mind. Don't forget I was a young guy and still learning how the urban political world worked. I realized then that organized labor could be very flexible and very pragmatic. If you're a friend of theirs, and support their policies, bottom line, you're always a friend.

6

BRAZIL TO CHICAGO

N THE SUMMER OF 1967, a few weeks after Mayor James H. J. Tate's victory in the Democratic Party primary, I left Philadelphia for a two-month tour of Brazil. The trip was funded through the American Institute for Free Labor Development (AIFLD), an organization established by the American government to help foster democratic trade unions in Central and South America. This trip was my first time out of the United States, and, more than any other experience I had up to this point, it changed my views of what it meant to be a labor leader, as well as my views on America's position in the world. During my stay, I visited most of the major cities in Brazil and met with workers, politicians, and unionists in the provinces and through the Amazon, and I was a different man when I returned to Philadelphia. I don't think any single experience in my life changed me more than that trip to South America.

I was one the first of many U.S. labor officials to visit South America in the years after 1960. This region was a hotbed of the global Cold War, and, from Harry Truman on, presidential administrations interceded here to try to shape local conditions and loyalties away from Soviet influence. These policies were intensified after the 1959 Cuban revolution, which posed a major threat to U.S. dominance with a Communist stronghold so close to the mainland. The political orientation of the trade unions in nations like Brazil were closely monitored, since Marxist revolutionaries were always grounded in workers' organizations and, if they held leadership positions, could determine how resources were used and had the potential power to call massive strikes that could paralyze the government. Brazil's labor movement was one of the best organized in South America, with almost twelve million workers in the various labor federations, and, as such, wielded a lot of political power if well directed.

The Cold War directives of the U.S. government, which had the full support of the American labor movement, made perfect sense to me. All through these years, the anticommunist struggle was a basic fact in my life. When I was in college, I served in the ROTC, was very active on the drill team, and for a time seriously considered enlisting in the Army full-time after graduation. I was so upset by what the Communists were doing around the world, especially their espousal of atheistic, anti-Church views. My father and mother were adamantly against me enlisting, but I felt the same way about the Soviet Union as I did about the Third Reich in World War II. These were sentiments shared by almost everyone in the labor movement, and AFL-CIO president George Meany backed President Lyndon Johnson's decision to increase U.S. military operations in Vietnam in 1965. Before I left for Brazil, there was a banner outside the Retail Clerks Union office on Broad Street proclaiming, "We support President Johnson's and President Meany's Vietnam Policy." There is a photo of me with some staff members pointing to it, which was printed in Local 1357's monthly newspaper.

Such sentiments about the Communist threat were shared by almost everyone in the labor movement, both in Philadelphia and across the nation. The AFL-CIO took this matter of fighting Communism seriously because they understood that radicals would always try to take over the labor movement. The fear was that the Communists were infiltrating democratic unions to spread their ideology, and if not checked, could lead to revolutions similar to the one led by Fidel Castro in Cuba.

In early 1967, James A. Suffridge, the top leader of the RCIA, invited me to go to Brazil on what was known as the Union to Union program, which was just starting up with the AFL-CIO. The program was modeled after President Kennedy's People to People program where the United States exchanged cultural figures such as musicians, artists, writers, athletes, and students with other nations to establish personal ties and to demonstrate the U.S. way of life, all as a way to preach democracy.

While I'm sure I could find Brazil on the map before I went there in June 1967, I knew very little about its history or social conditions. Not much coverage was given to South America in the local news, and I wasn't really up on what had been happening. One thing I learned in the training sessions I had before the trip was that there were stark divisions between the very rich and the very poor. This was made worse due to high inflation, which soared out of control in the early 1960s, and these conditions made the country a potential powder keg for popular unrest. The Brazilian labor movement, especially its left wing, was organizing people in the cities and countryside, and in the 1950s could mobilize half a million people into the streets as a show of force. There were worries of a left-leaning rebellion, and with the recent events in Cuba in mind, the military stepped in. In 1964, a military coup assisted by the United States overthrew President João Goulard, who fled to Uruguay. The State Department recognized the new government immediately, hoping it would prove a stable, anticommunist ally. Marshal Humberto de Alencar Castelo Branco, whom Brazil's congress chose to serve as the country's new president, immediately began a purge of the unions, with anyone with known communist connections or even suspicion of leftist sympathies thrown out. From this point on, the military government directly determined all matters pertaining to wage rates and workplace conditions, and because of this the labor movement was severely weakened.

This was the state of affairs in Brazil when the Retail Clerks Union delegation arrived in the summer of 1967. I spent most of my time in Brazil hosted by the *Confederação Nacional dos Trabalhadores no Comércio* (CNTC)—or in English, the National Confederation of Commercial Workers—which represented over three million workers in hotels, coffee distribution, and across the retail sector in over three hundred locals. According to reports, the CNTC had some leaders who were aligned with the Communist Party in the 1950s, so there was a lot of focus on reforming them. The RCIA was a conservative trade union, a model for what the Brazilian union might be, and was heavily invested in this program, which was subsidized through our foreign relations program. The union's foreign relations programs allowed delegates to go around the world representing the United States and give seminars in various countries to promote trade unionism and democracy. It was well known that the guy who ran the foreign relations committee for the RCIA was a former CIA agent. There were about fifteen unionists who were part of the delegation that the RCIA sent to Brazil, mostly staff from the international office in Washington, DC, as well as Herschel Womack, the leader of the RCIA

Figure 6.1 A delegation of members from Brazil's National Confederation of Commercial Workers visiting Philadelphia, 1968. (From the collection of Wendell W. Young III.)

Local 876 out of Detroit, one of the largest sections of the union at that time. (See Figure 6.1.)

In June 1967, the Retail Clerks Union delegation flew from Washington, DC, to Rio de Janeiro and were met at the airport by a bunch of union officials, mostly from the CNTC. From the moment we got there, we were treated like rock stars, with cheering crowds everywhere we went. Hershel was older than me, but he didn't like to give speeches, and we arranged it beforehand that I would do most of the talking at the scheduled assemblies. There at the airport reception, and in all the towns we went to, I'd give a short speech, usually about the role of trade unions in U.S. society and would always end the speech with a "thumbs up" sign. I'd always get great applause and—to my confusion—a considerable amount of laughter.

We're like a week into our trip and at a stadium rally in the city of São Paulo, which had the championship soccer team that Pelé played for at the time. There were about one hundred thousand people at the stadium and I'm with the U.S. ambassador to Brazil, a lot of embassy staffers, the governor of São Paulo, and all these other high-ranking officials. Right at the beginning they ask me to get up and give a speech. It was the largest crowd

I'd ever spoken in front of. I gave this real dramatic speech about the United States and the labor movement and I give the same sign at the end—holding my thumbs in the air. The crowd went crazy. I sat down next to Hershel and the ambassador's wife turns to me and says, "Mr. Young, do you know what it means in Brazil when you give the thumbs up sign like that?" I said that I didn't. She told me that the gesture was tantamount to giving the middle finger. "You are becoming very popular in Brazil. In fact you are all over the television, you are becoming a real star to the young Brazilians, they think it is great that you come down here and give the finger, so to speak," she said. I was mortified, remembering all the places I had done it already. Later on during the trip some of the Brazilian union guys I met who saw me on television said, "Boy, did you really tell us to go fuck ourselves. We really like that coming from a guy your age. A lot of us would like to tell you the same thing."

THERE WERE MORE SERIOUS MATTERS that confronted me and the delegation during this time in Brazil. The AFL-CIO officials overseeing the trip tried to limit my interaction outside of the selected and approved labor representatives and state department officials. Even with them trying to do this, in a country as big as Brazil, and with such a stark division between the classes, they couldn't hide everything from me. I had never seen poverty like the kind I was seeing in Brazil. You walked into the favelas up in the mountains around Rio de Janeiro and see the shacks people lived in, no windows, just tin and cardboard. Very few places had indoor plumbing, and you could see and smell the human waste in the streets and alleys. It was the stark smell of poverty. You can imagine how this impacted health conditions, resulting in high infant mortality, outbreaks of deadly diseases like typhoid fever and cholera, and food contamination and shortened life spans. The guy who was the ambassador told me to just ignore it, but how could I? In one area of hillsides I visited, there had been mudslides, and people lived in what remained of their former houses. I just couldn't believe the conditions.

One of the most shocking incidents I remember was when a group of us went to eat at a restaurant in a favela up in the hills. Young women holding babies were banging on the windows begging for food. To this day, I remember the faces of the mothers outside the restaurants, the desperation in their eyes. Their children were so thin, just like dolls. As I was waiting to go in to eat, some of the women came up to me; I couldn't understand a word they were saying, but I didn't have to. It was worse than anything I'd ever seen in Philadelphia. There was poverty in Philadelphia, but if you sat for lunch in a downtown hotel like the Bellevue-Stratford, you didn't have poor women with babies banging on the windows because they were so hungry. In Brazil, I saw infants clinging to their mothers, hardly any clothes on, and walking barefoot down the streets. There were some AFL-CIO guys there with me that day. They told me to ignore them, that we couldn't feed these people, but I couldn't sit there and eat with all those people starving there. I wanted to give my food to them but I was warned that they would rush me.

Both the American State Department and the AFL-CIO representatives tried to keep me from seeing this dark side of Brazilian life. If it were up to them, I would never have ventured beyond the pleasant world they had set up for me to take in. The State Department people who hosted us were well to do, and they highlighted their affluent lifestyle. They had what seemed like mansions, back garden sections with well-maintained pools, air-conditioned apartments with views of the mountains and ocean, afternoon cocktail parties with beautiful women in bikinis and bossa nova music playing, always six or seven servants on hand—a far extreme to what I had seen on the streets. There were elegant dinner parties at the end of the day, and plenty of opportunities for going to the beach and recreation. They really tried to sell that side of Brazil to me.

Before going on the trip, U.S. officials warned me that even with the recent purges, there were Communists in the labor movement. In all of my speeches in those first few weeks traveling across the country, I spoke about the way the American labor-management system worked with unions and that it was a democracy. I soon realized that some of the labor leaders that I met in Brazil were appointed to their positions by the military government rather than through direct election. Once they got to know me a little, some of the labor guys would open up to me about how bitter they were about the conditions that had developed since the coup, of the crackdown on workers and leftists. None of the basic labor laws were being enforced. If they made any kind of protest, they feared they would be thrown out of the union or even sent to prison. That didn't sound like democracy to me. Listening to these workers, it woke me up completely.

As I listened to the Brazilian unionists speak so frankly, I had insight into the conditions I was witnessing. In contrast to what the American officials were doing, I saw the Communists and the church helping people. I'm making all these trips around to poor villages, all I saw helping the poor were the Communist Party and the trade unions affiliated with them. The Catholic Church was also involved in basic ways. There were numerous Catholic leaders, such as São Paulo archbishop Dom Paulo Evaristo Arns who spoke out for the rights of the poor, and priests and nuns who were involved in the communities, connecting the teachings of Christ with the uplift of the poor and oppressed. In stark contrast, the Brazilian dictatorship and U.S. government officials were hampering any efforts to help the poor.

Of course, there were reasons why I was chosen by the RCIA international to go on this trip, although I was too naive to realize it at the time. I am pretty sure I was sent to Brazil with the plan that I would be recruited into the union's program to work for the CIA, which, if I accepted, would remove me from my union position in Philadelphia. They figured I was very young and idealistic and that I could be easily influenced. But what I saw in Brazil got me too emotionally involved, and the opposite happened. These Third World conditions I witnessed were the direct result of American policy, which supported corporations and permitted maximum profits to be taken from the country. Everywhere I went, there were so many gas stations with the names of American companies. They were there maximizing their profits; it was one of the reasons why there was so much poverty. When the trip was over, the AIFLD directors who coordinated the program gave me a debriefing session and I let them have it. I was emphatic that they didn't give any attention to the poor and that the poverty was made worse because of the way our companies were doing business there.

The more I witnessed the contradictions between American rhetoric about encouraging a free society and institutions in Brazil, and the reality of economic power, I started to rethink my opinions of broader U.S. foreign policy, especially in Southeast Asia. Since 1965, President Johnson escalated the war in Vietnam, justifying the actions as a needed response to Communist aggression. I now questioned this premise. I figured, if we're doing the kinds of things I saw in Brazil, a country that supposedly was a friend of ours, no wonder the Vietnamese were fighting us. American policy was aimed at maximizing the profits of corporations and enriching the elites at the expense of the poor. I started reading more about what was happening in Vietnam, and I reconsidered everything I previously believed. It hit me at a gut level. The issue was brought home to me also because some of the boys I taught at Northeast Catholic High School had been drafted. I realized that working-class kids from places like Northeast Philly were fighting the war. I couldn't wait to get home and speak out against what was going on.

I was really a changed man by the time I returned to Philadelphia in August 1967. The morning I got back to the union office on Broad Street, I saw the sign that said how Local 1357 supported President Johnson's policy in Vietnam. "Take that sign down," I ordered. "As long as I'm president of this local, that sign stays down."

FROM THE SUMMER OF 1967 on, I became an unusual figure in the U.S. labor movement: an antiwar activist. When I returned, I thought that I owed it to my members to explain what I had seen in Brazil, and at the next general membership meeting, I spoke for almost two hours. My staff was taken aback. They didn't support my antiwar position and warned me that if I continued to speak out as I was doing, it might lead the international union in Washington to put the local into trusteeship. I knew they were right, too. Many of the older labor leaders in the city didn't like me to begin with. In the two years prior to my trip to Brazil, my support of the civil rights movement and work with local figures like Rev. Leon Sullivan set me apart, and now, by joining the antiwar movement, some would say I had gone too far. Philadelphia's AFL-CIO supported the war unequivocally, and unions across the nation were closer to President Lyndon Johnson than perhaps any other administration in history. They stood behind his entire program, domestic and foreign. Even Joe Schwartz, the outspoken liberal leader of the ILGWU, who I really considered a progressive figure in the Philadelphia labor movement, was an out-and-out hawk, in total support of Johnson's Vietnam policy. He even resigned his membership with the liberal political group ADA after their executive committee came out against the war, something I found really shocking.

There was only a tiny antiwar movement in Philadelphia by mid-1967, but as combat operations increased and more men were drafted, national sentiment against the war got more vocal and took on more significance.

The first antiwar protests in Philadelphia came about in early 1965, called together by the local chapter of the National Committee for a Sane Nuclear Policy (SANE) and Women Strike for Peace. Volunteers from both groups set up petition tables outside City Hall, distributing literature calling for a negotiated settlement with the North Vietnamese and an end to U.S. military involvement. More people started showing up at these protests and by the end of the year, a new organization, the Philadelphia Area Committee to End the War was formed. Most of the energy for this movement came from college campuses and religious groups like the Religious Society of Friends—the Quakers—who constituted an outspoken minority in the Philadelphia region. Students at Temple University, the University of Pennsylvania, Haverford College, and Swarthmore College formed chapters of SDS and organized teach-ins and protests on campuses. High school students across the region joined this protest too, hundreds showed up for candle vigils outside City Hall and Rittenhouse Square.

The student-led antiwar movement in Philadelphia was part of what was being described around the nation as the New Left. Emerging in the early 1960s around antinuclear protests and based on a critique of modern society, I felt very much at home with their social critique. Less sectarian than the old left, this youth-led movement emphasized individual expression and called for breaking down social barriers that limited people because of their race, gender, and sexuality. For me, these concerns paralleled the reform spirit of Vatican II, challenging entrenched authority and encouraging lay involvement to forge a more open and just society. The kinds of priorities that guided me since taking leadership of the Retail Clerks Union in Philadelphia perfectly fit with the New Left. As a student-based organization, the SDS was sometimes understood as the critical mouthpiece of the New Left. When I read the Port Huron Statement, the set of principles on which the organization was founded in 1960, I agreed with everything in it. The way it addressed the problem of alienation, pointing out that modern, bureaucratic institutions isolated individuals away from a shared sense of community, resonated with me, and I saw this as a struggle in the lives of the retail store workers I represented. I wanted the clerks and cashiers to know they have a voice, rather than feel that they are cogs of a machine. Although I had graduated from St. Joseph's College in 1960, and it had very little student movement to speak of, I considered myself part of this movement. I believed young people could and should make contributions in the political arena and could remake society along more humane ideals. Over the coming decade, I would be a leader in this new movement and connect it to both the labor movement and the Democratic Party.

Most of the members of the Retail Clerks Union did not agree with me on the war, and as such, I didn't have much to bring to the antiwar coalition: no financial resources, or even bodies to bring to rallies—it was just me expressing my independent view. Some of the younger members joined me at the antiwar protests around the city, but that was it. I was one of the only antiwar voices that came out of Philadelphia's labor scene, but even this token of labor support that I represented was highly valued in the movement, and I was often billed as a speaker at public rallies and asked to serve on various committees.

The one Philadelphia labor leader in the region who joined me in the peace movement was Dave Neifeld, a rare remnant of the old left who, ironically, came out of the Retail Clerks Union. Dave got involved with the labor movement in the 1930s when he was still in his twenties as an organizer with Local 18 of the United Retail, Wholesale and Department Stores (URWDS-CIO). This union broke with the CIO and formed an independent organization that eventually merged with the RCIA in the 1950s, as Local 415. Dave led this small four hundred-member local that represented workers in some variety stores around the city, and we became friends. Dave understood the world of left-wing politics in ways that I did not, and I relied on him to navigate it.

Dave and I joined a new national organization called the Labor Leadership Assembly for Peace (LLAP), an antiwar organization founded by a section of progressive labor leaders that included the Meat Cutters Union national president Patrick Gorman, Hospital Workers leaders Moe Foner and Leon Davis, and Emil Mazey of the United Auto Workers. At its peak, the group had about five hundred members and hosted roundtables and sent literature to union members, mostly focusing on the fact that working people were fighting the war against their own interest. One of the LLAP's main spokesmen was Harold J. Gibbons, a Teamsters leader who came out against the war early on. To me, he was really the force in this group, and he became a kind of role model for me in these years. LLAP's connections to union rank and file were important in showing that not all men and women in the unions went along with the AFL-CIO positions on Vietnam. It was important to give them a voice and

Figure 6.2 Wendell W. Young III with Teamsters leader Howard J. Gibbons at a Labor Leadership Assembly for Peace meeting, 1968. (From the collection of Wendell W. Young III.)

to encourage politicians to represent their views. In November 1967, Gibbons invited Minnesota senator Eugene McCarthy to speak at one of their national sessions. That's how I found out about him and his antiwar campaign message. (See Figure 6.2.)

It was important for me to have these personal connections with other antiwar labor leaders around the country because in Philadelphia, I was taking a lot of flak for the position I'd taken. Within the labor movement, a lot of people started calling me a Communist, especially from guys in the building trades. I would never let that go. I always used to say back, "I'm either a lousy Communist or a lousy Catholic. But I'm a Catholic, so I'm a lousy Communist because one doesn't go with the other." It could get pretty ugly. But by far, the worst pushback I received came from my own members in Retail Clerks Local 1357. Before 1968, most of the workers in the food markets supported the war, and this was especially so among the many World War II and Korean War combat veterans who were clerks or meat cutters. I started getting anonymous letters from union members, physically threatening me. My father saw one of these letters and told me he thought I was taking a lot of chances. He was even worried I might get killed. Only a few months after I returned from Brazil there was a drive to impeach me as union president. The members voted—it wasn't a secret ballot; it was a standing vote—and I stayed in office by just one person. A year later, the prowar delegates brought it up again and that time I passed by two votes. I was extremely anxious about this, but I figured I was doing the right thing, and if they get rid of me, they get rid of me.

It wasn't easy for me to take such an unpopular position, but I believed that the war was against the real interests of working-class men and women. Public opinions on the war were changing, too. In January 1968, the Communist Vietcong launched a major offensive, and although defeated, the televised broadcasts of the street fighting led a lot of Americans to question the administration's policies. It was working-class boys who were being killed, kids just out of Philadelphia high schools like North Catholic, Cardinal Dougherty, Father Judge, Overbrook, and Edison. Many of the people in the stores I represented had sons who were drafted or had enlisted and were in combat operations. The antiwar movement on the campuses was coming into the streets and almost nightly there were television images of marches, students burning draft cards, and confrontations with police.

In early 1968, the antiwar demonstrations were gaining more support, with hundreds and at times thousands of marchers showing up to rallies coordinated by the resistance. I was often at these rallies in Philadelphia, at City Hall or Rittenhouse Square, with a small section of Retail Clerks Union members, mostly young part-timers. As much as I thought these mass rallies were important, I was still a Democratic Party ward leader, and I believed that significant change could come only through the formal political process. The main way to break the cycle of war was to change policy at the top, and getting involved in the 1968 presidential election was the most important way to push for this. It was obvious that President Johnson was not going to shift his position on the war, especially after bombing raids of North Vietnam intensified. Even though he had such close ties to the AFL-CIO, I couldn't support him.

Johnson had so much power and the backing of the entire labor move-ment, it didn't seem likely that he could be defeated. In early 1968, the an-tiwar coalition was uniting behind Minnesota senator Eugene McCarthy, who by January was the only candidate challenging President Johnson in the primaries. I knew about McCarthy because he had spoken before a gathering of the Labor Assembly against the war, and I liked him right away. McCarthy was Catholic, and like me, had thought seriously about the priesthood in his youth; but unlike in 1960, when I was drawn to Kennedy because of his religion, it was McCarthy's antiwar position rather than his Catholicism that attracted me to him. It didn't hurt that he was one of the most liberal senators in Washington and had a strong prounion voting rec-ord. Gene was committed to legislation that provided livable incomes, ex-panded medical care, education, and housing and was a cosponsor of the 1964 and 1965 Civil Rights Acts. There was nothing about him to not like as far as I was concerned.

No one thought McCarthy could seriously take on President Johnson, but after he almost beat him in the New Hampshire primary on March 12 with 42 percent of the vote, everyone on his campaign knew things were changing. A few weeks later, Johnson went on television and an-nounced he was not seeking reelection. I knew it was now feasible that Gene could win. If he was to do so, Pennsylvania would be a critical state, and I got involved in the campaign. Most of the support McCarthy had in the Philadelphia region, as elsewhere, came from college students. The first meeting for him was held at the University of Pennsylvania, where eight hundred students showed up.

Gene McCarthy's campaign in Philly was a pretty small operation, with a meager budget that didn't allow for radio or television ads. A cen-tral campaign office was set up in the Victory Building, 1001 Chestnut Street, and it was always busy with young volunteers who were focused on mobilizing other college students to support the antiwar position. Into the spring, I was determined to get his message out in Northeast Phila-delphia, to move it beyond the college campuses, to meet working-class people who had so much at stake. A door-to-door campaign was started in Northeast Philadelphia, mostly in the Mayfair and Oxford Circle sec-tions where I had teams of stewards and some younger members from the supermarkets join me on the weekends, dropping McCarthy campaign brochures in mailboxes and getting petitions signed. Most of these young volunteers had never canvassed a neighborhood before, and weren't ready for hostile responses from prowar people. One of the canvassers said, "Mr. Young, I had about six doors slammed on me today." I'd say, "Listen, how many didn't?" "Eight or nine." "Good. Then we're ahead of the game." These neighborhoods were where many men and women had sons who'd been drafted or enlisted to fight in Vietnam, and it is sometimes overlooked, but a significant number of people in Northeast Philadelphia were against the war, especially the mothers.

Pennsylvania's primary was scheduled for the last week of April, and the presidential race was quickly changing. After President Johnson announced he wasn't seeking reelection in late March, Vice President Humphrey immediately got in, followed by New York senator Robert F. Kennedy, who had a large following with young voters as well as the support of Congressman Bill Green. Under Mayor Tate's direction, the regular Democratic Party machine in Philadelphia was solid for Humphrey. Whenever I'd go to the monthly Democratic central committee meeting with the other ward leaders, guys would make speeches for him, and pledged to get out the vote for him in their divisions. I kept quiet, though, and never came out publicly for McCarthy. Humphrey was labor's man, no question about it. I liked him too, but he was in Johnson's pocket and prowar, and I wouldn't support him. I knew Humphrey had the resources to win in Philadelphia, and it would be difficult to work against that tide. McCarthy was the only candidate registered on the ballot in Pennsylvania primary on April 23 since the other candidates entered the race so late in the game, and even with many write-ins for Kennedy or Humphrey, Gene got seventy-five thousand votes in Philadelphia, and almost half a million votes across the commonwealth, far more than we had dreamed possible.

With that kind of showing in Pennsylvania and elsewhere, I knew that Senator McCarthy was no longer such a dark horse, that he actually stood a chance at securing the nomination that summer. After Robert F. Kennedy was assassinated in early June, it seemed possible that his supporters would move to support Gene. With so much uncertainty, I knew that the Democratic National Convention scheduled in Chicago later that summer would decide the ticket. I felt it was important to be there, to get on as a delegate to represent the antiwar position. Since I was a ward leader, I had no trouble getting the votes I needed to do so, and in late August, my old friend from St. Joseph's College Nick Clemente and I went out to Chicago together, staying at a room in the Conrad Hilton Hotel where a lot of the action would take place. Over the course of the week we were there, I witnessed things that I could hardly at times believe. I had been a delegate to the 1964 Democratic Convention in Atlantic City, where it was a sure thing that President Johnson would get the call, but the week I spent in Chicago was without question the most tense political gathering I had ever been part of.

Most of the Philadelphia delegation flew out together the day before the convention started, and Mayor James H. J. Tate met us at the airport. He was there early since he was on the credentials committee and he had been in meetings with Vice President Hubert H. Humphrey all week, making plans to get him nominated on the first ballot. He and Humphrey were very close friends, and there was some talk about Tate joining his administration as a cabinet member. Humphrey was all Jim talked about, explaining how good he would be to the big cities if he were elected. Tate was so certain that all of the ward leaders were on the same page with him that he never even asked who we supported leading up to the trip to Chicago.

The next day, Jim calls together a meeting of the Philadelphia section of the Pennsylvania delegation to get his house in order. A roll call vote started, each member calling out whom they were committed to. Of course, my name being Young, I'm at the end, the very last delegate. As names are called, every single delegate declared for Humphrey, until they get to me. I stood up and shouted, "McCarthy!" Tate glared over at me, and said, "What do you mean, McCarthy?" I said, "Eugene McCarthy. That's who I'm for." The mayor wanted to make the Philadelphia contingent's vote unanimous and he was absolutely livid. I could see him turning red. He actually started yelling, pointing his finger at me, calling me a kid. Had he known I wasn't for Humphrey, he probably would have fought to get me out of the delegation, but nobody ever asked me who I was for. He was really angry with me.

It wasn't easy for me to go against Mayor Tate. I liked him personally and knew he was an important ally, but I believed too much was at stake. It was a moral issue for me. The war in Vietnam was wrong, and I was going to support anyone who said they would work to end it. I was one of the few McCarthy delegates from Pennsylvania, and most of my time there on the floor was spent with a group of his supporters from the Pittsburgh area. Despite the fact that Humphrey's delegates outnumbered us, we had a considerable say in how the convention proceeded. At any national convention, state leaders usually pay delegates some token money to serve as sergeants-at-arms and McCarthy supporters, mostly college students, gobbled that up. Half the people who took these positions were McCarthy backers and when a debate began over a resolution to have the convention support an end to the bombing of North Vietnam and a negotiated settlement of the conflict, some Humphrey delegates, who were against the resolution, were pushed off the floor. At one point, Jim Tate came over and screamed at me that my people were controlling the proceedings. He couldn't even get to the microphone sometimes, and he was the head of the delegation. They never dreamed that the peace movement would be this organized and by the time the convention began, it was too late for them to do anything about it.

Jim was all upset with me. I overheard his wife, Anne Marie, talking to him, trying to calm him down, reminding him that I'd been one of the few ward leaders who had been loyal to him the previous year, and urging him not to overreact. I hate to say it, because I really liked him, but Tate was ugly at that convention, the way that he responded to the opposition. Maybe I was ugly, too, but I thought I was right. People were so locked into their position it was very divisive. I was very emotional about it. I didn't care if I got killed doing it. I mean, that's how most of us felt.

As I mentioned, one of the primary objectives the McCarthy supporters had was the adoption of a peace plank calling for the end of bombing raids in North Vietnam, and a negotiated settlement, where troops from both the United States and North Vietnam exited South Vietnam. The convention was divided on this point. Tate stood with Humphrey and opposed the measure, and, on the other side, Senator Joseph S. Clark and Congressman Green worked with us to get it adopted. A fierce debate ensued on the convention floor the evening of August 27. We were in the middle of the delegation as the television cameras rolled, yelling "Peace now, stop the war!" It was chaotic. I remember seeing Chicago's Mayor Daley screaming at some of the McCarthy delegates, turning red. He had ordered Chicago police in there; he wouldn't move—it was an ugly situation. The peace measure failed, and, with it, McCarthy's challenge seemed at an end. Later that night the deciding votes for the nomination were counted, and it was obvious that Gene McCarthy didn't have enough to win. On the streets, police beat protesters with nightsticks, in shocking images televised across the world.

When I got back to Philadelphia, the AFL-CIO mobilized for Humphrey with the same all-out blitz they had given to the Tate campaign the year before. The AFL-CIO's COPE raised $250,000 to fuel the get-out-the-vote efforts. Right before the election, Eugene McCarthy came out and endorsed the vice president, even though Humphrey had not changed his war position. I wasn't sure if I could support Humphrey at first but thought that Richard Nixon in the White House was an even worse scenario. I was busy through the autumn, working as cochair of the Eilberg for Congress committee. On Election Day, Philadelphia had a massive turnout for Humphrey, and he won the city by a 270,000 majority, enough to put Pennsylvania in the Democratic column. The same wasn't true across the country, though, and Nixon was elected. I knew we would face very difficult days ahead. The man who John F. Kennedy had beaten in 1960 would be president after all.

7

REFORMING THE RETAIL CLERKS

ITH ALL THAT WAS GOING ON, 1968 had to be one of the busiest years of my life. Not only was I leading Local 1357 and involved with the McCarthy campaign and the antiwar movement in Philadelphia but I also was in the thick of a major drive to take on and remove the existing national leadership of the Retail Clerks Union. In many ways, this effort took my local reform efforts to the national union, in a campaign to make an autocratic organization into one that gave the membership more of a say. Although this reform struggle has been mostly overlooked in labor history, the campaign we launched was one of the most significant grassroots efforts in a U.S. labor union from this period, one that would have an impact on how the union functioned well into the future.

The RCIA was, by 1968, one of the fastest-growing labor unions in the United States, beginning to rival the Steelworkers, Teamsters, and United Auto Workers. Some believed that the clerks were on the way to representing the largest number of workers in the nation, perhaps as soon as the end of the decade. Despite the fact that we were a potential force, I didn't consider the RCIA very democratic. It was a very top-down organization, ruled by the leadership in Washington, DC, with very little input from the members in the stores. Since the union's founding, there had been few attempts to change this, but there was some dissent brewing among the union's rank and file, especially from younger members who were making up a larger percentage of the dues payers. In 1968, a national movement emerged to reform the way the union was set up. The name of this reform group was the "Three R's" (RRR), which stood for Reformation, Revitalization, Reconstruction. I was a leader of this movement, slated on the ticket to run for one of the union's ten national vice presidential slots.

My involvement with the reform movement was driven, in large part, by the bad experiences I had with the international union. When the Meet the Challenge slate came in back in early 1963, we kept the office staff that had served the previous administration. I kept on all of the secretaries because I wouldn't know how to train new ones and had no idea how to run an office. This, I soon realized, was a mistake. I started noticing some things that seemed a little strange. One of the secretaries used to take a cab every day from South Philadelphia. That wasn't a ride around the corner. In morning traffic, it would have been like a twenty-minute commute. I knew that if I lived in South Philly, I wouldn't be able to take a cab each day, and here she is, one of our secretaries—with the money we're paying her? Something didn't seem right.

I began an investigation into the union's finances, looking through the records we had on file and asking questions about how things were being run. One of the girls from the office came to me and spilled the beans. She told me that for years, there had been a lot of stealing going on. The setup was simple: members would come in with cash to pay their union dues, but the money never got deposited. Both the office secretaries and the union's top officers were in on it, everyone taking a share. They were open about it, with the old president Henry Highland even explaining to everyone how to cover it up.

I called up our accounting firm, which I also had retained from the Highland administration, and told them to do an official audit; but, as I should have known, they were more interested in covering their own ass. I was reluctant to bring this issue up with the RCIA international officials in Washington, DC, since I felt I wouldn't get a fair shake because they were always fighting everything I did. So I did something a little unusual. I went down to see the Philadelphia district attorney James Crumlish, whom I had gotten to know over the previous few years from my political involvement in the city. Since I was a Democratic committeeman, I was an insider with the party leaders and knew that I could get fair treatment. I leveled with Crumlish about my concerns and he said he would help me get them straightened out with an audit. He called in Chief County Detective Francis J. Lederer, who agreed to come back with me to the office to begin an investigation that very afternoon. He said he'd see what's wrong and do the right thing for me. That's when I really got to know him.

I made one big mistake the day I went down to see the district attorney: I told some of the people in the office that I was going to do it. I realized my blunder when I was coming back to the office, driving with Franny down Broad Street. We noticed that a lot of smoke was coming from the direction of the union office, like the building was on fire.

"Holy shit, what is that?" I blurted.

Franny said, "I bet I know what it is. It's your records being burned!"

As soon as we pull into the back driveway, we see several metal trash cans, fires roaring out of all of them. Franny was right. The girls had destroyed all the local's financial records.

I hadn't expected this and realized how naive I had been. I knew right then that I had underestimated how bad the scheme was. All the women denied doing it, and we subpoenaed the other secretaries and the district attorney's office talked to them. The secretaries didn't even get a lawyer. They just didn't say anything, or swore they didn't know anything about it. The DA's office recommended an outside accounting firm to do a full audit, and, after it was completed, it was determined from the few records that were left that at least three hundred thousand dollars had been stolen over a fifteen-year period. That's just with the records that didn't make it into the burning trash cans—it was probably worse than that. I was sick about it, and I turned it over to the insurance company because I didn't have anything to do with it. The union was reimbursed for about 75 percent of what was taken by Highland and the others who were in on the scheme, but the RCIA international wrote me a nasty letter, essentially saying, "Who the hell goes to the DA to help them with an internal theft problem?"

There are some other stories that detail the ways that lines got crossed between me and the RCIA's top leadership in Washington, DC, in the first years after I came on as president of Local 1357. For one thing, the way I got behind the civil rights movement, specifically the demands to open up more jobs for African Americans in the region's supermarkets and warehouses, was a point of tension with some top leaders in my organization. Since the 400 Ministers campaign in Acme Markets, I remained close to Rev. Leon L. Sullivan, and followed what he was doing. In 1963, he founded the Opportunities Industrialization

Center (OIC), an organization that trained young African Americans to succeed in the job market. With federal aid and support from local businesses, OIC had a headquarters in North Philadelphia where participants took classes in vocational programs in math and literacy and learned the basics in such areas as office work, food services, construction trades, and textile and machine operators. In its first year, Sullivan's program trained over a thousand men and women, and it expanded in the following years.

WITH THESE INITIAL ADVANCEMENTS IN the City of Brotherly Love, Rev. Sullivan called me up sometime in 1967 because he wanted to take the OIC national and he figured all of the Retail Clerks Union chapters all over the country might be as supportive as I had been and help him out. He wanted to make the organization union, and I thought that was great, and I told him I would talk to James A. Suffridge, the RCIA's international president, to see if we could encourage the program and get it some publicity. I called Suffrage up and asked him for a meeting telling him there was a gentleman here in Philadelphia who's going to go national with the OIC and he wanted them to be unionized. I gave some background and explained that his organization helps black people in urban areas. I didn't mention that Sullivan himself was black, and didn't think of it. Looking back on it, maybe with an Irish-sounding name, Suffridge assumed he was white. At any rate, Suffridge told me to bring the minister down so he could meet him. He even suggested that Rev. Sullivan might be a good person to schedule to speak at the Retail Clerk's national convention that was planned for later that summer.

To put what happened next into some context, keep in mind that to me, James A. Suffridge was a really big man, very powerful. Even though he was a Republican, he was very close to President Johnson, and there had even been some speculation that he might be named secretary of labor in the president's cabinet. Some also thought that one day he might replace George Meany as president of the AFL-CIO. So to me, as this young labor leader, it was a big deal to have this conference with him. On the day of the meeting, Rev. Sullivan and I took a red-eye flight to Washington, DC, and got to the RCIA building bright and early. Suffridge's receptionist told him we were here for him, and, a few minutes later, he calls me into his office and the first thing he says to me is, "Why'd you bring that nigger down here? You think I'm going to put him on the convention floor? You're crazy! The convention this year is in Florida. Besides, I don't want to make business with any nigger." I stood there and looked at him, dumbfounded. I was almost beginning to cry right there in the office. He ordered me to get out, saying, "You take him back to Philly, you play with him back in Philly." That's exactly what he said to me.

When I came out of Jim Suffridge's office, Rev. Sullivan looked at me, and he must have read me right away. He said, "Wendell, I know what you went through. It happens to me all the time. Don't worry about it. You tried your best." But it affected me very, very deeply. On the plane back to Philadelphia, I sat next to the reverend with my eyes pouring out. He tried to console me, "Please Wendell, don't worry about it. This is what we go through all the time. It's a very rare person in the white community who gives a crap about us, whether in the North or the South." I had known about this. I wasn't blind to the way things were; but it was very hard for me to see how ugly a person can be—Suffridge, our great president, had turned a good man away just because of his skin color.

The way that James A. Suffridge treated us that day was not an isolated incident. I had another taste of this kind of behavior later that summer when I took some of my staff down to the RCIA national convention in Miami, Florida. It was my first trip to the South, and the Philadelphia local was one of the few in the nation that had black delegates or staff members. The facts of Jim Crow were felt that very first day: I couldn't get Local 1357's African American delegates into the hotel where the convention was booked. They turned us out, telling us it was a white-only establishment. I refused to stay, and we all wound up going somewhere else. I made a point of this at the convention, but Suffridge and the rest of the RCIA international board were pissed off at me because I had brought black delegates into the convention in the first place. They didn't offer any help and didn't speak out against what had happened. My hostility to James A. Suffridge, Jim Housewright, and the rest of the top-tier Retail Clerks Union leadership hardened like a diamond.

WITH THESE STORIES IN MIND, to say that I had started off on the wrong note with the RCIA international in the days after coming into union office would have been an understatement. In 1964, RCIA District

Council 11 chairman John T. Haletsky, who I was friendly with, left Philadelphia and became a regional director with the RCIA international in Southern California. Replacing him in the middle Atlantic region was James T. Housewright, who I already got to know. As I had mentioned before, because I was seen as an upstart and a radical, Housewright right away did not like me. He did everything in his power to put me in short pants. I know that Housewright's stance against me had the tacit approval of many of the older leaders from RCIA locals in South Jersey, Baltimore, and Washington. Some of them felt threatened by how outspoken I was and worried that I might encourage other young members and part-time guys to get involved and run for office and take over their positions, just as I had done to Henry Highland.

Sometimes I bucked the way things were done in the RCIA, often without knowing it. This brought the ire of the higher-ups down upon me. After 1962, I made a lot of changes in Local 1357, hiring a new organizing director and bringing on a new legal firm to handle arbitration, since the lawyers we had seemed more connected to the international than the local. Housewright decided that I had overstepped my authority since I didn't seek the international's approval on any of these measures. He waited until I was away at a conference and sent a letter to the Local 1357 executive committee, informing them that the RCIA international was initiating an investigation to see how the union was being run in Philly. A committee was formed, and, under the direction of a lawyer from the international union in Washington, DC, a new set of bylaws and constitution were handed down, basically stripping me of all power. Under the new rules, I no longer had the authority to hire or fire staff without the approval of the majority of the executive board. A lot of this was political: there were a few members on the board who wanted more staff jobs for people they were close to and because I didn't give those to them, they were pissed off at me.

Jim Housewright directed all of these moves to block me, and because of that I knew I couldn't trust him. He represented everything I thought was wrong with the international union, but he was James A. Suffridge's right-hand man and a rising star in the organization. In early 1968, Suffridge called me up and said that he wasn't going to run for reelection that year and asked me to support Housewright as his replacement. I had real reservations, but I didn't say no to him outright; I told him I'd have to think about it.

I thought it was a little odd that James A. Suffridge, who knew I didn't like him, called me up to ask for my support personally. I didn't know at that time that there was a rising dissent movement within the Retail Clerks Union and that there already was a movement to challenge the old guard leadership that year. Others in the union were as unhappy with the status quo as I was. John T. Haletsky, the former president of Local 1393 out in Reading, Pennsylvania, and the organizing director of the RCIA's Southwestern Division called me from California soon after to tell me he was going to run for president. I knew John pretty well, I told him right away that I would support him. He then told me he and some of the other reformers wanted me to run with them as a vice president, since a lot of members around the country knew my name and had heard that I led a successful reform effort in Philadelphia. I said no, but he told me to think about it. After a couple days, I called him back and accepted.

The one problem was that I was slated to run against one of the incumbent international officers, a guy named Jim McGuire, whom I happened to be very friendly with and thought was a good union representative. I told Haletsky that McGuire was the only guy in the international I got along with. So, naive me, I get off the phone and I search for McGuire's number, thinking I ought to call him and tell him myself, in all fairness, no hard feelings. So I get him on the phone and tell him I was running against him and he screams, "Fuck you, Wendell! I tried to be nice to you and you run against me!" Click!

I called him back but he called me "a fucking whore" and hung up on me again. I had never heard him use that kind of language before and I was really upset about it. I called John T. Haletsky and told him what had happened, and he said, "Wendell, what did you expect?" I said, "But he's taking it personal." John was silent for a moment and then said, "It is personal, Wendell. You're running against him. Don't you understand how politics works? You're a Philadelphia ward leader; you ought to know that stuff. You ran against Henry Highland didn't you?" I said, "Yeah, but he was doing a lousy job. McGuire's doing a decent job." John just told me to be strong. "That's politics. Just get over it and mature over it." It was one of the toughest things I ever had to do.

By the time I was on board, the reform movement had a name: Reformation, Revitalization, Reconstruction, which was known as the "Three R's," or RRR. Just like the Meet the Challenge campaign changed Local 1357, the RRR movement wanted to give power back to the members. Our platform pledged to make the union's governance less autocratic by having members participate in general elections and to encourage more dialogue. We were going to make officers of the international union be local union people and shorten the times between elections, down to three years from five. Rather than receiving directives from the international president, the reformers called for more local autonomy and, reciprocally, allowing regional council to have more say in how the international office was run. We also believed that the RCIA needed to prioritize organizing new workers, to move beyond what it had been doing to mobilize for this at an unprecedented level, to bring in more than a million members over the coming decade. To do so, we would also have to strengthen the union's political power, both in the communities where we lived and in Washington, DC. I knew of the kinds of real changes that had happened in Philadelphia and was confident it could be done at the national level.

Of course, once the reform movement made its move, the RRR leaders became targets. With my opposition to him out in the open, Jim Housewright tried to force me out through intimidation. The RCIA had sought a few years before to weaken me by changing Local 1357's bylaws and constitution, but now an all-out effort to remove me from office began. During a meeting in Washington, DC, I was tipped off by Chuck Lipson, director of the RCIA Active Ballot Club (ABC), that the international was going to put Local 1357 into trusteeship on an allegation that I had misused political funds. He said I had illegally appropriated ten thousand dollars of political action money for Jim Tate's 1967 reelection campaign without prior authorization of the international union. According to the ABC's rules, individual locals were supposed to forward all money collected to the international, which would then channel back a portion to the local union. It was true—I overstepped this process and kept all of the money to spend on the mayor's campaign, considering how important the race was.

When I heard what was planned, I immediately went back to Philadelphia, called all of Local 1357's business agents in off the street, and told them what was going on. I got a leave of absence for two of the biggest men we had in the local and I told them that for the next two weeks or more, they were going to stand guard at the union office front door. "No one gets in this office unless I say so," I instructed them.

I knew I would have to call on some of my political allies in Philadelphia if I stood any chance of winning this fight with my international union. Luckily, I had some pull with the police department because of my ties to Mayor Jim Tate. He was able to give some directions to the top brass about what was going on and get them to go along with what I needed. On top of that, the father-in-law of Joe Kelly, one of our business agents, was in charge of the district police office, where our union head-quarters was, and he agreed beforehand to send out a patrol wagon to arrest anyone we said was trespassing on our property. This was import-ant, because sure enough, the very next day, three vice presidents from the Retail Clerks Union international showed up at our office to take over operations. I called the police district office and a squadron car showed up minutes later to escort them off the premises. Some union official from James A. Suffridge's office called me up, absolutely furious. I held my ground. That was the first time they came after me, and, in many ways, that skirmish at Local 1357's headquarters marked the beginning of the RRR campaign. Round one, I won.

James A. Suffridge and his old guard alliance did not want to concede their power, and they were worried because the RRR campaign wasn't just a single, isolated local challenging their authority but a national, coast-to-coast movement. This was the first real power struggle in the union going back to the early 1940s.

The real force behind the reform movement was Joseph DeSilva, one of the most far-sighted leaders, not just in the RCIA, but the entire American labor movement. Joe was born in New York City and had gone out to Hollywood in the early 1920s with the hope of becoming an actor. He didn't get onto any movies but took a job as a clerk in a supermarket, and, in the 1930s, he organized his store into the Retail Clerks Union Local 770. Within a few years, the local had eighteen thousand members and was one of the most innovative in the nation, with benefits that no one else even thought of, including an alcoholics' recovery program, educa-tion benefits, and full dental and mental health coverage. Joe understood the power of media in getting a prounion message out to the public, and he hosted a radio program and eventually a weekly Sunday night tele-vision show that highlighted union achievements and the lives of working people across the region. Despite these innovations, Joe found the inter-national union difficult to work with and too top heavy and politically conservative to think ahead. He believed, as I did, that the RCIA could be the strongest, largest union in the United States, but, for that to hap-pen, a lot of change was necessary.

I had directed a reform movement to take over control of the Retail Clerks Union in Philadelphia a few years before, but to pull off a similar challenge against the international union would require much more planning and aid. For one thing, we would need the assistance of an experienced lawyer, one who was versed in the labor movement and who wasn't afraid to get involved. At first, I reached out to a lawyer from Philadelphia named Joe Dougherty who had been the attorney for a dissident group from the Teamsters Union known as The Voice. I knew that Joe could do the job, but he told me he was too busy and recommended we reach out to a lawyer named Mozart Ratner. Just as Joe mentioned, Moe had a lot of experience going back to the 1930s, and I met with him and told him about our reform movement and asked if he would represent us. He told me he would consider it but made it clear that it would be costly—over a million dollars.

I reported back to the RRR committee and we decided that Moe Ratner would be our man. We then turned to raising the kind of money needed to get him on board and went right to our supporters by setting up the Committee for a Democratic Election to raise voluntary funds. All the RCIA locals that we knew were backing our slate formed these committees so we could pool resources to pay Mozart. In Philadelphia's Local 1357, we had our members vote on it, and they agreed to a dues increase just to raise money for the committee. From January to June we tried to get as many locals around the country to nominate the RRR opposition ticket, an important process since Suffridge's aim was to keep us off the ballot if he could. I started in on making sure the reformers were slated in District Council 11, which covered from New York and southeastern Pennsylvania down to Maryland and Delaware. Trenton's Maurice Doyle was sticking with Housewright and expected him to win the nomination early on in the process, but the RRR outmaneuvered him and won, which was mortifying to him. The reform win there was a shot across the bow to all the other locals in the area. I would go out to these nomination meetings and make speeches, and, along with John T. Haletsky, we won over RCIA sections in Allentown, Reading, and Harrisburg, as well as up in Scranton—Wilkes-Barre. In Delaware, Norman Tyrie, who was also committed to Housewright, wouldn't even let us in to speak to his members.

In Camden, New Jersey, RCIA Local 1360's president Joe McComb, whom I had a closer personal relationship with, responded to my request a little differently. I had heard that he was backing Housewright, but, when I called him up, he told me I could speak at one of his general membership meetings on behalf of the RRR ticket. He did so because he wanted it to appear that he was very democratic, but he was a clever old fox. A week or so before the nomination meeting, I got word that he was in the hospital with heart problems and that he probably wouldn't attend. Of course, everybody felt bad when they heard about Joe not feeling well, because he was a little older than most of us.

The night of the meeting over at the Camden union hall, the word was Joe was still in the hospital and we were all wondering if he was going to be there or not. I drove over with about one hundred Local 1357 members. I was scheduled to talk and went inside as most of my members campaigned outside, handing out brochures about RRR. To my surprise, in comes Joe McComb. I go over to say hello and ask him how he was feeling. He's like really sick, like he's just got off his deathbed, and says in a weak, shaking voice, "Why are you doing this to me?" Next thing I know, a fight starts at the other end of the hall. I found out later that McComb set that fight up himself as a diversion. "Get those people out of here! These goons from Philadelphia are here!" I hear him say. "A bunch of Philadelphia hoods!" someone else was yelling.

In this melee, all of the sudden Joe McComb—who was supposedly so sick—gets up and starts giving a very dramatic speech. "These guys from Local 1357 are coming over here from Philadelphia and beating up our members! A little local like ours, and these big city slickers coming over, doing this to us!" As McComb was launching into this speech, I was sitting there on the stage. A guy named Carl Huber, an RCIA international representative, was there, and he had glasses that were really thick. In the middle of a tussle, he loses them and someone tread on them, leaving them all cracked up on the floor. I could see Huber with his broken eyeglasses. I knew I had been set up, the brawl orchestrated to discredit me and the reform campaign. By the time it was my turn to give my pitch to the meeting, I was getting booed from all over the place. The nominations took place right after that, and the RRR slate was voted down by Local 1360's delegates by something like two to one.

WHAT HAPPENED IN NEW JERSEY that night was an indication of the ways our opposition was going to fight us around the country. If we stood any chance of winning, we needed to send out carloads of RRR people to campaign for the cause, to reach regular clerks and cashiers who might support us. Local 1357 sent twenty-seven cars out to Cleveland, Ohio, under the direction of a business agent named Ray Long. The night after their first day out there, just a couple days before the election, Ray called me and said they had run into trouble. When he was getting the groups together in the hotel lobby, men with guns suddenly surrounded them. One of them yelled out, "The big fucking nigger is mine!" Ray was pretty upset about it. "That's me they're talking about boss, that's me!" I told him to pack up and come home, that we couldn't do anything about it. We'll just write up what happened. They were guys sent over by a RCIA local supporting the Housewright ticket, and I don't think they had real intentions of using those guns, but that was the kind of stuff going on. In other cases, in Montreal, Canada, we had cars following us around and there was a lot of intimidation reported by others as well.

Probably the worst incident took place in Atlanta, Georgia. I went down with my friend and lawyer Nick Clemente. The guy who ran the Retail Clerks Union local in Atlanta was Bill Jenkins, and I was aware that he was for Housewright. I had always been friendly with him so I made a courtesy call to let him know I was in his area to campaign for the RRR ticket. When Nick and I walked into the union building, all of a sudden we were surrounded by business agents who brought us into Jenkins's office. He was standing at his desk, and he looked at me and said, "Boy, you had better get the fuck out of town. Nobody campaigns in my local union, you hear me, boy?" I said, "Bill, come on, it's an election. We have a right to campaign here under the law."

Jenkins wasn't buying it, and he was using the vilest language. "Don't give me any fucking shit," he said. "You'll get a bill up your ass that's what you'll get!" I tried to reason with him, but he wouldn't give an inch. "Listen boy, you're going to leave your way or my fucking way, and my fucking way is in a box as far as you're concerned. I told you to get the fuck out of town." Then, he turned to his staff and said, "Men, get him out of here!" They rushed us, and we were carried, literally, outside to the car. We get inside and Nick starts the car up quickly, just as they started shaking it, rocking it from side to side. They were shouting and I told Nick to put the windows down so I could hear what they were saying, and Nick yelled, "Wendell, you're nuts! These people want to kill us!" They were still shaking the car as we drove out of the parking lot, throwing all kinds of shit, which was bouncing off the roof and back window.

Nick drove me back to the hotel and I called the team together and told them to be careful because our opponents down here looked like they're a little tough. Even with the type of reception we got at Jenkins's office, we were determined to carry out our campaign and hit the stores and talk to Retail Clerk Union members. We were giving out literature asking people to consider nominating the RRR ticket, explaining who we were and how we wanted to change the union. I had to go back to Philadelphia and I left a couple people in charge of the campaign, having detailed a strategy about what stores to go to and what other cities to travel to after we left Georgia. As soon as I get home, I called the office to see if anything was cooking and they said that I had better call Atlanta. When I did, I got some troubling news. Two of Local 1357's representatives, Joe Kelly and Sal Barbedo, were in the hospital after being beaten up in a parking lot by guys with baseball bats.

Right away, I called Joe DeSilva in the RRR headquarters in California and told him what happened. He set up a conference call with John T. Haletsky and Frank DeVito, a reform leader on our ticket from North Jersey, to determine a proper response. Frank said we needed to respond in kind, to hit them back, to show them we're not weak. He said he'd send a busload down and get a hold of some of their business agents and let them know who's boss. "Wait a minute," I said. "You're from North Jersey. If you send a busload past Philadelphia down to Atlanta, there's going to be retribution, and the guys they send up from Atlanta aren't going to North Jersey, they're coming to Philadelphia. It's my local that's going to suffer." We should take another route, I reasoned: contact the Labor Department and tell them what happened. Others disagreed. President Johnson's secretary of labor was W. Willard Wirtz, a man with close ties to James A. Suffridge, and they didn't think anything would be done. I wasn't so sure, but in the end they were right. The U.S. Labor Department took our information but that was it.

There wasn't much we could do about the attacks against us in Atlanta. Nick Clemente hired a Georgia-based lawyer who, it turned out, didn't know too much about labor law; Nick went down to help him with the case and said he never saw anything like it. The judge brought an entirely regional bias to the incident. He heard the testimonies and finally stated, "These guys from the North come down and rough up our people. We ain't going to put up with this shit." Those were his exact words. They let Jenkins's guys off the hook, even though we showed them the hospital records that proved what had happened to Joe Kelly and Sal Barbedo, our guys who had been beaten up so badly when they were campaigning for the RRR slate. They even got an injunction forbidding us from ever returning to Atlanta. I talked to Nick Clemente who said he would file a suit against them, but most of the lawyers he talked to said it was a lost cause and none of them would take the case.

I wasn't daunted by all this and ended up going all over the country, campaigning for the RRR ticket. In California, most of the locals were for us, since John T. Haletsky was the organizing director there and he had become friends with many of the local leaders. I stayed a couple of months in California, living with Rick Icaza, a young business agent who would become a lifelong friend. I used to go around to each store and introduce myself to all the young part-timers, telling them how important it is that they vote for the reform ticket. I compared the RCIA to the Catholic Church, saying that the church had become very hierarchical, but, with Vatican II, the windows were opened and fresh air and sunshine were let in—my standard line. The same thing needed to happen in the Retail Clerks, as well as to organized labor more broadly. I used to say that the way the RCIA works now was even more conservative than the Catholic Church, both were hierarchies that were out of touch with the people. Many of the members out in California were Latina and Latino, a majority of whom were Catholic, and they really responded to this message.

The way that people were mobilized in places like California really scared the RCIA old guard who realized that this was the beginning of a major national reform movement. Even if we didn't win this time, we were a force that would keep coming back at them. Before the election, James A. Suffridge sent some of his people to speak to Joe DeSilva, to try to work out a deal. So we had this big meeting in California, and DeSilva urged us to meet them halfway, to make a settlement. He'd been offered an opportunity to go to Washington, DC, to negotiate some changes before this election, so that we can postpone it and declare them the winners. That kind of deal was the furthest thing from my mind. I told them I was against it in principle, that we had a chance at winning; but I agreed to go with them to meet the opposition. I remember it was at the Mayflower Hotel, we were discussing things with James A. Suffridge, and Joe DeSilva was pushing it. Joe was our spokesman and at one point he looked over at Suffridge and he knew he was blinking; he knew that Suffridge was starting to give in to our demands.

Joe DeSilva comes back with a settlement that gave four of our reform slate positions on the RCIA executive board as vice presidential seats. Of course, I wasn't one of them. First of all I didn't care if I was; I said I'm not for giving any concessions at all. I went into this to change the union; this is change I don't agree with. I turned it down vehemently. DeSilva said, "Wendell, why are you so far out?"

"Because you guys put me out there. Because you made all these speeches, you've got me so far out you can't get me back to Earth."

John T. Haletsky felt the same way I did. We refused to be part of any settlement. The election was going to proceed as planned, and I intended to win. Joe DeSilva had several thousand members, and he had arranged to have twenty polling places in the Los Angeles area, a huge jurisdiction that could swing the results. I said, "Mr. DeSilva, you can't do that. No one's going to vote. You need to have hundreds of polling places." I said this is how I won my election when I challenged Henry Highland in 1962. We had numerous polling places. "You think people in your suburbs are going to come into the city to vote in a union election? We've got to have multiple polls—in fact, you've got to have traveling polls." This is how you would do it: get a station wagon with one of the union election judges and schedule times that you would be outside the stores so that members could vote out in the parking lot at different times during the day. You can have a big umbrella in case it's raining. You've got to plan ahead. I reminded him that's how the Meet the Challenge slate won the election in 1962; we had all of these points worked out ahead of time so we could be sure people got to vote.

Considering all of the ways Jim Housewright's team had tried to block this election from taking place, I knew we would need plenty of poll observers to make sure nothing funny happened on the day of the vote. Just as I knew there would be, there were a number of voter intimidation cases called in. One of the most memorable ones happened in Chicago, where a number of young seminarians had been recruited to oversee the balloting for the RRR side. I helped line this up, after my friend Michael J. Stack Jr., who was a Philadelphia ward leader with me, told me about a priest he knew who ran a seminary in the Chicago area and had a number of young guys who wanted to make some extra money. All we wanted them to do was watch and write down what was happening, because we needed a record of anything our opponents did wrong. A week or so after the election was held, Stack gets a call from the head of the seminary, telling him never to ask him to do something like that again. The seminarians were scared out of their minds. Half of them couldn't even write things down because they were chased off store properties by some of Housewright's supporters. They were intimidated pretty bad. In fact, the priest told Mike that he hadn't heard from two of the seminarians since, and this was like two weeks after the election!

All of this voting was happening from coast to coast, with polling places set up inside stores and break rooms, in parking lots, and in trucks and cars overseen by observers and lawyers and interns from the American Arbitration Association. After the polls closed, these ballots from all over the country were collected and brought in sealed boxes to the union headquarters in Washington, DC. These stayed there for thirty days, until a selected committee began the process of counting the marked cards one by one. With these boxes stored somewhere in the RCIA headquarters building and kept there for thirty days, you can't tell me that they didn't tamper with them. The entire process was overseen by officials selected by the Suffridge-Housewright team and their final tally had their slate winning by just over forty-two thousand votes—just enough to make sure they had enough to get them over.

Our lawyers were present, reviewing the process and noting all kinds of irregularities. Joe DeSilva and the rest of us met with Mozart Ratner and he said we had enough evidence on hand to challenge the results. Everyone knew it would be a rough road, because President Johnson's labor secretary W. Willard Wirtz was tight with Housewright, and we knew it was preloaded. Again, we turned to the Committee for a Democratic Election to raise money for this legal challenge, and began scheduling hearings all over the country. I was called down to the Mayflower Hotel again to testify because I'd been all over the country, and I related all of the incidents of intimidation I could remember.

In the days following our challenge, Jim Housewright called a unity meeting to try to put the issue to rest. All of the RRR ticket was there, and we were offered a number of concessions, the same ones that had been floated before, in addition to five seats on the executive committee on the condition that we wouldn't challenge the election and take it to the Labor Department. I felt this was proof enough that Housewright knew that the election had been stolen. Moe Ratner was willing to continue the case because by this point, he had gotten emotionally involved too, but Joe DeSilva said that if we didn't settle, he would pull his money out. Only half the RRR officers were for compromise. There were a lot of personal issues to consider. John T. Haletsky, who was a regional director for the international, would be serving under Jim Housewright and was pretty sure that he was going to be fired. He really urged us to stay the course and fight, to continue the struggle for everything we demanded, whatever it took. We were divided, and some of the legal battles went on for another three years before it finally finished, without any resolution.

With Jim Housewright now in charge of the international union, I knew I would have zero influence over the kind of direction the organization would take. Housewright went along with the compromise he had made with Joe DeSilva and the other reformers and saw it implemented at the 1972 RCIA international convention. DeSilva was named chair of the constitutional committee and five of the RRR ticket officers were named vice presidents to oversee policy making. I was excluded from this new group, as I was a holdout to the final agreement. Because of my stand, it was pretty much etched in stone that I would never be involved in the inner circle of the RCIA international. Too many of the key figures hated me. Over the long haul, though, I believe the RRR campaign had an impact on making the Retail Clerks Union a more democratic organization. A tradition was instilled that encouraged members to demand a say in the union, and, in 1972, a caucus was formed to advocate for more minority leadership. What we started remained one of the progressive elements with what, in another decade, would become the United Food and Commercial Workers (UFCW). I hoped that these things would happen, and continued to push for these things from Philadelphia.

In 1972, right before the Democratic Party's national convention, I met with Housewright. I said, "Jim, I'm here to meet with you to find out who you like for president." He looks at me and he jumps out of his chair. "Who do you think I like for president? Me! I'm the one who's running for president!" I said "Jim . . . Jim, I'm not talking about president of the Retail Clerks Union. I'm talking about president of the United States." He thought I was coming down to tell him I was going to run against him. That's how paranoid he was.

8

ORGANIZING PENNSYLVANIA

THROUGH THE 1960S, workers were joining unions by the hundreds of thousands, and the power and influence of their organizations were on the rise. The Retail Clerks Union grew to half a million members, and by 1970 ranked sixth in total membership in the AFL-CIO, behind such giants as the United Auto Workers, Steelworkers, and Teamsters. In Philadelphia, Local 1357 organized six thousand new members over a seven-year period, and we were one of the largest unions in the city. This focus on membership growth continued into the new decade. In 1970, I oversaw a successful statewide effort to bring liquor store clerks into the union, part of a broader organizing surge of state employees that would have lasting impact on unions and political power in Philadelphia and across the commonwealth. While these gains did not equal the kind of surge that had happened in the 1930s, I believed that bold action could build the momentum, and union density could continue into the upcoming decade, and that, by building coalitions with consumers and the students and civil rights movements, the new decade could make good on the promise of the 1930s, to make America a true social democracy.

The most dynamic areas of union organizing of this era came in the public sector, as university grounds crews and clerical staff, state hospitals, sanitation workers, and crossing guards gained power by strikes. Teachers were at the forefront in securing collective bargaining rights and negotiating good contracts for higher wages and professional status. By the end of the decade, the nation's two largest teachers' unions, the AFT and the National Education Association, had one million members. With that kind of power, continued improvements in teachers' conditions seemed certain. The AFSCME was another major union behind the new public worker movement that was happening across the country. In 1964, Jerry Wurf was elected AFSCME's international president and applied the same kind of organizing drives, work stoppages, media campaigns, and aggressive political engagement that made New York City's District Council 37 a power, linking workplace struggles with the civil rights movement and the rights of the poor, immigrants, women, and youths. By the end of the decade, AFSCME was organizing about a thousand new members a week, flexing its political muscle, its goals and rhetoric embodying the kind of social justice unionism I wanted the Retail Clerks Union to be.

Since the late 1930s, efforts to organize Pennsylvania state employees had been poorly coordinated with very limited resources and almost nothing to show for it. Out of the small section they did sign up—a few state hospitals, school boards, and clerical employees—a weak statewide organization was formed claiming about two thousand members out of a possible one hundred thousand. The Quaker State was not unusual in this regard. Most government employees around the nation remained unorganized, in large part because they lacked the kinds of federal protections of New Deal era labor laws that oversaw the private sector. Pennsylvania state law also forbade any kind of formal recognition of unions for its state government employees, a measure that reduced any chance of success for union drives. Conditions were so bad for these workers by the late 1960s that they were ready to support a more militant campaign by AFSCME. Changes in public opinion also created new openings that AFSCME took advantage of.

EVEN THOUGH IT WAS A MAJOR manufacturing state, many of Pennsylvania's industries like textiles and anthracite coal were in decline by the late 1950s, and in some areas the only employer might be a state mental hospital or a corrections facility. Pay was so low that many full-time employees qualified for welfare benefits. Every state job placed peculiar demands on the workers because these jobs were considered political spoils and were distributed as patronage by whichever party controlled

Harrisburg. Although Pennsylvania had really been a one-party state after the Civil War and into the early twentieth century, with the coming of the New Deal, gubernatorial elections were hotly contested, and both the Democratic and the Republican Parties held the office from time to time. Whichever party won that office controlled the bulk of the patronage of the state and with every shift in the governor's mansion, thousands of state employees were fired en masse in the opening days of the new administration, opening positions for the victorious party's loyalists. Of course, with the lack of professional status and security, service suffered and reformers sought to end this patronage. In 1966, Raymond P. Shafer, a reform-minded governor, was elected and the Commonwealth shifted its policy to allow the state troopers' association to bargain for wages and conditions.

The new public support for bargaining rights for public employees in the 1960s sparked a more serious organizing effort by AFSCME. There were a sizable number of workers that, if brought into the union, would make AFSCME a political power. For instance, 14,500 blue-collar workers, mostly road crews and maintenance employees in the state Department of Transportation, were one group, besides 21,500 health service workers, about five thousand corrections officers, and 19,000 clerical employees. Starting in 1969, a statewide organizing drive was directed by Gerald W. "Jerry" McEntee, the son of Philadelphia's blue-collar AFSCME leader Bill McEntee. AFSCME pushed for a new state law—Bill 1021, the Public Employee Relations Act—that would secure collective bargaining rights for civilian state employees for the first time. For it to pass, a lot of lobbying was needed, and Jerry McEntee was seeking a coalition across the labor movement and citizen's groups to advance the issue with the voters.

I paid close attention to these developments because I was interested in organizing Pennsylvania's three thousand state liquor store clerks. Since the end of prohibition, a state government agency—the Pennsylvania Liquor Control Board (PLCB)—oversaw sales of wine and liquor across the commonwealth. In 1970, there were 780 liquor stores across the state, and, like it was for almost every other commonwealth worker, pay at these stores was miserably low and shaped by political rules that made them subservient to political bosses. In early 1970, I called Jerry McEntee up and told him I was interested in getting the Retail Clerks Union involved in lobbying for the new public sector bargaining act.

Figure 8.1 Pennsylvania liquor store clerk with customer, 1970. (From the collection of Wendell W. Young III.)

I promised financial support to buy radio and newspaper ads and to send out political organizers to meet with civic groups to explain why the proposed changes would be beneficial to state services. In 1969, Bill 1021— the measure that would be known as Act 195—was passed. It provided a structure to the public sector employment relations, mediation, and fact-finding in disputes and a seventy-five-day cooling-off period in case of impasse. (See Figure 8.1.)

When Pennsylvania's new public sector labor law was on the books, I went back to Jerry and told him I wanted my union to represent the liquor store clerks. I invited him to meet me at the Schwartzwald Inn and he showed up with Eddie Keller, his right-hand man and my old friend from the zoo employees' union, which had recently merged with AFSCME in Philadelphia. McEntee made it absolutely clear that AFSCME would represent all state workers, including the PLCB clerks. We discussed things and it got pretty heated. Jerry was drinking Manhattans, and, after about eight strong ones, he finally starts to give in a little. He said he'd agree, so long as AFSCME got all the office clerks in other state departments and that I'd promise to stay out of everything else. The next day, when he realized what he had agreed to, I think McEntee had some reservations. Eddie Keller told me years later that McEntee called him up the next day and said, "That son of a bitch got me whacked on those Manhattans and I went along with him." He asked Eddie if he thought I would hold him to all that he had promised, and Eddie said from what he knew about me, I would.

The campaign to organize state workers was gaining momentum just as the 1970 governor's race was getting under way. I knew that whoever won the governor's seat would determine the course of the organizing drive, so I looked closely at the candidates from both parties. Early on, I decided to back businessman Milton Shapp, a very liberal candidate from outside Philadelphia who had a lucrative electronic manufacturing business. I liked that Shapp had been an adviser to President Kennedy and worked on the Peace Corps program, and when I met with him he told me that he would support the unionization of the liquor store clerks. One condition he had was that there would be one statewide unit covered by a comprehensive master agreement rather than a series of regional locals. To do this, Local 1357 set up the Retail Clerks State Store Organizing Committee as the bargaining unit for all the store clerks across the commonwealth. Soon after we met, I joined his campaign team; Shapp campaigned hard and he pulled it off, with a lot of union support. He never forgot my work for him, and he invited me down to his inaugural and we became very friendly. All during the gubernatorial race, the liquor store campaign continued and the majority of the clerks voted to join the union in March 1971. Later that year, the members approved a twenty-one-month contract that gave an across-the-board wage increase of twenty dollars a week, overtime pay, a shortened workweek, and state-paid health and life insurance.

As the Retail Clerks Organizing Committee brought in twenty-five hundred clerks, other organizing and negotiations continued across the commonwealth. By April 1972, the Service Employees International Union (SEIU) had signed up ten thousand welfare caseworkers and supervisors, while the Pennsylvania Nurses Association organized registered nurses at state facilities. AFSCME got the bulk of the commonwealth workers, taking in seventy-five thousand members over a three-year period. Jerry McEntee led the first contract negotiations in 1971, securing modest wage increases, health insurance—and, most important, a job security clause—finally ending the patronage system across a dozen bargaining units. In 1973, McEntee crafted a master agreement covering all AFSCME members across the commonwealth. Soon after, AFSCME Council 13 was formed, with Jerry McEntee elected president. What Jerry had coordinated in Pennsylvania became a model for how AFSCME would grow over the course of the decade, eventually reaching the one million mark in 1977.

THE CHANGES FOLLOWING THE PASSAGE of the Pennsylvania Public Employee Relations Act had important implications for organized labor in Philadelphia. AFSCME expanded to include white-collar city employees such as social workers, parking authority managers, restaurant inspectors, and other technical positions, forming a two thousand-member District Council 47, in 1969, that acted as a central body that coordinated the program of the various locals it represented. Many of the early members of DC 47, especially the social workers who made up the union's most militant base, came out of the civil rights and students' movements, and infused an activist spirit to the organization. Women made up a sizable portion of the union, and in the coming decade pushed for new kinds of contract issues, including flextime scheduling and child-care provisions, contraceptive coverage and expanded health benefits, and pay equity across all municipal job categories. Although a small union at first, DC 47 wielded a lot of power and was a force for social justice unionism by the end of the 1970s.

Another serious development of the new legal environment to organizing in Pennsylvania happened in the health care industry. Philadelphia was a national center for hospitals, but, despite the union power in the city, only the municipally run Philadelphia General Hospital (PGH) was unionized by 1969. Conditions in these hospitals were horrible. These workers did all the dirty, rotten jobs that nobody else would do: handling infectious waste, removing, hauling, and cleaning hospital bed sheets, and emptying bedpans. Despite the fact that they worked the front lines of health services, almost no workers had any health care benefits and they could not afford hospital care for themselves or their families. Average costs of an overnight stay at most hospitals were about one hundred dollars, more than what most workers made per week. Almost all of these low-wage workers were minorities—a majority African American and Puerto Rican—and the lack of access to better-paying jobs relegated them to the ranks of the working poor. Not much success had come from union campaigns in the industry, but by the 1960s a series of highly publicized, victorious strikes emboldened workers to form unions. Such efforts paralleled the black freedom struggle, and connected citizenship rights with economic advancement.

In 1969, the National Union of Hospital and Nursing Home Employees Local 1199c sent Henry Nicholas, one of their key organizers from New York City, to start a Philadelphia campaign. Henry estimated that there were forty thousand potential members working in the eighty-six hospitals in the region, including service and maintenance workers; nurse's aides and orderlies; dietary, laundry, and housekeeping staff; receptionists; and technicians. The hospital workers organizing campaign began in early 1970, and Henry set up a meeting with me to see if I could help him because I had a reputation for being on the left wing of the labor movement. Local 1357 had a couple of units representing clerical staff in some of the hospitals in the area, including the AFL-CIO hospital and all the pharmacies and diagnostic centers affiliated with them. I told him after he organized his first hospital, he could take over all the medical office employees that the Retail Clerks Union had. He asked if he could borrow some of my business agents to work as part-time organizers. I told him I could loan him some people but that he would have to train them. In addition, I got him in touch with some of the more activist members I knew who worked in the stores and he offered them positions as organizers. He trained them and they got to work.

Over a two-year period, Henry Nicholas and his staff brought in ten thousand members, making 1199c one of the largest unions in Philadelphia. The union was militant, calling strikes at Hahnemann Hospital and other health centers, and engaging in direct actions, blocking traffic outside facilities, and maintaining noisy pickets. In the initial contract at Philadelphia College of Osteopathic Medicine, the union negotiated a minimum salary of $125 a week, a standard soon adopted at area centers such as Einstein Medical Center, Temple University Hospital, and Jefferson Medical. Similar deals for other hospitals secured raises, paid holidays, and sick days.

Although Henry's union was making real advances, it came only as the result of hard struggle. Hospital management fought against giving in to any demand. All through the summer of 1972, 1199c had been organizing a few dozen workers at Delaware Valley Hospital Laundry at 9th and Jefferson Street, and the owners wouldn't budge. Most of the workers there were women, and they had some of the hardest jobs you can imagine, coming into contact with all kinds of filthy linens, bed sheets, and hospital gowns, which they disinfected in huge vats. None of the hospitals could function without this kind of labor, but the women took home less than eighty dollars a week, which qualified most for food stamps. Pickets were set up outside the plant gates, and protesters were out there demanding a sixty-cent raise. On August 28, 1972, 1199c organizer Norman Rayford was shot and killed in the hospital parking lot by a security guard. Claiming that Rayford had pulled a knife on him, the guard was released without charge. This was the first time a union organizer had been killed in Philadelphia since the 1930s, and Henry Nicholas called out for union support for a citywide day of mourning. I joined Earl Stout and some of the textile union leaders at a prayer vigil at the site of the shooting the following morning. I thought it was a disgrace that so few unions came out. Not even Philadelphia's AFL-CIO Central Labor Union president Ed

Figure 8.2 Workers picket outside Delaware Valley Hospital's linen service plant, 9th and Jefferson Street, August 3, 1972. (Special Collections Research Center, Temple University, Philadelphia, Pa. Photograph by Frederick A. Meyer.)

Toohey showed up, even though a labor organizer had lost his life. After the vigil, about three hundred hospital workers organized a protest march, proceeding from 8th and Vine over to City Hall where they had a rally to bring attention to all that had happened, and to demand justice. (See Figure 8.2.)

The vision of labor's role in society that Henry Nicholas and I shared was in sharp contrast to the conservative business unionism of George Meany, and most of the Philadelphia labor movement. By organizing workers in retail and health care, we sought to improve the economic and working conditions for our members, but we wanted something more. We believed that the trade union movement was a force for making important changes in society, to make it a true social democracy where everyone had security, decent wages, and equality and opportunity. We wanted this for all people, not just our members. I liked Henry because he was young and very ambitious and he became a man to be reckoned with because he was there not just to get members but to make real social change. That's the thing that impressed me; he wanted to be an instrument of change, which is what I wanted to be, too. I felt that I had a powerful position and I should use it to make change. A lot of labor leaders didn't think this way, but it was what we should have been doing, and if we were doing what we were supposed to do, there wouldn't be so many problems.

A S THE 1970S STARTED, the union campaigns for social justice were gaining the sympathy of many young people across the region. Often, students from local colleges and high schools were joining union activists on picket lines. This new coalition connected progressive trade unions with the antiwar and the civil rights movement and I believed that these kinds of connections were needed if broader social changes were going to happen. One of the most important campaigns connecting labor rights with broader social causes was the fight for decent conditions waged by the United Farm Workers (UFW). These men and women were some of the lowest-paid workers in the United States and lacked basic legal rights since federal labor statutes didn't cover them. In the early 1960s, Cesar Chavez and Delores Huerta helped form the UFW, reaching out to the mostly Mexican American migrant workers in California. In 1965, the union called a strike against the largest grape firm on the West Coast and gained a lot of media attention and sympathy across the nation. Cesar was connected to social Catholicism, and used terms that promoted the farm workers, cause along moral terms. This caught the public's imagination and became the most iconic union campaign of the period. Since I represented workers in the food industry, I was directly connected to the UFW's grape and lettuce boycotts into the 1970s and saw its impact across the region.

At first, the grape boycott didn't have much attention in the Philadelphia area, but, as it gained momentum, it joined in the movement in support of the farm workers around the country. I was very active in the AFL-CIO Food Council of Philadelphia and Vicinity and, in 1967, put forward a resolution in support of the strike. The real impetus behind the effort to aid the strikers came from ordinary people who shopped in the stores and put pressure on management to not shelve nonunion grapes from California. In Philadelphia, the most significant organization to back this campaign was the Consumer Education and Protective Association (CEPA), which was founded in 1967 to give consumers more power in their dealings with corporations. CEPA was organized by Max Weiner, an accountant and real estate broker who had deep ties to left-wing politics going back to the 1930s. Through his work with people in West Philadelphia, he saw how people's lives were hurt by certain business practices and he campaigned against tax increases on installment purchases, for the end of real estate transfer taxes, and for consumers to gain more say over prices. For the grape boycott to succeed, Max believed that it had to happen through ordinary consumers' refusal to buy and that only the mass power of selective patronage would have an impact, and, to help educate people about what was at stake, he organized pickets outside the stores.

In 1968, CEPA intensified its picketing campaign outside local supermarkets to gain support for the farm workers. Before they did so, Max called me at my office to let me know what was happening and that he understood that the retail clerks weren't being asked to stay off from work but that the union could help him in the campaign. He would bring pressure on Acme, Food Fair, and A&P through the informational pickets outside the stores, but as an extra point of pressure he wanted me to authorize the produce crews in the stores to not put nonunion grapes on the shelves. To do so was a secondary boycott, a tactic that was outlawed by the Taft-Hartley Act, and I knew it was risky since the stores and grape companies could sue the union. This was a serious matter, and I organized a meeting in the back room of one of the Acme Markets, and about fifteen union stewards from some of the area stores were there to talk about what we were going to do. I remember these guys were standing there wearing their service aprons, talking about what a boycott would look like and what our risks were. They all decided that it was important to stand with the farm workers. After that, we refused to take nonunion grapes off the trucks if they came in; and, if anyone did, the stewards would refuse to shelve them: if a customer asked for grapes, the produce staff told them that they didn't have any in the store, even if they did. Because of this kind of militant action across the Philadelphia region, Acme Markets stopped buying nonunion grapes, and I feel this played a role in the eventual UFW victory.

Just as the grape boycott was ending in the summer of 1969, the UFW launched another major boycott, this time against iceberg lettuce. This strike was ultimately a struggle between the UFW and the Teamsters, which had signed a sweetheart deal with the growers that provided a raise of a measly two cents without even consulting with the workers in the fields. Since the unionized stores had already been supporting the grape strike, we automatically got behind the new struggle. Max Weiner organized protests again and contacted me because he thought it was important to bring Cesar Chavez to Philadelphia, to mobilize even greater mass support for the campaign. On October 6, 1969, the AFL-CIO Food Council sponsored an event at the Unitarian Church at 2125 Chestnut Street, and three hundred people showed up to hear Chavez speak. I introduced him and made a speech promising support from the Retail Clerks Union. Most of the people there that night were young—teenagers and students from around the Delaware Valley—and in the days that followed, even more support for the farm workers was apparent with pickets outside stores, fund-raising events on campuses, and letter-writing campaigns. Over the coming year, scores of young UFW supporters joined farm workers in hunger strikes, setting up tables at Independence Hall and outside Acme Market's headquarters. These actions gained a lot of newspaper and television coverage and brought pressure on the stores. (See Figure 8.3.)

Behind the scenes, the Retail Clerks Union did our part. With control over what got put on the shelves, our produce workers had a lot of power and the union stewards in the stores had my backing in making sure no

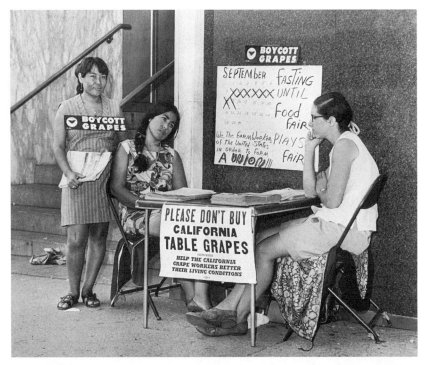

Figure 8.3 Mexican American grape pickers fast in front of Food Fair Building, 32nd and JFK Boulevard, September 15, 1969. UFW members Carolina Franco and Tona Salvdado of Delano, California, are joined in the fast by Temple University student Lilli Sprintz. (Special Collections Research Center, Temple University, Philadelphia, Pa. Photograph by Sonnee Gottlieb.)

iceberg lettuce was for sale, just as we did during the grape strike. I would go around to the stores in the city looking for the union symbol on the lettuce boxes. I ordered the clerks to keep the nonunion lettuce in the back and say it wasn't available if people asked for it. As I mentioned, this was an illegal secondary boycott—an action banned by the 1947 Taft-Hartley Act—but I told my members in the produce departments that we had to do things different, to show we were a militant union. Acme threatened to sue me for hundreds of thousands of dollars, but we didn't back down. I called Mayor Tate, and he pressured the store's top management to change their policy and got them off my neck. Hundreds of dollars' worth of lettuce was purchased by the city of Philadelphia each week for use in school cafeterias, hospitals, and lunchrooms, and the mayor directed all city agencies to purchase nothing but union lettuce. To me,

my access to Tate and his willingness to go to bat for this cause underscored how important it was to have a mayor who understood the needs
of working-class people. This is why Jim Tate was labor's mayor. He made
a real difference.

This coalition between the unions, students, religious leaders, house-
wives, and consumers had an impact. It brought enough pressure on the
stores and politicians and, along with similar kinds of actions in support
of the boycott around the nation, helped lead to a victory for the UFW.
Acme Markets realized this and shifted their position and issued a press
release that they would no longer purchase boycotted lettuce from California. The Retail Clerks Union was allowed to go around and inspect the
warehouses to see what was coming in, because even though the company said they were doing one thing, that didn't mean they were seeing it
through. Because of our actions, Philadelphia was one area of the country
where the lettuce boycott had real consequences.

A S I SAW IT, THE CAUSE of Cesar Chavez and the UFW in the late
1960s and early 1970s was purely in line with the principles of social
Catholicism, which called for fair wages and representation on the job
and a basic affirmation of human dignity. Many clergy supported Cesar
around the country, but Philadelphia's conservative archbishop Cardinal
John Krol was not one of them. Most of the city's parish priests fell in line.
At St. Martin of Tours church, where I was still a parishioner, I had a run-
in with its very conservative pastor, Monsignor Walter A. Bower. On Sun-
days, I often served as a lectern, helping with the readings and responses
during mass, and assisting with communion. One time, when I was on
the altar with him, Monsignor starts giving a homily attacking Chavez,
along with the nuns and priests who were out in California picketing
with him. I was so disgusted that I got up, moved to the center of the aisle,
genuflected, and walked off the altar. I heard polite applause from some
of the parishioners who supported the farm workers. I was supposed to
help with communion, but I didn't come back; I waited behind in the
sacristy. Bower comes storming in after mass is over, yelling at me, "How
dare you do what you did out there! That was an affront to this parish!"

I looked at him and said, "Let me tell you something, Monsignor. You
can talk all you want about church law, but when you're talking about

labor, you're wrong. You insulted Cesar Chavez this morning. He is a very decent man. You don't know him. He's a good Catholic and you shouldn't talk about him like that. That goes for the nuns and priests who are out there with him too. If I had the money, I'd be out there with him, also. Don't you dare talk about him like that as long as I'm on the altar, I'll walk off every time."

My willingness to place Cesar Chavez's and the UFW's demands on the forefront of the Retail Clerks Union's dealings with the stores made me even more of a pariah among store managers and supermarket top brass across the region. There were consequences for my support of the grape and lettuce campaigns. An example of this was with the St. Joseph's Food Marketing Institute. Founded in 1962, it was intended to be a training center for leaders in the food industry. I was an early board member, selected because of my position as a union officer who represented thousands of workers in this sector. I was also named to this board, I am sure, because I was an active alumnus. Meyer Marcus, the executive director of Food Fair Markets, was outspoken about not wanting me involved in the institute, arguing that they didn't want a union position impacting the decisions they made. St. Joseph's Business School didn't want me there either, and Jim O'Conner, the program director, gave in to their pressure and asked me to leave.

I was really disappointed by this, but not everyone at St. Joseph's College agreed with how I'd been treated. Father Michael Smith, who taught a popular course on ethics and was then head of the Philosophy Department, was livid and saw my removal as an affront to intellectual freedom and the church's teachings on labor. In response, he arranged for me to teach undergraduate courses on the church encyclicals three mornings a week. I taught in the physics amphitheater, with about 120 students a semester. These were forums where we could speak about the problems of the farm workers, and other contemporary topics such as the student's movement, the Vietnam War, and the future of politics. One of the things I liked to do, besides the assigned readings, was to have forums where outside guests could come in to give their views on how the theory we covered in class applied in real-life situations. I tapped my connections in the local political scene, and labor leaders, and I brought in Teamsters officials like Frank Keane. The students loved it, and our classes often went beyond the scheduled time.

There were still many tenured academics there that were skeptical of what I was doing. One professor in the Philosophy Department came up to me at some faculty gathering and said, "Mr. Young, how is it possible to be an honest labor leader?" I looked at him and said finally, "Professor, how is it possible to be an honest philosophy professor?" He turned and walked away, puffing on his pipe.

9

PHILADELPHIA LIBERAL

A S I HAD ALL THROUGH MY WORK with the labor movement, I believed that labor and politics involved a struggle for the heart of America and the kind of future we would have as a society. Labor must be involved in shaping the bigger issues; it was more than advancing its own interests. Labor and politics are tied together—they can't be separated—and this was what social justice unionism was all about. There were campaigns that connected labor to community alliances, and I continued to build coalitions in Philadelphia. As the new decade of the 1970s opened, I was hopeful that the social changes that had started would continue and reach new levels.

Since my late teen years, politics had come very naturally to me, and I enjoyed being part of that world. Following Mayor Tate's reelection in 1967, I was well positioned in the city's Democratic Party because I had been one of his staunch supporters at a time when so many had refused to back him. This continued even after I went against him when I was the only member of the Philadelphia delegation at the national convention to support Eugene McCarthy when he ran for president the following year. I was close to the mayor and could call him at any time. He also recognized me and appointed me to a very prestigious job on the Board of Trustees of the Free Library of Philadelphia. I must have been the first labor person in the city's history to be appointed to this position. It was all blue bloods and myself. One time, someone picked me up at the Retail Clerks Union office on Broad Street in a stretch limousine to attend a board meeting. I got in but was embarrassed to ride in the damn thing. I'm a guy from Philly's Mayfair neighborhood, what the hell was I riding in a limo for?

The position, as the mayor had made clear, was mostly ceremonial, but, in 1970, there was a minor controversy that the library board played a role in addressing across the region. The biggest decision to come before the board that year was whether or not to shelve Jerry Rubin's book called *Do It!: Scenarios of the Revolution* in the city's libraries. The issue came about after a Northeast Philadelphia housewife saw the book in her local library and complained to the board. The local Chamber of Commerce and the American Legion got behind her effort and lent their support behind a drive to remove the book.

Rubin's book was no literary masterpiece, believe me. From what I recall, and it has been years since I've seen it, it had a lot of sex in it, full images of naked hippies, a man urinating in the street and other vulgar scenes, as well as the prolific use of the F-word. I think Rubin, who was a countercultural radical and founder of the Youth International Movement, made it gross and sensational on purpose. Based on the predictable outcry, there were many people who wanted the book banned, both from local bookstores and all branches of the Free Library of Philadelphia. The issue eventually worked its way up to the board for a decision. I agreed it was a lousy book, but I argued against banning it. That would be exactly what Rubin would want us to do. Everybody's going to buy the book then because they want to see what's being banned.

I think the point of the book actually was to show that people get more upset about that kind of nonsense than they do about the war. That's what Rubin was trying to do, showing that people get more upset over the use of a vulgar word than the fact that the government was supporting policies that were killing civilians in Vietnam. I'm making his case and some of the others on the board accused me of being with Rubin. Sure enough I got outvoted, and the book became a best seller in the Philadelphia area. Later I got to know Jerry Rubin from the antiwar movement and he agreed with me that it was a lousy book, but he said he'd made a lot of money on it.

LABOR STRIFE involving Philadelphia sanitation workers was the first major local news story of the new decade. In late January 1970, Philadelphia streets commissioner David M. Smallwood resigned and Mayor Tate miscalculated the politics of finding his replacement when he appointed Joseph F. Halferty, a chief police inspector who had zero background in civil engineering, to fill the post. The city's four thousand sanitation men, who were over 95 percent African American, were enraged that a white police officer with such limited experience was put in charge to oversee their daily operations. Within a day of the announcement, the sanitation union called a slowdown, leading to trash pileups all over the city.

The bitterness of the sanitation crews over Halferty's appointment was rooted in years of conflict between the city's African American community and the police department. This sense was magnified because of the politics that seemed to shape the decision. It was pretty clear that the man behind the move to boost Halferty was city police commissioner Frank L. Rizzo, who many believed had aspirations to become mayor. Naming a police official loyal to Rizzo sent a message to the sanitation union—AFSCME Local 427—one of the city's most militant sections, that they would face harsh consequences for any bold actions. The trash slowdown continued through the month and divided the city, with only the African American community rallying behind the trash crews. The union's main spokesman was Earl Stout, a 48-year-old trash truck mechanic who was brash and outspoken—all over the news promising a yearlong slowdown if changes weren't made. On February 26, 1970, Joseph F. Halferty finally resigned, a major victory for the sanitation workers.

The sanitation showdown of early 1970 was proof that direct action on the streets could effect political decisions at the top levels. To me, this was an important part of bringing about social change, in mobilizing broad coalitions, and showing mass support for labor's causes. There were plenty of social problems to address, but I felt that the most important single issue facing working-class people was the war in Vietnam. I wanted it ended immediately and spoke out about it every chance I had. This was an especially strong feeling for me after four student protesters were shot dead by troopers from the Ohio National Guard at Kent State University on May 4, 1970. The following day, three thousand college students boycotted classes around the city and joined a procession down Broad Street from Temple University to meet students marching from Penn and Drexel at City Hall. Later that week, the largest antiwar protest in Philadelphia from this era was held, with fifteen thousand convening at

Independence Hall. At both of these rallies, I was the only representative from the local labor movement present. AFL-CIO president George Meany still supported the war and was now even moving closer to Nixon's economic program. Later that year, at the convention of the Pennsylvania AFL-CIO, I gave a speech calling for Meany's resignation on the grounds that, by supporting the nation's military aggressions, he was out of step with the real needs of union members across the nation.

The divisions within organized labor reflected the same splits of row house working-class voters across the region. This was a major concern for the party leadership by the end of 1968. After Bill Green stepped down as Philadelphia's Democratic Party chairman in December 1969, the leadership went to Joseph J. Scanlon, a state legislator and tavern keeper from the city's Kensington and Allegheny section. The party chairman was the ward leader selected by all of the other sixty-six ward chieftains in the city to be their central spokesperson and liaison between them and the mayor and all other politicians, a very important position. Joe ran the party for about a year, but he died unexpectedly of kidney failure at just forty-six. Since I was close to both Governor Shapp and Mayor Tate, who by this time had gotten over my support for McCarthy in 1968, there was talk about naming me to the position. If I had been asked, I would have accepted, but instead Peter J. Camiel, a ward leader from the city's Roxborough neighborhood, was appointed.

Camiel was a tough man, a light heavyweight boxer when he was younger, and he brought a fighter's attitude to everything he did, especially the political realm. He was a good businessman, and by the time he was in his forties had made a fortune through a beer distribution business. Like Joseph Scanlon before him, Camiel was well liked by everyone in the Democratic Party but didn't have too much ambition, didn't want to run for national office or anything. He didn't have much of a profile. His taking over the city chairman position I think was a reflection of the times, an indication of how divided the party was. Pete was what I would call a liberal conservative, an all things to all people kind of guy; but he would do what he had to do to keep the Democrats in power. I was friendly with him even though I was on what was considered the party's left wing.

Pete Camiel's main challenge as the decade began was to keep the city's traditional blue-collar working-class white people from bolting the party. Philadelphia had gone for Hubert H. Humphrey in 1968, but as far as local races, especially the mayor's office, things were now up for grabs. A lot of this had to do with racial politics. Through these years, there was a sense that advancements were being made by black people, and that white people were being left behind. Many working-class white people were turned off by television images of Black Panther militants with their fists in the air and holding rifles, which was a challenge to their security. Many white people blamed increases in crime on black people. Through the 1960s, home break-ins, auto theft, muggings, and rape were on the rise, and although I didn't see this as rooted in racial causes, many white people did. The law-and-order political response championed by Alabama governor George Wallace and President Richard Nixon had a powerful appeal and was the main issue that split traditionally Democratic voters into conservative ranks. In 1970, the main focus of the Democratic leadership was to hold on to City Hall, something that was not to be taken as a given, since Arlen Specter had come to within eleven thousand votes of winning in 1967.

Although neither one of them liked him personally, both Mayor Tate and Pete Camiel believed that police commissioner Frank L. Rizzo was the only Democrat who could win and keep the old coalition together. Lots of white working-class voters around the city liked Rizzo and the blunt law-and-order politics he represented. Rizzo was working class and took pride in his background. He was born and raised in South Philadelphia, the son of a homemaker and police officer. After high school, he took a job as a crane operator at the Midvale Steel plant, and after a brief stint in the Navy, he came on the Philadelphia Police Department as a motorcycle cop.

Frank Rizzo had a reputation for toughness. From his early days on the force, there were many accounts of his mistreating suspects. In one famous incident, Rizzo and other officers beat up some rowdy Navy sailors, who sued him for his actions. Instead of changing, Rizzo actually boasted about his hard tactics, saying it was the only way to fight crime. Despite this, in 1952, Rizzo was named captain in charge of the nineteenth district at 12th and Pine Street, and his brash reputation grew. In 1959, Rizzo directed a series of highly publicized raids on coffee shops in downtown Philadelphia, targeting anyone he considered part of the counterculture. Some of the individuals who were accosted and the shop owners filed civil rights suits against him, accusing him of discrimination. These kinds of actions defined his career. After Jim Tate appointed him police commissioner in 1967, Rizzo continued to act this way. In November 1967, hundreds of public high school students held a protest demanding black studies courses as part of the official curriculum. When police showed up, they moved in on the students with their billy clubs, with Rizzo shouting an order to "get their black asses!" He denied saying it, but it was caught on television footage.

Rizzo's reputation for being tough on black militants was again in the news in the summer of 1970 when the Black Panthers assembled in Philadelphia to convene the Revolutionary People's Constitutional Convention. Following the shooting of a Fairmount Park police guard on the evening of August 29, 1970, Rizzo ordered a raid on Panthers headquarters in a North Philadelphia row house, wrongly assuming that they were the ones behind the attack. The arrested men were brought out on the sidewalk and made to strip naked. Photos of these arrests were on the front pages of the newspapers the next morning, and spread around the world.

I had my first interaction with Rizzo a few weeks after this raid when he came to an AFL-CIO Political Action Committee banquet. There was a lot of talk about Rizzo running for mayor, and even though he hadn't announced yet, he was acting like he was already on the campaign trail. He knew he would need labor's support to win and was courting the unions hard. At the start of this banquet, I'm sitting on the stage with some of the other Central Labor Union vice presidents, the group that determined organized labor's policies in the city, and Rizzo comes over to us and starts bragging about how he literally took the Panthers' pants down. He's standing there on the stage with a bunch of white labor leaders, leaning over to us, saying, "Boy, did I straighten those niggers out. They ain't going to get away with shit so long as I'm commissioner. I'll beat the shit out of them." Everybody was like "go get 'em Commissioner, give them what they deserve." I'm sitting there and couldn't believe what he'd said. Most of the other white guys were sucking it all in, guys I liked, and that really disgusted me.

From that point on, there was no way I would ever support Frank Rizzo, no matter how popular he was with the other labor guys. He was anathema to me, totally philosophically the direct opposite of what I believed. He purposely appealed to white racial prejudice. Rizzo's campaign had signs all over the city that said "Rizzo Means Business." It didn't mean business in the sense of supporting mom-and-pop stores in the neighborhoods or promoting economic growth more generally; it was a not-so-subtle message that he would deal harshly with black people, who many white people believed were responsible for all the crime and problems in the city. Accordingly, Rizzo had virtually no support in black sections of the city because he didn't campaign in any of them.

Once Rizzo formally announced he was running in the 1971 Democratic Party primary, he called up Ed Toohey to set up a meeting so he could address all of the city's labor leaders. Just about everyone went to hear him speak. I still had what he said previously, his use of the N-word, in my head, and I was fuming as he was at the podium. He's ranting and raving, asking for the support of the AFL-CIO. I stood up and said to him, "Most of labor in this city is behind you, but I want you to know I'm not supporting you. I think you're a racist and I don't agree with any of the stuff you're doing." For all his bravado, Rizzo actually wasn't accustomed to dealing with this kind of direct confrontation, and he got all bent out of shape. He started yelling at me, and said to the others that I should be thrown out. The other labor guys said they couldn't, that I represented the biggest union in the city, which I did at the time. At least they defended me. "We don't agree with him, he talks this way all the time," I overheard some of them saying to him. Rizzo, who knew about me already because of my activities against the war in Vietnam, called me a "leftist pig."

I said, "I'm not a pig, the pig I look at is you!" Everybody was horrified that I was talking that way and that there was such open sparring between me and their candidate.

There was no doubt in those early weeks of 1971 that Rizzo was the front-runner, but he had some formidable opposition. In early 1971, Congressman William J. Green III announced he was running for mayor. He was rising quickly as a congressman and had been appointed to the House Ways and Means Committee, one of the most powerful in Washington. I cautioned him that he ought to think twice about giving that up, since, in another few years, he could be chair. Bill said he needed to expand his opportunities, had always wanted to be mayor, and believed he could win. I agreed right away to support him and saw him as the most viable option against Frank Rizzo. Most of the Democratic Party chieftains were against Bill Green running, including Mayor Tate and Congressman Bill Barrett, who were adamant, saying that he was already congressman and should stay put. In March, the city's Democratic Policy

Committee, the group I served on that approved candidates and determined who would get the official backing of the party machine, met and
endorsed Frank Rizzo. Right away, I stood up and declared that I could
no longer serve on the committee if it endorsed Rizzo. That's how strongly
I felt about it.

By the time this happened, I was already active in Bill Green's campaign. I had been treasurer of his congressional races since 1964, and he
asked me to be involved as an adviser. I met with him to discuss strategy
almost every day in his house on Herbert Street, a few blocks from where
I lived in Northwood. Dick Duran, another St. Joe's man a year ahead of
Bill and me, was part of a kind of informal Kitchen Cabinet of advisers
who met regularly. Bill was a very powerful man by this point, but I was
concerned because many people said he came off aloof. I told him he had
to connect with people, go to ward meetings, know and talk to every
committeeperson, shake their hand, let them know you're a human being
and not just come in and walk through and leave. That's what he used to
do. Some of the other advisers in that kitchen group didn't agree with me,
and told Bill that he was already dignified, already a congressman, and to
be confident in that. But I kept reminding him that he needed to show he
was no different than the people in the row houses across Philly, the
people he represented.

Some of the changes I urged on him early in his 1971 campaign even
came down to the way he dressed. Bill wore an overcoat that was really
long; it went down to his socks and had a belt around the waist. It was
very Chestnut-Hillish, very upper class, not something you'd see too
many guys in Northeast Philly wearing. I confronted him on it. "Bill, you
shouldn't be wearing that," I said. "It makes you look old." I thought he
should wear a suit coat and forget about the overcoat. "If you're going to
an event, get somebody to drop you off at the door, you shake some hands
and you go inside. John F. Kennedy never wore an overcoat or hat. What
you are wearing is not going to fly in South Philly. You're a young guy.
People compare you to Kennedy. Make yourself look like Kennedy," I
advised him. Dick Duran and others, they must have thought I was too
negative, because, all of the sudden, I stopped getting invited to these
kitchen bull sessions. I would still set up meetings for him with labor and
talk to him, but I wasn't really part of his inner circle any more. I kind of
lost that closeness to him after that exchange about the overcoat.

According to most political observers, the primary this year was a race between Rizzo and Bill Green, both of whom had campaign money and volunteers due to sizable union support, and promises from ward leaders who pledged to back them. Bill appealed to the city's sizable liberal base who were for a strong economy and social programs, while Rizzo's message was mostly law and order. Another liberal was former city councilman David Cohen, who briefly ran, but dropped out because I think he realized he might take votes away from Green and aid Rizzo. State representative Hardy Williams, who along with John White Sr. had founded the Black Political Forum to coordinate black empowerment in the city, started the first serious mayoral campaign by a black candidate, with a platform to address issues like gang violence, unemployment, and improvements in mass transit. More than anything, Williams focused on registering black people to vote, and through his campaign, thousands did.

Polls showed a close tie between Green and Rizzo, and many Philadelphians said they were unsure whom they would vote for the week before the elections. Rizzo won with almost half the votes cast, taking most white working-class areas in Northeast Philadelphia, Kensington, and Roxborough, and his base in South Philadelphia. Congressman Green got 35 percent, outperforming Hardy Williams in the predominantly black wards, where Rizzo got only the smallest number of votes cast.

With Frank Rizzo's primary win, for the first time in my life, I decided that I had no other option but to turn to the Republican Party. The GOP's candidate in 1971 was Thacher Longstreth, a true blue-blood politician from the city's Chestnut Hill section. Longstreth was a known figure in the local political scene, as he had previously run as the Republican standard-bearer against Richardson Dilworth in 1955, and was now head of Philadelphia's Chamber of Commerce. Longstreth had an Ivy League pedigree, a graduate of Princeton University who had served in the military during World War II, and came home to get involved with business. His personal style reflected his upper-class background, a point that Rizzo hit him hard on. He was famous for wearing argyle socks and bow ties, which I thought was over the top, but he was good on the issues as far as I was concerned. Thacher stood up against Rizzo in his press releases and in public debates, characterizing his opponent— appropriately—as a bully. I campaigned for Thacher, and Congressman Bill Barrett and the Democrats in South Philadelphia and all over the city were disappointed with me because I didn't back their candidate, but I felt so strongly, I couldn't back down.

Meeting after meeting, I would be one of the only voices challenging him. In October 1971, the AFL-CIO delegates met to endorse a candidate for mayor, and I brought all of the people from the Food Council to try to stop the vote going to Rizzo. There were some of the guys, including Frank Keane of the Teamsters, who were adamant for Rizzo and refused to back me, but I convinced the others in the Meat Cutters and Bakery Workers to take a stand against him. I had a lot of respect in this section of the movement, and they all voted with me against the Rizzo endorsement. Of course, I got slaughtered in the vote, and Rizzo got the endorsement of organized labor. The Teamsters Joint Council broke with their long-standing custom to stay away from political endorsements and backed Rizzo. Even AFSCME, which had been so adamant against him in the primary, got on board with the rest of the labor movement and backed him now.

In the November election, Frank L. Rizzo won by seventy-eight thousand votes, hardly a landslide by Philadelphia standards, but decisive enough. Pete Camiel and other party bosses were happy to maintain Democratic control, but thousands of conservative Republicans had crossed over to vote for Frank, a fact that the new mayor was keenly aware of. The election map showed starkly how racially polarized the city was over the new mayor. Only one predominantly black ward—Congressman Barrett's 36th ward in South Philadelphia—gave Rizzo a majority. The day after the election, President Nixon called Rizzo to congratulate him. I was aware of the fact that Rizzo was part of Nixon's new working-class strategy, one that would tap white ethnic voters in the big cities as a foundation for a new majority conservative political party. Rizzo represented this demographic perfectly, and Nixon nurtured a relationship based upon law and order and promises of federal monies to the city. Rizzo's victory was a bad omen for how Philadelphia might go in the upcoming presidential election; it wasn't a good thing for working people, let alone the retail clerks in the supermarkets and department stores.

THESE THOUGHTS WERE PARAMOUNT in my mind as I continued my work in negotiations for my members in the stores. The mayoral election wasn't the final battle I waged in 1971. Our members who worked in the retail sector were particularly vulnerable. In August 1971, Nixon unilaterally declared a price and wage freeze. Although this would impact union members around the country, the president didn't even consult with AFL-CIO chief George Meany. Because of this, it would be next to impossible to get wage increases in our contracts. For retail workers who were already struggling to pay bills and make rent and mortgage, this made it very difficult. These were still lower-paid workers, and a wage freeze impacted them and it made the union's abilities to advance their cause more difficult. Such a decision proved to me the reasons why we fought against Nixon's election three years earlier and the need for labor to remain in opposition.

This was especially true for the majority of women workers Local 1357 represented in the department stores. In early 1967, the department store local merged with 1357, with the majority of their membership coming out of Lit Brothers, one of the main department stores in downtown Philadelphia. The main building was at 8th and Market Street, built in 1890, a staple of downtown architecture, employing hundreds of cashiers, cafeteria staff, wrappers, perfume and cosmetic ladies, and commissioned salespeople.

Department stores employed a lot of women and there was a myth that they worked these jobs only as a supplement to their husband's paycheck. From what I saw this was not true. Just like the women cashiers in the supermarkets, the majority of the women were there because they had to be, they needed the money to take care of basic necessities, not as pin money. A sizable number were elderly, and some took these jobs to add to their social security checks after their husbands died. The women worked there year after year and they'd get themselves all dressed up to come into the store every morning, it was their whole life. As employees, they got a 10 percent discount and a lot of the money they made channeled right back into the store. After they merged with Local 1357, I don't think the women who worked at Lit Brothers really knew what to make of me. I was just twenty-eight years old, and looked a lot younger, and some of these women saw me like a kid brother, or little nephew. I could tell because they would give me hugs and kisses when I came in. (See Figure 9.1.)

Even though they treated me like this, I couldn't overlook the precarious economic position they held. Most of these people were making just a little better than minimum wage, less than four thousand dollars a

Figure 9.1 Wendell W. Young III speaking to striking Lit Brothers' workers, December 1971. (Reprinted with permission from the *Philadelphia Inquirer.*)

year, which ranked below the city's sanitation workers. Any effort the union made in this period to bargain for raises was wiped out by President Nixon's price and wage control policies in 1971. To try to get some support from other unions and to raise awareness of our concerns, I got a resolution passed with the Philadelphia AFL-CIO against the president's economic program, along with a call for a march of low-wage workers on Washington, DC. On October 14, 1971, Local 1357 chartered ten buses and brought about a thousand men and women to the nation's capital. About half of the people who went down for the protest were from Lit Brothers, joined by five hundred more who weren't even represented by the union from Strawbridge's, Gimbels, and John Wanamaker's. The action we coordinated that day was the first of its kind since Nixon's new economic policy had been announced that summer, and I hoped it would encourage bigger gatherings in the days that followed.

As soon as our buses arrived, we had a big rally at Rayburn congressional offices where Congressman Bill Green met us, along with New

Jersey senator Clifford P. Case and Philadelphia's representatives Josh Eilberg, William Barrett, and James A. Byrne. I remember that Bill Barrett gave an impassioned speech. It was a hot day and we were so overcrowded in this place, all of us sweating profusely. Bill always wore a toupee, and as he was giving the speech, I noticed that it was sliding off to the side of his head. It was slipping off, almost down to his ear. He didn't realize it, and I was sitting behind him and could see some of the people in the audience starting to smile. I got up and whispered in his ear, "Congressman, your toupee is sliding down." Bill left the stage, and Congressman Josh Eilberg got up and finished the speech for him. I know that some of the people might have thought it was kind of funny, but actually our members had even more respect for Congressman Barrett. They were like, "He's out here fighting for us, and look at him, even his wig's falling off."

After lunch, we walked over to the White House, carrying our signs calling for an end to the wage freeze and for a living wage for all workers. I felt our mobilization could start a wave of similar gatherings to put pressure on Nixon by showing that ordinary working Americans were against his wage control programs. I wanted to make the problems of low-wage retail workers visible in the media and to influence how decisions were being made. This tactic could work. I was convinced of it. I believed it could have been the start of a mass movement, but the labor movement under George Meany was sour on it. Following the speeches at the congressional offices, our delegation walked by the AFL-CIO building, but, even though he was there in his office, Meany refused to have anything to do with us. In fact, some of his aides came down to say that he disapproved of our march and was very upset that we had gathered there. They told me he said that I was nothing but a "troublemaker." I said, "Yeah, I'm pointing out there's trouble for working people." We had a different reception when we went over to the Retail Clerks Union main office, where some of our top officers even came down and spoke to the crowd.

If this had been a European capital, there'd be thousands and thousands of people marching with us, members of different unions, across sectors of the economy, retail and otherwise, along with student groups, consumers, and activists of all kinds, in a show of solidarity—but this small rally was the best we could do here. It showed me how disengaged the labor movement was in the United States, each union focused only on its own narrow needs, rather than all of society's problems—the concerns of all working people—at large. It disgusted me. It was very obvious that the national labor movement was drifting, disconnected from the needs of their members, not to mention potential members. Still, the march was a sign of our militancy. We were in negotiations with the Lit Brothers's management and the contract expired in the summer but I had decided to extend the negotiations into the fall, because I knew if we struck in the holiday season, it would be more effective. In this range of talks, we wanted to gain health and welfare and pensions, and importantly, a guarantee that management wouldn't close the stores and a provision that stated, if they did, the members would be transferred to other Lit Brothers outlets in the region.

On November 15, 1971, a week before the Black Friday sales bonanza, 850 members from Local 1357's Department Stores section went on strike, the first time in Lit Brothers's eighty-year history. The strike was memorable for me because it was the first one I ever brought my oldest son, Wendell, to. He was just ten years old then and was very effective on the picket line. He got on a bullhorn and declared, "Don't shop here! My Daddy is the president of the union. Please don't shop at Lit Brothers!" Even with Wendell on the picket line, Lit Brothers president J. P. Hansen kept the store open for a few days with managers operating the registers, but they eventually had to close down. We had hundreds of pickets down on Market Street. Right across from the store at 8th and Market was an H&H dinette and our members would go over there from the picket lines to get coffee. I remember joining some of them over there, and some of the older ladies stood there looking up at the store, just stood there on the sidewalk looking up, like they were thinking, realizing what they had done: "I'm not working; I've worked there all my life. I'm on strike." They seemed mesmerized, looking at the store. Just standing there, looking up, I'll never forget that.

Lit Brothers had a number of unions representing workers in the stores, and they joined us on the picket lines in solidarity. This was my first interaction with John P. Morris, the president of Teamsters Local 115, which represented the heavy stock guys, the men who moved refrigerators and washing machines in all the stores. John was a legend in the Teamsters organization and would come to be one of the most powerful leaders in the region. He took over Local 115 in 1955 when it had exactly seven members; over the years, he added almost three thousand more in an industry that was very difficult to organize. Johnny—as almost everyone called him—grew up around Scranton, Pennsylvania, and while in high school he was involved in a serious electrical accident that caused him to lose some of his fingers of his right hand. Even with this, he won a scholarship to play football at the University of Scranton, but he eventually dropped out and moved to Philadelphia to take a job with Lit Brothers' shipping and receiving department. It was here that John got involved with the Teamsters and built that local up, eventually organizing prison guards, independent trash haulers, township police, and the cleaning crews and staff at the University of Pennsylvania.

In the beginning Johnny Morris and I got along fine, but what happened during this strike soured our relationship. When I knew we were getting weak, about the beginning of the strike's second week, I called this big meeting at the Ben Franklin Hotel and over a thousand people packed in. I invited Morris, whose men were supporting us, along with Frank Keane, the head of Teamsters Local 169, which represented drivers and warehousemen who service the store. Morris agreed to give a speech in support of the strike, but when he got to the microphone he started ripping into Lit Brothers executive, J. P. Hansen, in a way I hadn't expected. "This Jew kike bitch, we've got to get this Jewish bastard in line!" he started yelling. I was horrified—not only was Hansen Jewish, but so were the majority of the women who worked there in the store! Morris didn't know that, because most of the guys who worked heavy stock were Irish. After his speech, I almost had to call in the Army's tank division to keep my members in the Retail Clerks Union from going back to work. We were begging the women not to give in, but even before his speech they were losing their resolve. Now Morris had given them an excuse to rush back.

The next morning, Local 1357 members in the five stores on strike started going back to work, just as I suspected. Frank Keane was out there with me at 8th and Market Streets trying to reason with them, to convince them not to cross, but to everyone's shock, guess who's leading his men back in? Johnny Morris! He crosses the picket line, and when our people saw that, even more decided the strike was over and that they had better go back too if they were going to keep their jobs. The majority stayed put, but enough went back to damage our cause irrevocably. The strike continued for a few more days, but, on the seventeenth day, Lit Brothers secured a federal injunction that effectively ended the walkout. If we had continued, it would have destroyed our finances, and so we entered into mediation to try to work out a better deal.

On December 7, 1971, the twenty-day strike was settled with a new three-year contract providing a raise of thirty-six cents an hour across that time. In addition, pensions were increased and our members were given a guarantee that they would get transfers to other regional outlets should the downtown Lit Brothers ever close. But I knew that the raises were still low. Even with the gains we had made, I knew we would have some difficult struggles in the days ahead.

10

THE NEW POLITICS

BY EARLY 1972, I had a mustache, my hair was a little longer with sideburns, and the clothes I wore were more informal. I would have a paisley tie or sometimes went to meetings with no tie at all, something unheard of from a labor leader ten years prior. Many of Philadelphia's older labor leaders considered me a full-blown hippie. It was true in that I was a young leader and part of the New Left in Philadelphia, but I also came out of the ward system where I still had a lot of pull and friendship with the city's Democratic Party leadership. This gave me an unusual position in the city at a transitional moment in its political history.

The 1960s saw the political empowerment of groups previously on the margins—African Americans, women, Hispanics, students, gays, and lesbians—and just as gains were being realized, there was a reaction against these developments. A lot of Philadelphians didn't like these changes that were happening. Frank Rizzo's election in 1971 was, in many ways, a reaffirmation of an older way of doing things. He put a lot of emphasis on the fact that he was a guy from South Philadelphia and had a very personal way of doing things. He was known for returning phone calls to his office personally. He oversaw basic services such as making sure streets were maintained or replacing bulbs in alley lights. He attended the funeral of every city worker who died while he was in office. It didn't matter if you were a supervisor, a detective, or a street repairman. In this way, Frank was a lot like an old-style ward leader; he got personally

involved, and everything he did was a favor he expected people to remember, to tie them to him politically.

RIZZO'S APPEAL TO ROW HOUSE Philadelphia voters was also a reaction to a new kind of politics that was emerging after the late 1960s.
Coming out of the 1968 presidential campaign, there were two opposing
segments within the national Democratic Party. On one side, there was
the old-style urban politics that for years had controlled the nomination
process in the party and was represented by politicians like Jim Tate in
Philadelphia and Mayor Richard Daley in Chicago. The power centers of
the party were in the wards and precincts, and patronage, personal loyalties, and influences were key to which candidates were named for office
and the platforms they ascribed to. Organized labor played a critical role
in this setup, channeling money and volunteers to street campaigns. In
1968, labor saw Hubert H. Humphrey as their man. After 1968, a new
section of the party was emerging—the New Politics—and it was more
committed to participatory democracy and reforms that would strength-
en the roles played by women, minorities, and young people. These were
the coalitions building around Eugene McCarthy and George McGovern.
One of the criticisms of the old style of politics was that it had no diver-
sity, being dominated entirely by white men. In contrast, the New Politics
was built on a promise of a greater variety of voices represented in the
party organizations, based on a more open primary system that encourage new kinds of candidates that reflected the voters.

I agreed with a lot of the issues that were put forward by the advocates
of the New Politics. Those who came out of this wing of the party were
against the war, supported more democracy, and encouraged youth involvement and women's representation, all things I had pushed for in the
labor movement. They wanted to put an end to important decisions being
made in back rooms and wanted everything out in the open. They called
for more women and minorities to be involved in the political process
and for more young people to have a voice. This turn in Democratic Party
politics was shaped by a number of new social developments. First of all,
a lot of young people were coming out of college, and they may have been
a little more financially able because jobs, especially in technology, education, finance, and other white-collar fields were plenty in the 1960s and

into the 1970s. People were buying cars and had more pay and education, and, as a consequence, they didn't need to rely on neighborhood ward politicians the way their parents or grandparents often did.

I had come up through ward politics and knew its flaws, but I knew that, at its best, it allowed participation from the neighborhoods because the committeepeople were accountable to the people they lived near. It also had obvious flaws. By the late 1960s, most of the ward leaders were too old, and, with one or two exceptions, they were all white men. It was this way in big cities across the nation. On the heels of the 1968 convention, there was a push to reform the Democratic Party, especially in how it selected its presidential ticket. South Dakota senator George McGovern came out of Chicago as a prominent figure in the party and he oversaw a rewriting of the party rules. In 1970, the McGovern-Fraser Commission, a twenty-eight-member body set up by the Democratic National Committee, restructured the presidential nominations process, calling for more involvement from members, especially women, minorities, and youths, and a strengthening of the primary system where actual voters, rather than political insiders, determined who the candidates would be. I had seen how the political bosses controlled things in Chicago in 1968, and, when they couldn't, they tried to shut things down. It showed me that the big city mayors and ward leaders had too much power and that they should open it up and let people run in the primaries.

Maybe more than anyone else in Philadelphia's political scene, I could bridge these two very different worlds. I was part of the old neighborhood-centered system, having come up through the 35th ward organization; but I was also part of the New Left, the antiwar movement, and supported the demands coming from both the black freedom struggle and the emerging women's liberation movement. I believed that the various reforms were necessary if the Democratic Party was to continue to be a force in the new era. The new rules outlined by the McGovern-Fraser Commission were a step in the right direction for the Democratic Party, because it would make it more representative of its support base and more transparent in its operations so that the kind of infighting and chaos that had happened in Chicago would be avoided. I thought the ward system could be changed for the better: allow more participation in the neighborhoods, while appealing to young professionals and the college educated, and when they did, a stronger party would emerge.

ALL OF THESE DISCUSSIONS AND movements about the future of the Democratic Party had an eye toward the upcoming 1972 presidential contest. Hubert H. Humphrey wanted another chance at the White House, and most of Philadelphia labor backed him. I liked Humphrey's domestic platform because he put labor's concerns at the forefront, but I didn't think he could win. Mostly, though, I still didn't think he was an adamant antiwar candidate. Looking at the developing field by the end of 1971, I was more attracted to Maine senator Edmund S. Muskie who had run as Humphrey's vice presidential candidate four years earlier. Everybody liked the way he handled himself, and his liberal point of view. Since joining the Senate in 1959, he had a strong record of support for labor and backed both the repeal of state right-to-work laws and the establishment of pay standards for Mexican farm workers employed in the United States. Most important for me, this time around, he was speaking out against the war in Vietnam and promising to work to get U.S. troops out as soon as possible.

Philadelphia's Democratic Party chairman Pete Camiel was also an early Muskie backer, in part, I think, because they were both Polish American. A number of influential people from the 1967 Tate campaign, including my friend John Elliot, also came out for Muskie. Camiel told me that he was going to mention to the Muskie people that I was the kind of guy they should work with in Pennsylvania. In late 1971, Marciarose Shestack, a local television news personality, and her husband Jerome had a gathering at their penthouse apartment atop the Philadelphia, a fancy apartment building. I met the senator there for the first time and, at the end of our conversation, Muskie asked me if I would be state chairman for his campaign for president in 1972, and I agreed.

Going into 1972, Muskie had a lot of support, and he was clearly the front-runner in the pack of Democratic Party hopefuls. He had some serious backing in Pennsylvania, with Governor Shapp coming out early for the senator. In the Keystone State, labor had proven essential to any presidential campaign since the days of Franklin D. Roosevelt, and if he were to have any chance, Muskie needed endorsements from the Steelworkers, Teamsters, and other unions. I lobbied hard on his behalf. I called up various labor leaders, set up introductions, and had them come out to the rallies. Of course, since the Retail Clerks Union represented the state liquor store clerks, we could back him in sizable sections all across the state, in the rural districts as much as in Philadelphia and Pittsburgh. But toward the end of the trip, flying back with him to Philadelphia, I began to have serious doubts about him. I'm sitting on the plane and we were going over some issues and he asked what issues were big in Philadelphia. I said, "Now listen Senator, the big issue is definitely the economy. We're getting killed with the 5 percent wage freeze that Nixon put in. And for all workers, we need to up the minimum wage."

He looked at me and said, "Wendell, what is the minimum wage now?"

I looked at him dead silent. Is he asking me what the minimum wage is? I guess I was naive; I never dreamed that a senator wouldn't know what the minimum wage was. I looked at him and said, "The minimum wage? Are you talking about state or federal?" By the way he looked back at me, I could tell that he didn't have a clue what either of them was. I gave them to him. The retail clerk at Acme and A&P is trying to get along on these really minimal scales, and he had no way to really relate to that. It took the wind out of me. I realized that most of the others running for president weren't much better. As we were getting ready to land, Muskie was thinking about trying to break the ice with the crowd and he turned to me and asked, "Wendell, you've got any jokes I can tell?" I said, "Yeah, I'll give you a couple about Philadelphia." We got into the airport and drove out to a meeting at some union hall, and I don't know if he could read my face or not, but my enthusiasm was gone. I had to introduce him at the rally; I used to give these real barn burner introductions for people, and I did my best. The crowd loved him, but I was in crisis, and I bet it showed.

Ed Muskie was the kind of politician who was out of touch with the average working man or woman in the stores. I came across a lot of politicians like that. There were always a lot of upper-class politicians and people who worked as lawyers and in business, rather than in the trades or on the factory floor, and this was a problem since they were often unfamiliar with the everyday needs of people they represented. This had been the case in Philadelphia, too, but there was a certain kind of politician that had come out of the New Deal period who was different. This hadn't always been the case, as many of Philadelphia's leaders had been working class, and didn't forget the people they came from. Congressman William A. Barrett is a perfect example. When he was in his early twenties, before he got into politics, he worked as a boilermaker at Atlantic Refinery: he punched the clock at the plant gates every morning; he knew what overtime meant; and he saw men get injured on the job and knew what a union did for people. The problems of working-class people weren't something he had a hard time understanding. Bill never lost his connection to ordinary people. He flew home every day from Washington, DC, to see his constituents in South Philadelphia, something I always admired about him.

I didn't stew in my doubts about Muskie for too long because his campaign imploded a week or so later. While in Maine, as he talked about a newspaper editorial that had insulted his wife, it looked like he was choking up and beginning to cry. Muskie's press conference was held in the middle of a snowstorm, and the tears were snowflakes, but this was the final straw for his weakening campaign, and he got out. In April, with the full backing of organized labor across the commonwealth, Hubert H. Humphrey won the Pennsylvania primary by 169,000 votes.

I was already elected as a delegate for Muskie, but he had dropped out before the convention, and I then shifted my vote to South Dakota senator George McGovern. He had a very strong labor voting record and had overseen the important changes in the Democratic Party's structure after 1968. McGovern was one of the most liberal politicians in the country. He was committed to tax reforms that would close loopholes that allowed the rich to write off luxuries, was for full employment that would send federal monies to local states and cities, and had sponsored a National Health Insurance Act that would give medical care to all. He was against Nixon's wage program but would focus on consumers by keeping consumer prices reasonable. The major point, though, that turned me toward him the most was that he was against the continuation of the war in Vietnam and supported a total and immediate removal of U.S. troops.

Most of organized labor was turned off by the cultural politics of McGovern's supporters. I got a full sense of this at the 1972 Democratic Convention in Miami Beach, Florida. McGovern was popular with a lot of countercultural figures like the Beat poet Allen Ginsberg, who was there at convention gatherings, in his long hair, beads, and a poncho. That really turned off guys like Ed Toohey. Add to that other controversial activists like yippie leader Abbie Hoffman and civil rights spokesman Jesse Jackson, plus the various feminists and gay activists who were there as well. They resented the new rules that gave people who were not party regulars from the ward committees and the labor unions more say over the kinds of candidates that were to be selected. I'd been to the previous

Figure 10.1 Philadelphia AFL-CIO Central Labor Union president, Edward F. Toohey, 1965. (From the collection of Wendell W. Young III.)

two national conventions, and, from what I saw there from the floor, this one was very different. (See Figure 10.1.)

I remember the reaction Ed Toohey had watching the types of things we saw. He was a big Humphrey supporter, and a loyal Democrat, but he completely despised George McGovern. I remember the kinds of conversations I had with Toohey during the 1972 convention. As part of the new rules of the convention, everybody who had something to say was given a chance to speak. One time, I was down there on the floor sitting next to Toohey when there was someone up there at the microphone who, if I am remembering correctly, was a transvestite. Toohey blurts out, "My God, this is a disgrace!" He was literally tight lipped, almost shaking.

I said, "Ed, what are you sitting here listening for?"

"I've got to see what's happening," he said. "The country's going to pot. Jesus Christ, this is what the Democratic Party has come to? They've got these fags up there talking about their rights. What's going on here?"

I said, "Ed, get with it. This is what's happening. It's a new society."

As much as I was open to a lot of the new cultural stances that were happening, I have to admit that from a purely strategic standpoint, the convention was poorly run. The 1972 proceedings were completely disorganized, and the nomination process took longer than anyone had expected. On the night of the state-by-state roll call that boosted McGovern over the top, he gave his acceptance speech at about two in the morning. I remember his speech. A sizable portion of the delegates had returned to their hotel rooms, and, because of the late hour, most people around the country weren't watching on television either. That was too bad, because it was really one of the best speeches I've ever heard. The theme of the speech was "Come Home, America," which I agreed with completely. America had lost its way, had forgotten its position in the world, and needed to come home, to remember its better nature. Of course, it was also in reference to the disastrous policy in Vietnam, a call to bring our soldiers home. I thought McGovern had a chance that Americans would unite against Nixon because of the war but also because of their own economic interests. We needed as a nation to focus on our own social and economic problems.

A week after the convention, George McGovern sent me a handwritten letter inviting me to a conference in Hawaii and asking me to organize his campaign in Philadelphia. I agreed to do this because I knew how important this election was and because I believed that the best way I could help my members in the retail stores was to work to determine who would be in the White House overseeing the nation's economic policies. McGovern's nomination boosted me in the Philadelphia Democratic Party because I was his most outspoken supporter from our delegation. I had a strong position, because the old style ward leaders knew me and knew they could work with me, and I had links with the youth activists, college students, and black power sections in Philadelphia. The city's Democratic Party chairman Pete Camiel was glad that I agreed to take on these responsibilities especially since McGovern's state field director for Pennsylvania was a guy named Rich Chapman, who went on leave from his position as a philosophy professor at Penn State to help with the campaign. Someone like that didn't have any sway with ward leaders in Philadelphia, so it was important that I take on a major leadership role.

Right away, I realized that this would be the most difficult political campaign I had ever been involved with. Under George Meany's directive, the AFL-CIO for the first time did not endorse a presidential candidate and forbade local councils from backing other national candidates. This was a major roadblock for McGovern, since in any political campaign everything comes down to money. You need it to get your message out, to print campaign posters, lawn signs, and literature, to make campaign buttons, and to order takeout food for telephone bank volunteers and door-to-door canvassers. Raising money for George McGovern in Philadelphia was tough. To his credit, Pete Camiel raised a little on his own. Among the peace activist community, Joe Miller, one of the original founders of SANE, helped bring in thirty thousand dollars cash, hosting a cocktail party with Ted Kennedy at his house for one thousand dollars a person. Money came in from the more affluent downtown section where he lived, as well as Chestnut Hill and Germantown, but there were few neighborhood fund-raising operations in other sections of Philadelphia. It was very frustrating to me because I knew the kind of financial power organized labor had if they would only use it.

There were thousands of people around the city who hated Nixon and were ready to get out to support McGovern. But Nixon had his supporters, too, as most of Philadelphia's Teamsters and Building Trades unions and the city's firefighters and police organizations came out strongly for him. I knew that McGovern wasn't that popular among many of my own union membership in the supermarkets. Nixon's economic shock policies were crushing low-wage workers and the members in supermarkets and department stores. According to the federal regulations, no American worker could gain beyond a 5.5 percent wage increase, a rule that came into effect just after I had negotiated a 19 percent pay boost for thirteen thousand clerks and cashiers in stores. Because of Nixon's program, the members would have their twenty-six-dollar-a-week raise cut to just seven dollars. Similar to what I did with the Kennedy campaign in 1960, I got chance books, where members could sign their name, give two dollars, and become a member of the Dump Nixon Committee. Through this, I collected over one hundred thousand dollars for the campaign, but that wasn't enough. Pete Camiel and I sat down and he leveled with me, "Wendell, you've got to get some money from the AFL-CIO. They haven't done diddly." While stopping short of endorsing Nixon, Meany had forbidden any AFL-CIO council to contribute anything to McGovern. I knew we had a lot of money, almost three-quarters of a million dollars in the COPE treasury, and I went over to the AFL-CIO headquarters at 22nd and Market Streets to talk to Ed Toohey.

"Eddie," I said, "the McGovern campaign needs some money. I need at least one hundred thousand dollars from the COPE fund."

"Well, I can't do that," he says back.

"What do you mean you can't do that, Eddie? You have almost one million dollars in the fund. I'm a Vice President on the council and I know what you've got."

He said, "We've got to save that for a rainy day."

"Ed, it's fucking pouring out! What the hell's a rainy day, this is it!"

He said, "He can't win, anyhow!"

"Yes, he can win, he can win Philadelphia. He can win all of Pennsylvania!"

I pressed him to give the campaign some money, even if it would piss off George Meany. In the end, Ed Toohey wound up giving Philadelphia's McGovern campaign forty thousand dollars, period. That might seem like a lot, but for a presidential race in the nation's fourth largest city, it wasn't. But that was it, and I was lucky to get that. On the other side, Nixon's attempts to sell his campaign to conservative labor leaders and much of labor's rank and file paid off. In Philadelphia, the Building and Construction Trades Council, along with the Fraternal Order of Police (FOP) Lodge 5 and the majority of the various Teamsters locals in the region came out with strong statements of endorsement for Nixon.

For me, the problem of organizing George McGovern's presidential campaign in Philadelphia was made more difficult by the fact that Mayor Frank L. Rizzo, despite the fact that he was an elected Democrat, was actively supporting Nixon. The president had been seeking Rizzo's endorsement and had made promises of federal support for the city should the mayor do so. In a press conference, Rizzo brought a plucked chicken that had a McGovern-Shriver sticker on it, and held it up in contempt. This was the start of the open feud Pete Camiel had with Mayor Rizzo in the years that followed. By now, Pete felt that Rizzo was a Republican all along and he didn't want him in the Democratic Party. More than that, Rizzo believed in Nixon's cultural program against the antiestablishment and thousands of row house Democrats in Kensington and South Philadelphia were on the same page. As I said earlier, the McGovern campaign was the most difficult I have ever worked on. Anonymous threats were made against me and my family. Random people would show up at my house wanting to argue with me about my support for McGovern. Sometimes they would harass my next-door neighbor, mistaking him for me.

It got so bad that he put a sign up on his lawn, saying that Wendell Young lived one house over, not here.

Rizzo intervened to disrupt our campaign efforts every chance he could. George McGovern's Philadelphia campaign headquarters was in the Keystone Building at 220 South Broad Street and beginning in early September, every day I would park my car in a lot behind the headquarters, and every day a police officer would order it towed. Eighty-seven times my car was towed. I had to go get it each day, but I refused to budge on it. That's the way Rizzo got back at me, and he would laugh about it. I would call up the police and say that I had a permit, and they would say the mayor said that the car shouldn't be there. I would have to send someone down there to get my car at the auto pound down by the river. There were other ways he would try to get at me. Often, when trash was collected, the private haulers forgot to take it away from our dumpsters. If a driver or delivery truck came to drop off literature, or office supplies, he'd get a ticket. Every other truck was fine, but cops harassed us with Rizzo's approval. He would orchestrate harassing stuff like that.

Despite the difficulties faced, I had great hopes that in the end, George McGovern would sweep to a narrow win in November. Voter turnout meant everything, and there were good reasons to think Philadelphia would be the groundswell that pushed Pennsylvania all the way over for McGovern. Thousands of people were coming out to campaign rallies, some of the biggest public gatherings I had ever been a part of. The most memorable was a massive lunch hour rally in downtown Philadelphia on September 13, 1972, when a crowd of five thousand blocked off Broad Street right outside the Bellevue-Stratford Hotel—a sea of people for three blocks that jammed intersections all the way to City Hall. I was on the podium with McGovern, Senator Ted Kennedy, Pennsylvania senator Joseph S. Clark, and Pennsylvania governor Milton Shapp, and I could feel the energy from the crowd. I had reports that the campaign was picking up ground across the city and surging in the surrounding suburbs. (See Figure 10.2.)

On October 20, 1972, events in Philadelphia were the major news story of the presidential campaign. Nixon made a promise to come to Philadelphia's Independence Hall the week before the election to sign the State and Local Fiscal Assistance Act, a measure that increased federal funding to state and municipal governments. When word got out that the president was going to be in the city, the Philadelphia Peace Action

Figure 10.2 McGovern campaign rally in downtown Philadelphia, September 13, 1972. From left: Senator Joseph S. Clark Jr.; Pennsylvania governor Milton Shapp; Democratic presidential nominee and senator George McGovern; Senator Edward Kennedy; Wendell W. Young III. (From the collection of Wendell W. Young III.)

Coalition representing various antiwar groups planned a major protest. The night before Nixon arrived, a group of Quakers had an all-night vigil on the steps of Independence Hall, the start of what would be a large action planned at 5th and Market Street the following day. Unions opposed to Nixon's economic policies organized and joined the action—which besides the retail clerks included the Hospital Workers, Textile Workers, the Meat Cutters, the UFW, and AFSCME. Besides a big downtown rally that was planned, the unions called a partial work stoppage across the city because of wage and price control board freezes and all that stuff Nixon had done against working people.

Around noon, a thousand people, some with labor and others with peace groups convened on Market Street and marched down to Independence Hall. Nixon had just arrived by helicopter, and I'd never seen anything like it before—there were Secret Service men everywhere and snipers had taken positions on the rooftops. Other major dignitaries were there including Vice President Agnew, New York governor Nelson Rockefeller, and Mayor Frank Rizzo, as an official who would be a beneficiary of the federal act, which promised to send money to the city.

Police had set up barricades outside the grounds, and, as protesters arrived, things got ugly. The protest had been well planned, and an injunction had been issued to the police by U.S. District Judge Daniel H. Huyett III reaffirming the constitutional rights of picketers to access the area. But as I was walking, I saw that some of the protesters were being beaten. As I got closer, I saw a police officer dragging a woman by the hair down the steps of Independence Hall. Another young man was sucker punched in the face by a Nixon supporter. He was knocked out cold on the sidewalk. It was in full view of the police, but no one made a move to arrest the man who punched him. The abuses I saw that day sickened and angered me.

I saw all of this, being in the thick of the protest out on the streets around Independence Hall that day. I was leading a group of marchers, walking down the sidewalks along the route, and there were hundreds of cops all over the place. Inspector George Fencl, who was in charge of Rizzo's Civil Disobedience Squad sees me and blurts out, "You want me to arrest you! You think I'm going to arrest you, Wendell? You'll be all over the papers on me." I said, "Fuck you, George. You're right, I do want you to arrest me, and you don't have the balls to do it." All of a sudden, a line of police on horseback came at us while we're standing there, backing into us. I remember one of the horses literally started to take a shit on us. That's when we pushed back against them. What were we supposed to do, let a horse take a shit on us? We pushed back hard, and the cops came in and arrested some of us. They pulled me out of the crowd, and took me away. There were plenty of reporters around on the streets, and I was talking to as many of them as I could as I was led to the police wagon. Down at the Police Roundhouse, there were about forty of us who'd been taken in—and they held us in the cells for ten hours, even though we were never charged with violating any laws.

These were the kind of abusive and threatening actions that characterized the climate in the days before the 1972 election. There were other dirty games. Rizzo was threatening ward leaders that if they helped get out the vote for McGovern, they would lose their jobs. A lot of ward leaders still had city jobs with the Office of Register of Wills and the courts, and Rizzo had virtual control over these jobs, even with civil service. He sent word that they were to get as many people as possible to split their ticket—go for Nixon at the top, but support Democrats locally. With the party split, the underlying point of the election was who was going to control the Democratic Party in Philadelphia. I watched the results come in at the Bellevue-Stratford Hotel with Pete Camiel and those guys. Of course, Mayor Rizzo wasn't there. We were up in the room and despite the polls, I was confident that McGovern was going to win. Results came in, first from Philadelphia, and McGovern won the city by 80,000 votes. This was a clear victory, no doubt, but considering that John F. Kennedy had won by over 320,000, it wasn't a good sign. Out in the western parts of the state, where I thought McGovern was strong, he got beat badly, and lost the state by 600,000 votes, the first time a Republican had taken Pennsylvania in a presidential race since Eisenhower's win in 1956. I walked over to the McGovern headquarters at the Keystone Building and the mood was so bleak, everyone watching television. Many of the volunteers were in tears. About nine o'clock, I got up to give a speech, and I tried to remind everyone that this was part of a longer fight, to not lose faith. "I don't think this is the end," I said. "You know, Christ was the biggest loser of them all—he got crucified, and that started it." I did my best there that night, addressing everyone who was there, but it was one of the most difficult speeches I'd ever have to give.

For years after, I remembered that night as one of the low points of my life. It was so depressing. But on another level, I felt vindicated, because I had won the city of Philadelphia, not Rizzo. "He's the guy that should go to the Republican Party where he belongs," I stated to reporters. I said that the dead chicken with a McGovern sticker that Rizzo held up at an infamous news conference earlier that year should be for Rizzo. The night of the election, I sent Channel 3's Eyewitness News anchor Vince

Leonard a dead duck. He's holding a dead duck on TV, saying, "Well, this was sent by Wendell Young, chairman of the McGovern campaign committee, to Frank Rizzo to hang up on his office wall."

Nixon's reelection only convinced me to stay in for the long haul. You don't back away from a fight. Many of the people arrested at the Independence Hall rally got together and sued the city for false arrest and won the case. Eventually, I got a check for five thousand dollars. I never cashed it though. I didn't want to profit from the protests. I just framed it and hung it in my office.

11

FIGHTING TIBERIUS

WITH RICHARD M. NIXON in the White House and Frank L. Rizzo running Philadelphia's City Hall, no question, it was a difficult time to be pushing for liberal causes. Rizzo was always at the center of local news, and the city was polarized, either loving him or hating him. At times, I could hardly believe the way he acted, the kinds of things he boasted that he could do as mayor seemed outrageous and out of step with the way previous mayors had acted. Rizzo was such a powerful personal figure and so domineering, acting like no rules applied to him, like a modern-day version of a Roman emperor, but from a South Philadelphia row house. I used to call him Tiberius, because he reminded me of the corrupt and power-crazed emperor who once ruled Rome.

In these years, Rizzo's policies and personality galvanized a local opposition movement that brought together a coalition of neighborhood-based civil rights activists, the antiwar movement, and thousands of young people who had a different vision for the city. Although many in Philadelphia's organized labor backed Rizzo, a significant bloc of unions did not, and I was a leader in this section. After Rizzo won reelection in 1975, this liberal coalition remained intact, and in response to what many believed was an overreach of power, would start a movement to remove him from office, just as President Nixon had been after Watergate. Although this reform movement came short of recalling him from City Hall, its message had a real impact that would shape the city's politics for years to come and show the ways that popular coalitions that had progressive labor at their center could reach their goals.

The political struggles that I focused on after 1971 happened at a time when Philadelphia's Retail Clerks Union was the strongest it had ever been. With aggressive organizing campaigns through the 1960s, RCIA Local 1357 now had almost eleven thousand members, the bulk of them in the Philadelphia-based supermarkets and state liquor stores. By 1973, I had been president of Local 1357 for ten years and I was proud of some important achievements. Through the negotiations I had headed, the rates of pay for clerks and cashiers in the region's unionized supermarkets had advanced by one hundred dollars a week. In 1964, clerks made under one hundred dollars. In 1974, they were making $190. Also, through collective bargaining agreements, the unspoken racial discrimination that blocked access to certain positions in the region's supermarket sector was overturned. Nonwhite people had advanced to assistant manager positions and as cashiers rather than being relegated to maintenance and janitorial jobs that had been the norm. Women's pay was equalized with that of male clerks after 1965, and there were more women who were managers and deli supervisors, which meant higher wages. (See Figure 11.1.)

Through the 1960s, more women around the country were joining unions in large numbers and becoming more active. Even though the national Retail Clerks Union had one of the largest female membership bases in the American labor movement, by the end of the decade, women still only had a limited voice in the organization and held no leadership positions. This was true with Local 1357 as well. All of our secretarial staff were women but in all of the stores the union represented in the Philadelphia region, there wasn't a single woman business agent or steward, and not one on the executive committee. This changed gradually in the early 1970s. When Local 1357 merged with Retail Clerks Union Local 1390 in 1967, there was an assistant to the local's president Joe McLaughlin named Sylvia Zimmerman who basically ran the local as an administrative assistant, handling all the problems that came into the office and sometimes going down to Lit Brothers to resolve grievances. With the merger, Joe was worried that Sylvia might lose her job, since I already had an assistant working for me. I suggested that we make Sylvia a business agent, since she already managed a lot of that work anyway. Joe didn't think we could, since she was a woman, but I disagreed.

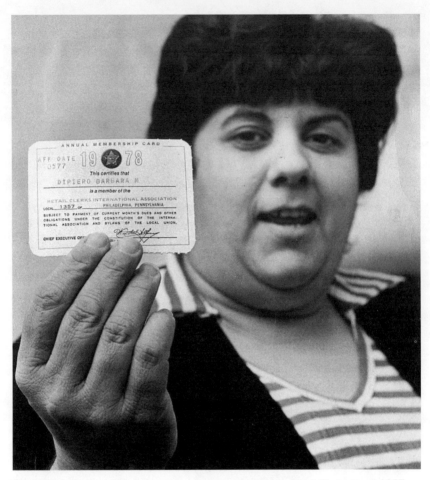

Figure 11.1 Barbara DiPiero holds her membership card to Retail Clerks Local 1357, December 17, 1978. Women were joining unions in increasing numbers in the 1970s. (Special Collections Research Center, Temple University, Philadelphia, Pa. Photograph by Jon Falk.)

Sylvia and I met for a coffee at the Horn and Hardart restaurant on Market Street across from Lit Brothers in Center City Philadelphia and I told her my idea. At first she was against it and said she couldn't do it. She said she didn't drive, and that there were no women business agents, but we talked it over and I convinced her. The funny thing was, in a lot of the stores, it was our women members, not the men, who had a hard time accepting her. To them only men could do the job. I just didn't understand this. I was brought up in a family that recognized women's abilities, with my aunts running hospitals and universities. Within a couple of years the attitude started to change and our members at Lit Brothers were 100 percent behind Sylvia. She would go into the stores with a list of grievances and she would resolve the ones that the men could never crack.

Besides the Retail Clerks, unions like AFSCME were organized in the health care fields, welfare agencies, and nonprofits where many women worked as clerical staff and nurses. With women now serving on committees and at the negotiating table, new kinds of concerns were up for discussion, such as childcare, flexible work schedules, contraceptive coverage, and maternity leave. Job classification studies were initiated in many public sector environments to encourage pay equity between the genders, which had an impact in the private sector as well. Union women were stepping up and talking about how they needed to gain more power in these organizations, many of which continued to resist their innovations. In 1974, the Committee of Labor Union Women (CLUW) was formed in Chicago to encourage a network to make women's issues known in organized labor, and, immediately, the Retail Clerks Union passed a resolution in support. Pat Halpin, who was out of the Philadelphia Federation of Teachers (PFT), was president of Philadelphia's CLUW chapter and, soon, over two hundred women joined, making it one of the largest and most active sections in the country.

One area where women were making the most impact in the labor movement was in the teachers' unions. The most militant job action in the city during Rizzo's first term was the 1973 teachers' strike, which shut down all public schools across the city for over a month. Going into negotiations, the union called for a 5.5 percent wage increase over three years, while the school board wanted to lengthen the school day by forty minutes. The PFT strike began on January 8, 1973, and almost immediately Common Pleas Court Judge D. Donald Jamieson issued an injunction forbidding the action, citing Pennsylvania's Public Employees Relations Act. Union leaders John Ryan, the chief negotiator, and Frank Sullivan, PFT Local 3 president, refused and were arrested for contempt of court and sentenced to six months to four years in prison. There was so much public outcry with 285,000 children missing almost a month of school, and no signs of resolution. Rizzo was in over his head, and he asked President Nixon to help by sending U.S. Assistant Secretary of Labor Willie J. Usery Jr., who set up meetings in Philadelphia, to try to reach a settlement. Even with this kind of pressure, the strike continued on.

By the fourth week, the strike had gained national attention, and the Philadelphia labor movement decided to take a stand for the teachers. There was some talk about staging an illegal general strike, one that would stop work in every union worksite in the city. Such an action was risky, and instead, a Day of Conscience was decided on, which would bring out thousands of union supporters in a major public rally in a show of force. Wednesday, February 28, 1973, was set aside as the day of the action, and scores of unions announced a one-day work stoppage. None of the city's trash would be collected; all buses, subways, and trolleys would halt; and the port would close. I met with the union stewards in the state stores, and they decided to shut down, too. The plan was to start gathering our people in the morning at three meeting points, at the intersections of North Broad and Girard Avenue, from South Broad and Washington Avenue in South Philadelphia, and from the steps of the Philadelphia Art Museum up the Parkway. At ten o'clock, all would begin walking toward City Hall for a noonday rally that would bring everyone— over fifteen thousand people—all together, for one of the largest labor rallies in the city's history.

Plans for this massive march and rally were ready to go but it was called off when a tentative agreement between the teachers and the school board was announced the day before. After thirty-nine days, the public school teachers returned to work on March 2, 1973, with slight salary increases, a reduction in class sizes, and no increase in the school day. The school board agreed to amnesty for all of the teachers who had joined the walkout, and PFT leaders Ryan and Sullivan were released from jail.

Frank Rizzo's labor troubles in 1973 showed that he was not invincible and that not every section of organized labor supported him. The progressive section of organized labor, the teachers, hospital workers, machinists, public sector, and retail workers were the core of a powerful liberal opposition that had developed in the city, a movement that was growing stronger. Nineteen seventy-three was marked by more worker militancy and strikes than I had ever seen in all my years as a labor leader. In June, about two thousand Retail Clerks Union members from Two Guys Department Store walked off over wage disputes, and a month later, my members in Pennsylvania's state liquor stores called a strike. In September, clerks at Acme, Food Fair, and A&P went on strike for three days.

Figure 11.2 Wendell W. Young III addressing Local 1357 members at the Arena, 46th and Market Streets, September 13, 1973. Members voted to accept a new contract, ending a three-day strike. (Special Collections Research Center, Temple University, Philadelphia, Pa. Photograph by James J. Craig.)

Across the region, thousands of other workers in dozens of industries had job actions, too, showing the power unionized workers wielded. (See Figure 11.2.)

Politically, unions mobilized enough voters to decide election outcomes. This was a critical point that I kept in mind. It was easy to feel discouraged after George McGovern's loss, and because the Democrats were in disarray at the national level, but, to me, this wasn't a hopeless time. Protest had results and change was possible. The antiwar movement had shown that ordinary Americans were turning against government policy, and, in the summer of 1974, President Nixon resigned as evidence of his corruption mounted, and after years of street protests against his programs. These kinds of popular protests had consequences, and I believed that the labor movement must take a lead to shape the kinds of coalitions that make such social change possible.

Those in the city of Philadelphia who had rallied against Frank Rizzo since his mayoral campaign remained opposed, and, by 1973, even a section of the regular Democratic Party organization was turning away from him. Rizzo's vocal support for President Nixon the previous year grated on a lot of the party's leadership, including Congressman Bill Barrett, and some questioned if he was really a Democrat at all. Democratic Party chairman Pete Camiel had really soured on the mayor, mostly over Rizzo's personal style in how he handled politics. Rizzo micromanaged everything. He would personally call up ward leaders and feel out where they stood and pressure them to support things he wanted. Mayors weren't supposed to do that. Camiel thought the ward leaders were his turf and didn't like the mayor overstepping this boundary. Other mayors had ways of dealing with ward leaders but they were more discreet about it. Jim Tate would go through Congressman Barrett, for example. When Joe Scanlon was in charge of the city committee, Tate would go through him, too.

These tensions were brewing beyond the public view since Rizzo's first weeks in office, but a more public break occurred in 1973 when the mayor and Camiel split over who they would support for district attorney. Rizzo insisted on having his Managing Director Hillel Levinson for the position, since he would be more loyal to him, but Camiel pushed for F. Emmett Fitzpatrick. When Camiel's guy won the primary, Rizzo urged ward leaders to get behind Republican incumbents Arlen Specter for district attorney and Tom Gola for controller's office. When the Democrats won, the party was in open feud, just as it had been when Democratic Party chairman Francis Smith refused to back James H. J. Tate in 1967.

All of what transpired in 1974 set the stage for the mayoral election coming up the following year. Before this political season got under way, Pete Camiel had come out and said that he would not support Rizzo. To rebuild a new party faction loyal to him, he was hoping to get Congressman William J. Green III to challenge Rizzo in the primaries. Even though Bill had always wanted to be mayor, he was eyeing a senatorial race in 1976 and just wasn't interested. At one point, Camiel came to me and urged me to run in the primary since he thought someone from the labor movement would mobilize a lot of people and put up a good fight. I said I wasn't interested, as I had too much going on as head of the Retail Clerks Union and, more importantly, had no desire to be mayor. Camiel looked elsewhere and, in the early weeks of 1975, Louis G. Hill, a state representative and the stepson of Richardson Dilworth, announced he would challenge Rizzo in the May primary. Hill was independently wealthy, and Camiel knew he could fund much of the campaign out of his own pocket, but I thought he was a weak candidate and didn't have a chance.

Even though many progressive union leaders disapproved of Rizzo, for every one who was against him, there were three who were for him. Rizzo was tremendously popular with the building trades. He was macho, right from the ranks of the white working class, a regular guy from South Philadelphia. Just as it had been for Jim Tate, organized labor was Rizzo's primary support base. To show just how much he understood this, he named former Building and Construction Trades Council president Jimmy O'Neill as his campaign manager during the primary race. Rizzo had also gained some additional labor backing going into this election, one that many of us found puzzling. Even though they had always hated one another, sanitation union leader Earl Stout and Frank Rizzo patched things up and developed a very pragmatic relationship. Earl had taken over as president of the seventeen thousand-member AFSCME District Council 33 in 1974 and, going into contract negotiations, had worked out a deal that guaranteed a 15 percent wage increase for the city's blue-collar sections. In exchange, Stout mobilized his union members on Election Day to get out the vote in African American sections of the city, gaining the mayor important support among voters who normally would not have given him a second look. This paid off as Rizzo took a substantial portion of the city's black vote in the primary, routing Lou Hill in every section of the city. (See Figure 11.3.)

With these results in, Camiel was pretty much isolated as the Democratic Party chairman and sat out the campaign while the majority of ward leaders backed Rizzo. Facing Rizzo in the general election that November was Thomas Foglietta, a popular city councilman from South Philadelphia. Tom was what you'd call a liberal Republican, open to working with organized labor, socially liberal, and sympathetic to many progressive programs. I liked him and knew I could work with him. After the primaries, he and GOP chairman Billy Meehan asked me to consider running for city council as a Republican. I remember they took me to a restaurant in a high-rise building overlooking city hall, and Meehan laid out a plan in which Foglietta would be mayor and I could be in city council as a key ally. Billy promised he'd back me in the election. I remember

Figure 11.3 Mayor Frank L. Rizzo waves in front of a crowd, May 14, 1974.
Philadelphia Building and Construction Trades Council president Thomas J. Magrann
is behind Rizzo to the right. (Special Collections Research Center, Temple University,
Philadelphia, Pa. Photograph by James J. Craig.)

I said, "But I'm a Democrat." I couldn't figure how they could do it. I
considered it, but I didn't take them up on it.

Even without the support of all the city's ward leaders, Rizzo boasted
he couldn't be beat, even if Foglietta had control of all of the voting
booths in South Philadelphia. In a characteristically vulgar statement
that became infamous, he told a *Philadelphia Magazine* reporter that
after the election, the way he would deal with those who stood against
him would "make Attila the Hun look like a faggot." But even with that
confidence, no one can ever take an election in Philadelphia for granted,
and Rizzo knew this. This was especially so because in April, Charles W.
Bowser, a lawyer and community activist who had served in Jim Tate's
administration as the city's first African American deputy mayor, announced a mayoral run on an independent ticket he formed called the
Philadelphia Party. Many of the city's black political class, clergy, and
business leaders were supporting him, including 1199c Hospital Workers
president Henry Nicholas. A massive registration drive was launched in

black wards in support of Bowser's program, and, even though he dismissed his campaign, Rizzo knew he posed a serious challenge.

I had gotten to know Charlie Bowser pretty well by this time and I liked him, but I didn't think the independent Philadelphia Party had any chance. I never thought that third parties could get very far, since we are so steeped in the two-party system. He campaigned well, though, pressing the important issues, and building a bipartisan coalition of working-class black people and white liberals. This wasn't enough, though, as Rizzo got 57 percent of the popular vote on Election Day, tallying huge margins in the city's white working-class neighborhoods, and winning in some of the black wards, too. Bowser ended up getting 138,783 votes, about 35,000 more than what Tom Foglietta pulled in. Tiberius's reign would continue, having won the greatest landslide victory in Philadelphia mayoral history. Even so, Bowser's showing proved something. An independent black political movement would be a powerful force in all-future elections, and if an African American candidate had the backing of the Democratic Party's policy committee and ward leaders, they would win, no question. The coalition Charlie Bowser built block by block, in West and North Philadelphia, in Germantown, and in Mount Airy would not melt away, it would remain a force to be reckoned with—a point that would be an important fact in the coming year.

One of the most important black leaders to rise in the city's Democratic Party in these years was Lucien Blackwell, who took over as leader of West Philadelphia's 48th ward in the mid-1960s. Lu dropped out of high school in 1950 to start working as a longshoreman on the Delaware River Port and joined the Army a few months later when the Korean War broke out. After his years in service, he came back to the docks and became a crew leader of the men who loaded boxes onto trucks and trains. He was eventually elected president of International Longshoremen's Local 1332, a small local of about four hundred men, mostly African American. As the result of his political engagement and his service to people who lived in his district, he was elected to the Pennsylvania legislature in 1972 and divided his time between Harrisburg and Philly. Even after Lu was elected to state office, he would be down there with his men as they started their workday in the mornings by the Walt Whitman Bridge. It wasn't some kind of a desk job for him.

I first met Lucien when he and I were both ward leaders when he first came on the Democratic city committee, but I really got to know him

after 1972 when he was a state legislator in Harrisburg. Lu was a devout
Baptist and never drank alcohol, and he didn't like the idea of young
people getting served alcohol illegally. He was a strong supporter of
Pennsylvania's state liquor stores, as he believed the system cut down on
juvenile drinking and drunk driving. We became allies and worked together against Rizzo. Early in 1975, he announced a run for city council
and asked me to help him line up labor support. I agreed right away, but
I had a tough time getting many other union leaders to back him. He
wasn't too well known to most in the Philadelphia labor scene, in part
because he had such a small local. Some of the white labor officials did
know of his support of the poor and those on welfare, and that he had a
lot of community activists and men and women connected with the Black
Power movement who were behind him. Because of this, they thought
he was too radical. I remember we had an executive board meeting of
the AFL-CIO COPE, and I confronted Ed Toohey on why he wasn't
backing Lu.

"How can you not support him? He's a labor leader."

"Yeah, he's from labor," he said, "but he's one of your kind." He said
that right to my face.

THAT DISAGREEMENT I HAD WITH Ed Toohey over Lucien Blackwell
in 1975 pretty much underscored the different understanding we had
of organized labor's role in society. My support for Lucien was about
more than helping my own members in the Retail Clerks Union but in
recognizing the needs and working toward helping the poor across the
city, something I believed the labor movement must do. This was what
was meant by social justice unionism. Even without the endorsement of
COPE, Lu won his race in a landslide, and over the next twenty-five years,
he and I were firm allies in trying to shape Philadelphia politics along
more progressive lines. For me, connecting this new coalition of African
Americans, liberal white people, and working-class union members was
critical if human needs were to be addressed in the city in any serious
way. As it had since the early 1970s, I believed that the progressive wing
of Philadelphia's labor movement needed to work to bring these groups
together in the last years of the decade, and I did all I could to make this
happen.

In the mid-1970s, Philadelphia, like many other American cities, had an uptick in crime and hundreds of factories and mills closed, leading to a swell in unemployment. Since 1950, Philadelphia had been losing population, as thousands of residents relocated to suburban communities in the surrounding counties and New Jersey, resulting in depletion in tax revenue. Philadelphia was close to financial collapse in 1976, in part because of Frank Rizzo's political maneuvering in the previous year's election. Rizzo had promised the impossible: although he had already offered Earl Stout's AFSCME members an unprecedented wage and benefits package, he also reassured residents that their taxes wouldn't go up. Frank knew this deal would cost the city, but he believed that Harrisburg would bail him out with some emergency funds. Despite some hard lobbying, this didn't happen. Rural legislators, and almost everyone outside of Philly, blocked any kind of boost to the city's finances. As a result, city financial director Lennox Moak announced that Philadelphia was near bankruptcy and that immediate hikes in water and home tax bills were the only possible recourse, along with service cuts. Reactions from citizens were swift. On the talk radio programs, people blasted the rate hikes. Letters in the newspapers expressed outrage and put the blame on the mayor.

The most controversial service cutback in 1976 was the move to close the municipally run PGH. This was the oldest hospital in the nation, and, although it had its share of problems, it had a strong reputation for serving the city's working poor, as it was one of the few medical centers that people could afford. More than a thousand jobs in maintenance, food services, laundry, and licensed practical nurses in the hospital—all positions predominantly held by black men and women—would be lost. This proposed hospital closure reinforced a conviction that many already had that Rizzo was against black people. Even worse, though, was the feeling that Rizzo didn't care about the people who would lose access to any kind of health care. Many felt that closing PGH would ultimately result in the deaths of some of the city's poorest and most vulnerable citizens, most of whom would be black. By advancing this closure of the city's only public hospital, the mayor was in direct violation of his oath of office to protect the welfare of the people of Philadelphia.

Almost immediately, a movement sprang up to stop Rizzo's proposal to shut down PGH. With President Nixon's 1974 resignation fresh in everyone's mind, the movement's main goal was to recall the mayor from office. To do this, movement organizers looked to a section of Philadelphia's 1951 City Charter allowing citizens to remove a sitting mayor through plebiscite. If 25 percent of voters who cast ballots in the previous election petitioned for a referendum to vote for a possible recall, removing Rizzo from office was a possibility. Few cities had ever successfully conducted such a recall, but sentiment against Rizzo was so strong that many wanted to move forward with the plan. By the end of January 1976, the Citizens' Committee to Recall Rizzo formed and began to mobilize to get the needed 145,000 signatures.

This recall coalition brought together a wide range of citizens who were opposed to Rizzo. At the lead were Hospital Workers Union Local 1199c president Henry Nicholas and 1975 Philadelphia Party candidate Charles W. Bowser, both of whom saw the mayor as little different from Bull Connor, the infamous white police chief who terrorized black people in Birmingham, Alabama, in the 1950s and 1960s. They reached out to African American clergy, business leaders, and politicians and started the campaign moving. Bowser's earlier mayoral campaign still had a strong volunteer nexus in neighborhoods in West and North Philadelphia, and this helped in the initial stages of the petition drive. White liberals and those associated with the city's reform tradition joined in. The ADA, whose executive director Shelly Yanoff was an outspoken liberal leader, raised money and started a media campaign. Henry Nicholas wanted the city's progressive trade unions to play a role and asked me to be one of the cochairs of the citizen's committee, which is how I became involved with the committee. The PFT and District 1 of the International Association of Machinists, whose leader, Norman H. Loudenslager, was an outspoken critic of Rizzo, took our side. By February 1976, we were setting up petition tables around the city, our volunteers a daily presence outside City Hall, supermarkets, and hospitals, on college campuses, and in shopping malls. I couldn't believe how many petition signatures our volunteers netted. I felt we were on the way, but, after that initial wave of signatures, things seemed to trail off. Even if a lot of people didn't like Frank Rizzo, they thought he had won the election fair and square and that it was too extreme a move to oust a duly elected mayor. (See Figure 11.4.)

I was realistic about the odds the movement faced, and, by the first week of March, I thought the campaign was over. However, an un-

Figure 11.4 Hospital Workers Local 1199c president Henry Nicholas, 1972. (Reprinted with permission from the *Philadelphia Inquirer*.)

expected development turned popular opinion toward our side. In March 1976, a violent protest by the Philadelphia Building and Construction Trades Council shut down the *Philadelphia Inquirer*. The action came about in response to a satirical piece written by the *Philadelphia Inquirer*'s Desmond Ryan, a beat reporter who covered local politics and who had a regular column called "The Skeptic." On March 14, 1976, he published a mock interview with Rizzo called "Our Mayor Speaks." In it, he parodied the mayor speaking in vulgar ways about his opposition to lesbians joining the police department, and using ethnic slurs. It was clearly stated that the article was a satire, although some people close to the mayor actually thought he had said these things. Word leaked to the mayor about the piece before it was printed, and he sued for libel in an effort to stop its publication, but he lost the decision, and the column was printed soon after.

Mayor Rizzo took Desmond Ryan's satirical article very personally and so did many of his supporters. To hit back at the newspaper, Thomas J. Magrann, president of the Philadelphia Building and Construction Trades Council, set up pickets outside the Inquirer Building at Broad and Callowhill Streets around noon on March 19, 1976. Magrann claimed the protest had nothing to do with Desmond's parody and that the pickets were responding to what he called the press's unfair coverage of union issues. It wasn't hard to read between the lines, though. The building trades were Rizzo's troops out there, forming a mass of pickets and shouting demonstrators, punishing the *Inquirer* for what it had said about the mayor. Magrann was determined to shut the newspaper down that day and things got ugly. With every exit blocked, none of the journalists, staff, or delivery trucks could get in or out. Anyone who tried got pushed around pretty hard. One press photographer who went out to document what was happening got beaten up badly. There were scores of Philadelphia police present, but none of them intervened. No trucks left the loading bays to deliver editions of the paper and, effectively, the presses shut down for the day.

These mob scenes at the Inquirer Building were broadcast across the nation on evening television programs that night and in all the major newspapers the following day. A federal injunction finally ended the pickets, limiting the number of protesters outside the building, but the damage had already been done. It was widely believed that Rizzo ordered the protest himself, raising the issue that the mayor was above the law and capable of extraordinary means to attack his critics, even if it meant trampling on the constitutional right to free press. I don't know if that is true, but it highlighted a kind of style that informed the way he operated, the kind of police state he oversaw, and seeing it on display that day on the streets of Philadelphia galvanized a lot of people. It didn't matter to me, because I was already against him, so it only underscored the things I knew. Rizzo defiantly stated that he would never send police to break up a union picket line, but I thought it was a disgrace to the city and a black eye on the city's labor movement.

After the confrontation with *The Philadelphia Inquirer*, thousands more signed the recall petition, enough to place the referendum item on the ballot that fall. Rizzo attacked his opponents any way he could. My position with the recall movement made me a target for retribution, just as my support for George McGovern's presidential bid had a few years before. I got arrested a couple of times during the recall campaign. One night, I ran out of gas as I was coming home from some political function and was riding up Broad Street. I got out of my car and walked all the way down to an all-night gas station about 1:30 in the morning to get a tank of gas. After I had walked back to my car and filled it up, I made a U-turn so I could drive back to the station to return the container. Suddenly, there's a police car behind me with its lights on. I pulled over, and next thing I knew, there were three police cars on the scene, lights flashing. Police surrounded my car and I got hauled off to jail, my car left there at the intersection. Incidents like this happened multiple times that year. There was no doubt in my mind these arrests were politically motivated, meant to embarrass and intimidate me.

Into the summer of 1976, the citywide recall campaign got over 210,000 signatures within the required sixty-day period, but it wasn't easy. Volunteers were harassed outside City Hall and many of the other places where we set up information tables. We had our opposition, which hated us, confronting us every day—cops ordering us to move our petition tables, even though we had the right to be there. In the end, we came pretty close to pulling it off, but we fell short. Rizzo's legal team challenged the validity of many of the signatures on the petitions, claiming that many of the names could not be verified as registered Philadelphia voters. In retrospect, there was truth to that claim. We were so intent on getting a mass of names on those petition forms that we weren't as strident as we should have been in policing the process. Only registered voters who had cast a ballot in the 1975 election were supposed to sign the petition. A lot of people from out of town who were visiting city hall, people passing through for the day, or who had not actually voted in the prior election put their names down because they didn't like Rizzo and what he stood for. I am not saying that a majority of the names were false but enough to call the process into question. In October 1976, the recall measure was scrapped and the vote never taken to the people of Philadelphia.

ALTHOUGH THE COALITION of progressive trade unions, liberals, and a large section of Philadelphia's African American community had come short of removing Rizzo, this bloc had proven itself again as a viable, and growing, political force. Organizing this coalition, and mobilizing Philadelphia's Democratic base would be crucial to the 1976 presidential race, which was on the horizon, and which I was getting more involved in. Having led the McGovern campaign four years earlier, many potential candidates contacted me to see where I stood and if I could build support among the unions, line up ward leaders, and help steer the candidates toward victory.

In early 1975, I went down to Washington, DC, to meet with Senator Hubert H. Humphrey who was considering another run for the White House. He had arranged this lunch because he knew I had led the Mc-Govern campaign in 1972, and he wanted to see if I would do the same for him in 1976. Humphrey was one of the most progressive lawmakers in the second half of the twentieth century and was proposing comprehensive labor law reform and a national health care system. I had first met the senator back in 1964, and had known him well since, but this time I was surprised when I saw him in person. He was only sixty-three, but he looked so much older, and very thin, and I left there wondering how his health was. I knew he wasn't going to make a national presidential campaign. Even though everyone in the labor movement loved Humphrey, others who met with him before 1976 also couldn't help but notice his physical decline.

In Philadelphia, AFL-CIO Central Labor Union president Ed Toohey and others were leaning toward Senator Henry "Scoop" Jackson, who had a lot of early backing from George Meany, in part due to his prolabor voting record but mostly because of his commitment to national defense industries and aggressive anticommunist foreign policy. I didn't like Jackson because he was a Cold War hawk, a very conservative Democrat.

By early 1976, I was already backing Jimmy Carter, the governor of Georgia, a real underdog. Very few people outside of the South had ever heard of him. In 1975, when he was beginning the campaign, he knew that he needed to build some support among Northern labor leaders, and he reached out to me, in part because of my previous success with running McGovern's campaign in Philadelphia. I called some labor people I knew in Georgia and they spoke very highly of him and said they were going to endorse him. I called Carter's campaign headquarters in Atlanta and told him the next time he was in Pennsylvania to let me know, because I'd like to meet him in person. Soon after, he invited me down to meet him at the old Sheraton Hotel where he was staying while on a brief trip to Pennsylvania.

I remember it was my son Scott's birthday, and, after the party, I brought him and my son Wendell to meet the governor. I wanted to make sure Carter would work with unions, support labor law reform, and, as much as possible, promote an anti-imperialist foreign policy. Union support in Pennsylvania would be crucial if he had any chance at winning, and he was very pronounced about his respect of the labor movement and that he wanted us to back him, although he knew it would be tough with Scoop Jackson running. He asked me to get involved in his campaign, and I agreed. He wrote Scott a note on a napkin saying that once he was elected, he could bring it to the White House and get in. He signed it and put the date on it.

Jimmy Carter stayed in touch with me and when he was in the process of putting his Pennsylvania campaign together, he asked me to take over the operation in Philadelphia. I had decided I couldn't do it, though, even before he asked me. I knew from 1972 how much work went into coordinating a citywide presidential campaign, and I just didn't have the time. With the state liquor stores threatened with privatization, and with tough supermarket bargaining sessions coming up, my first job was to work for my members in the stores. But still, I was one of the only Philadelphia labor leaders to back Carter through the spring of 1976. As I mentioned, most of Philadelphia's labor movement had by this point endorsed Senator Henry "Scoop" Jackson, and they believed he would pull in front with a strong win in Pennsylvania. Carter was his main opponent, having chalked up wins through the South and New England. There were others in the early primaries—including Senators Birch Bayh, Lloyd Bentsen, Frank Church, and Alabama governor George Wallace, who was anathema to me. Pennsylvania governor Milton Shapp also briefly ran, but he never gained any traction. By April 1976, most of these guys had dropped out, and it was really a two-way race, between Carter and Jackson.

Organized labor had not warmed up to Carter in part because he didn't fight Georgia legislation that made it a so-called right-to-work state, which allowed workers to opt out of joining unions that were already set up in their workplace. Many felt that the majority of Carter's supporters were drawn from white-collar professions and the college educated, rather than blue-collar workers who had always made up the bulk of Democratic Party voters. Both of these points didn't sit well with labor leaders in Pennsylvania. Jackson had won earlier primaries in New York and Massachusetts, and he was capitalizing on the sentiments held across organized labor's ranks, saying that Carter could never win in an industrial state. Pennsylvania would be a test case for this.

On April 27, Carter took the Keystone State decisively, beating Jackson by twelve points. Philadelphia was the only place that went for Jackson, just as labor leaders had predicted, but he only took it by a twenty-five thousand vote margin, which might seem like a lot, but by Philadelphia standards it wasn't considered a landslide. Carter did well in Pennsylvania's union households, despite all the predictions.

Jimmy Carter was a new kind of candidate, committed to principles of transparency that reminded me of George McGovern. His campaign manager in Pennsylvania was Joseph Timilty, a state senator from Massachusetts who had previously been mayor of Boston. The fact that he was an outsider to Philadelphia posed some problems right away. Carter had come out against Rizzo and said publicly that if the mayor gave him his endorsement that he wouldn't accept it. At another point, he refused to attend a fund-raiser with Rizzo, a snub that didn't gain him any ground with Philadelphia ward leaders who were for Rizzo. Despite these issues, Rizzo no longer had any connection to the White House now that Nixon had resigned and had nothing to gain from President Ford's election. Marty Weinberg, a staunch Rizzo loyalist from South Philadelphia, had replaced Pete Camiel as Democratic Party chairman earlier in 1976, and he pushed Carter with the ward leaders, feeling that it was in Rizzo's interest to show that he could bank a victory for the Democratic Party on his home turf. On Election Day, Jimmy Carter took Philadelphia by 250,000 votes, and that night I was at the Carter headquarters at the Warwick Hotel. Almost everyone I knew there were people from the recall movement, and when the election was called, Frank Rizzo wasn't on the podium to address the crowd.

Jimmy Carter really captured the American people's imagination in 1976. He was a true outsider, very honest and humble, and a breath of fresh air after Watergate and the Nixon years. After the inauguration, he invited me down to a big reception at the White House and while I was there, I ran into the new international president of the Retail Clerks Union, William Wynn. I don't think he realized how close I was to the new president. I remember, when he saw me, he gave me a surprised look, as if to say, "What are you doing here?"

12

GOING OUT OF BUSINESS

EVEN BEFORE THE END OF THE DECADE, my hope that the 1970s would be a period of unprecedented union membership gains and a parallel step toward the realization of a full social democracy in the United States turned out to be a bitter disappointment. Beginning in 1977, the Retail Clerks Union in the Philadelphia region faced a loss in membership, brought on by the closing of department stores and supermarkets across the region. My main concern in these years was making sure the local survived at all.

In the newspapers around the nation, there was a steady stream of reports about steel plants and auto shops and textiles and other factories shutting down. These changes came so quickly it was hard to make sense of why everything was happening. In the postwar period, the U.S. economy was thriving, growing every year, and, with unions, wage rates were increasing with productivity. This continued through to the end of the 1960s, but some fundamental changes came about in the 1970s. Increased global competition, especially with Japan and West Germany, cut into the share of U.S. auto and manufacturing, and placed companies in more difficult positions. Oil and gas prices spiked upward with the energy crisis, after 1973, and never returned to normal. Prices for basic goods increased, and it was harder for people to get by. For too many of the men and women who worked the registers, these long-term changes simply meant they had no job.

The decline of retail, especially the department stores that had been the hub of downtown commerce since the late 1800s, was an unexpected economic turn. Looking to the future in 1950, Philadelphia City Planners predicted a period of sustained growth, and a potential demographic boost that could bring the city's population to as many as three million people by 1970. New housing tracts in Northeast Philadelphia, improvement of regional rail lines and highways, and expanded educational opportunities would prove a basis of these hopeful predictions. However, a very different reality emerged. Over this period, Philadelphia faced a net population loss of close to half a million as white residents relocated to the surrounding suburbs and the city's diverse manufacturing base dwindled. Municipal tax revenues were depleted, leading to cuts in city services and reciprocal declines in the quality of life.

Traditional urban department stores showed the impact of such pressures by the end of the 1960s. John Wanamaker's, Gimbels, and Lit Brothers' all faced shortfalls from competition with suburban-based stores. During my first negotiations with Lit Brothers in 1969, I could see the company was turning its focus away from its original downtown centers and going toward a suburban trend. Within three years, they closed their Camden location and moved to the newly developed Escelon Mall in Voorhees Township, New Jersey. I knew that as the Philadelphia flagship store at 8th and Market Street struggled through the early 1970s, it might shut down, too.

The scale of the crisis facing the men and women who worked on the sales floor and in the stock rooms was clear by early 1977. Lit Brothers called all of the union representatives to a meeting at the Ben Franklin Hotel, and J. P. Hansen, the store's chief executive officer, gave a speech about how the company's finances were in bad shape. He blamed the union contracts, saying that no other department stores in the city paid the kind of wages that Lit Brothers did. He explained that he was going to write a new contract, one that had a series of major cutbacks—a 40 percent pay cut, along with the removal of every fringe benefit the members had previously gained. The terms were so extreme that, if enacted, some sales clerks' weekly take-home pay would come in at below federal minimum wage standards. Even with that, Hansen said that if we didn't accept all the terms outright, he was going to close the stores for good.

There were sixteen trade unions representing workers in the whole of Lit Brothers; some, like the elevator operators, the locksmiths, and plumbers, with as few as four or five members in the bargaining unit. With thirteen hundred members, the Retail Clerks Union had the largest section of workers in the stores, followed by Teamsters Local 115, which claimed a couple hundred heavy stock guys—the men who moved stoves, refrigerators, and other heavy appliances from trucks into the back storage areas. Hansen's ultimatum wiped out every gain the unions had secured in the forty years of representing workers at Lit Brothers. In the face of this, all the various union leaders met up to try to figure out our unified response. Not everyone agreed on what to do. Teamsters leader John P. Morris was there, surrounded by his men, literally screaming that he wouldn't take the contract. I countered, saying that Hansen's proposal was a ploy to pin the blame on the unions for having to close the store. We needed to outsmart him. If our unions were ever going to organize again in this region, we couldn't take the blame in the public's view for stores going out of business. Instead, we should call their bluff and accept the contract. Every union representative there agreed with me, but Morris was adamant. He stormed out, saying that he would lead the Teamsters on a strike.

On the evening of March 30, 1977, I called a meeting for Local 1357's department store employees, and about two hundred came out to the Ben Franklin Hotel ballroom. Going into this gathering, everyone there knew how dire things were because they had read about it in the newspapers. To give an idea about how bad the situation was, while I was onstage reading out the proposed contract terms for the commissioned salespersons, a guy in the front row vomited all over the floor. It was awful, but I tried a little humor, asking that not everyone do that, and continued on. But it was bad. Some of the members began calling out to reject the store's demands, but I said, "Listen, we've got to accept this, because we've got to outsmart them." I knew Hansen was going to close the stores, had been planning it for years, not because his employees were unionized, but because the store was doing lousy. By a very close vote, the members accepted the terms I had urged, but less than a week later, Lit Brothers closed its doors for good and that was it.

The shutdown of one of the city's most iconic downtown institutions was part of a disturbing trend in the city. Philadelphia manufacturing had been in decline since the end of World War II, with entire sectors of industry, such as the once-booming textile firms, folding up. Now it was hitting retail. The collapse of Lit Brothers' in 1977 was the start of a flood of retail closings in the Philadelphia region over the next few years. The trend seemed to speed up. Two Guys Discount Department Stores and Korvette's shut down and Food Fair and everyone under their banner— Pantry Pride, J. M. Fields, Best Markets, and Penn Fruit—filed for bankruptcy in early 1979, closing with only twelve-hours' notice, taking fifteen hundred jobs. New retail establishments such as Jefferson Ward, K-Mart, and Clover were opening, but they were all nonunion operations. A huge indoor urban mall known as the Gallery opened at 9th and Market Streets right next to the old Lit Brothers' building in 1976. It had 125 retail outlets and a food court built with connections to regional rail lines, and employed hundreds of retail workers, but not a single one was unionized.

With the severe economic upheavals and the continued set of urban problems, like increasing crime rates, crumbling infrastructure, and depleted tax revenue, Frank Rizzo presented himself as the one man who could save Philadelphia. He had thousands of supporters who agreed with him. Philadelphia's 1951 City Charter imposed a two-term limit on mayors, barring him from running again, but Rizzo refused to accept this and quietly pushed for efforts to change the city charter provision to allow him to run for a third term. At first I thought this was a pretty farfetched idea, but in early 1978, the Citizens Congress for a Modern Charter was formed and began a campaign to get the necessary twenty thousand petition signatures from Philadelphia voters to put a charter change referendum on the November ballot. Pro-Rizzo ward leaders and committeemen went around with petitions door-to-door in their areas, joined by hundreds of volunteers recruited from the Building Trades unions, and the police and fire organizations. By June, the petition drive had over fifty thousand signatures, assuring that the measure would be before voters in November.

I was appalled at Rizzo's effort to change the city charter, but after all the outrageous things he had done up to this point, I guess I wasn't too surprised. I wasn't against the notion of allowing a mayor more than two terms, in principle, but didn't think the change should apply to the current mayor who launched the effort to change the rules—just to suit his political ambitions. It was a ridiculous and blatant abuse of power. But, as far-fetched as his charter change plan might have seemed, I knew that there was a real possibility he would win. Liberals across the city really hated him, but Rizzo had just as many die-hard supporters lined up to cast ballots for him. People were calling into local talk radio programs, saying that they would vote for him no matter what and that they would be happy if he could serve as mayor of Philadelphia for the rest of his life.

Around the city, the liberal coalition that formed the base of the recall movement two years earlier quickly mobilized to stop Rizzo's proposal. Once again, the progressive wing of the labor movement—the Hospital Workers, the Machinists, Teachers, and Retail Clerks, all unions that had been a bastion against Frank Rizzo through the decade—played a key role, raising money, mobilizing our members, and launching an aggressive media campaign. If that same percentage of the black voting bloc that had come out for Charlie Bowser when he ran for mayor in 1975 could mobilize again, along with the votes of white liberals and trade unionists, the charter change measure would go down. Labor took up this challenge to expand the coalition into white working-class neighborhoods in Kensington, Port Richmond, and Northeast Philly. With the Retail Clerks Union joining, we formed an umbrella group called Trade Unions Against the Charter Change and through the fall of 1978 pooled our resources and set up meetings in neighborhoods around the city. My area was Northeast Philadelphia, where I educated members about the dangers of the charter change, saying that adoption of the new rule would threaten democracy since it would place too much power in the hand of one charismatic leader. I organized a petition drive where volunteers from the union set up tables outside the supermarkets, and eventually secured several thousand signatures.

As he had throughout his political career, Frank Rizzo looked to another section of the city's labor unions, especially the building trades and Teamsters, to back him. Rizzo supporters formed the Labor Committee of the Citizens to Reform the Charter, which joined with ward leaders to sign a petition to get the referendum on the ballot and then to get out the vote. Although he counted many friends in labor's ranks, Rizzo had, by this time, lost some critical support from some organizations and leaders who had backed him earlier. After the 1975 deal with AFSCME DC 33, which granted city workers a sizable pay boost, Rizzo announced some layoffs in the sanitation department. Earl Stout felt that Rizzo had broken his word, having promised the union that no city workers would be furloughed so long as he was in charge of City Hall, and because of this Earl severed all ties to him. In a show of independent power, DC 33 called a trash strike in the middle of the summer of 1978, a move that sent the city into chaos. For two weeks, garbage piled up, as people were dropping trash bags off on playground fields, into the Schuylkill River, and into the streets. On television, images of city bus routes blocked by hills of trash, and angry people venting about the mayor and Earl Stout showed how bitter the climate had become. This sent a message that Rizzo didn't have the kind of control over the city that he claimed.

The 1978 election was a midterm one when fewer people usually go to the polls, but the referendum issue was sure to mobilize voters. Along with the potential change to the city election rules, the contest was important in Pennsylvania because a new governor was being elected. This had particular importance to the Retail Clerks Union as it would determine the kind of policy that would affect almost two thousand liquor store clerks. Ever since the formation of the state store system after Prohibition ended, there had been calls to privatize the liquor store business in Pennsylvania, to open up the sale of wine and spirits to independent entrepreneurs, but this rarely had any serious support in Harrisburg since the system was such a major source of political patronage. When the store clerks unionized in 1971, this statewide patronage system was smashed, since the new contract provisions specified that all commonwealth employees obtain their jobs through an impartial civil service system, rather than from political backers. With this new setup in place, a push to scrap the state Liquor Control Board took on more traction. As early as 1971, Governor Milton Shapp told me of a plan to sell wine in private retail establishments, but I told him I was against this, and the clerks threatened a march on the capitol in opposition. Shapp backed away from this idea, but it soured my support of him in 1974. Even though we stopped the plan, the threat of closing the state stores remained a reality all through these years.

The privatization issue was raised around the state through these years, and by 1978 it was gaining bipartisan support. Since pricing competition between various liquor stores would spur more advertising, newspaper interests saw privatization as a major source of potential revenue and lobbied for its passage, their bias evident in their coverage of the topic, and especially in the editorials. I agreed that the liquor store system needed serious reform but that selling off the stores was ultimately against the financial interests of the commonwealth. In 1974, I had a list of changes that I wanted implemented. Up until this point, liquor sales were a cash-only transaction, and, to keep up with the times, I proposed credit card purchases or payment with personal checks. In addition, I wanted to lower the state's 18 percent tax on liquor sales; to have the state legislature change zoning rules to facilitate more store locations; and to shift to computerized inventory, better warehousing, and wider brand selection. Clerks should earn commissions on sales, I believed, as was the norm in appliance centers and department stores, because it would foster better servicing of the customers. Most of all, I wanted customer self-service, as only a fraction of the 713 stores in the system had that. In most of the stores, a customer had to come to a clerk at the sales desk, say what they wanted, and wait for the clerk to go into a back section and retrieve it. This was a major customer complaint, and I agreed.

With the rumblings to end state ownership, I needed to find out where the gubernatorial candidates stood. The two candidates that year were Richard Thornburgh, a lawyer who was not widely known, and Pittsburgh mayor Peter Flaherty. Because the Retail Clerks Union had a sizable membership across the commonwealth, I knew that our endorsement mattered. In the summer of 1978, I met with both candidates to size up their positions. In private meetings with Richard Thornburgh, he told me he was not committed either way but promised not to press the issue of privatization. Flaherty would not make a similar commitment, and I decided I could not support him, even though he was a Democrat. That fall, as the campaign went into full swing, Local 1357's membership remained divided and did not endorse either candidate. I made it known in the press, however, that I was voting for Thornburgh.

Although there was so much on the ballot this year, the charter change amendment was what everybody in Philadelphia was talking about. Rizzo and Philadelphia Democratic Party chairman Marty Weinberg were confident, boasting that they had it in the bag. Similar to the earlier political races, the measure divided the city along neighborhood and racial lines. In September, during a television interview at a community event in Northeast Philadelphia, Rizzo said that black people were being urged to cast their ballots along racial lines, and he predicted that in turn white people would "vote white" on Election Day. His comments sparked an immediate backlash. Henry Nicholas and Earl Stout called for a censure vote to repudiate all support the mayor had from organized labor at the city's AFL-CIO delegates meeting the following month, leading to some hot exchanges. I spoke out for the censure vote, but the measure failed to get enough support. Rizzo just had too many allies within the central labor council, but the fiery debate we had showed again just how much disagreement there was, a reflection of the general mood in neighborhoods across the city.

On November 7, 1978, Philadelphians came out to the polls in record numbers, and gave Rizzo a stunning defeat by decisively rejecting the charter change by over two hundred thousand votes. That night I was down at 18th and Market Street, at the Holiday Inn in Center City, with the Committee to Protect the Charter leaders Henry Nicholas and Charlie Bowser and other groups from around the city. As the results came in, it was pandemonium: the charter change referendum was defeated. It was a joyous night, with almost a thousand people and an assembled band of mummers celebrating what we believed was the end of Rizzo's political career. It was an especially good night for me, as along with the defeat of the charter change referendum, Dick Thornburgh won an upset victory over Peter Flaherty. Now, I felt the state store workers had a reprieve from the push to eliminate their jobs with privatization. I called Dick up the next day to congratulate him and to let him know I looked forward to working with him.

WITH THESE SIGNIFICANT POLITICAL VICTORIES at the end of 1978, I was feeling hopeful that better days were on the way, but this soon changed. In February 1979, I got notice that one hundred Penn Fruit and Pantry Pride stores, all of the stores in the Food Fair chain in the region, were closing for good. The problems in the food stores were replicated in the discount stores, the no frills sales establishments that Local 1357 represented across the Delaware Valley. A few weeks after the supermarket closures, J. M. Fields also announced it was going under, followed in the next year by Two Guys and Korvette's Discount Stores. As a result, Local 1357 lost 6,000 of 15,500 members in two years, a major hit on the union's finances that required the layoff of half the staff and all of our full-time organizers.

Food Fair blamed their demise on excessive capitalization expenses, claiming wages had reached such a level that they couldn't afford to pay workers and remain competitive. I knew this was an excuse to hide their poor decisions. A lot of a store managers' salary at the end of the year was based on a bonus calculated against the expenses of individual stores. Because of this, managers had an incentive to keep labor costs down and to give as little to in-store capitalization as possible. If a new air conditioning system was needed, they didn't put in for it. Many stores had damaged shopping carts, with busted handrails and wobbly wheels. In some stores, back room toilets backed up and needed replacement, but this too was skipped. If things were broken down, managers would try their best to do without them instead of bringing in maintenance, because the bill would be taken out of their yearly bonus. Everything was geared toward the manager's bonus, rather than servicing the customers. Shoppers noticed these problems, and employee morale suffered. Rather than pay for structural upkeep or changes, the top brass in the stores let things go. This kind of mismanagement was the key to why Food Fair failed.

Food Fair's problems were not occurring in isolation, however. Supermarkets were facing unprecedented economic pressure by the end of the 1970s. No one thing brought this about. With the 1973 oil embargo, gas and oil prices spiked up, and this rise in cost of transporting produce and meat from farms to warehouses and stores passed on to consumers. The plastic cellophane butchers used to wrap meat, and which was used in virtually all other kinds of packaging, is petroleum based, adding further to costs. With higher fuel prices, people made fewer trips to the market and spent less money there on average. People were saving every dime. More women were working outside the home now, and most didn't have the time to spend going to the stores as often, which hurt the bottom line of supermarkets around the country.

In the same month that Pantry Pride closed, the threat of privatization of the Pennsylvania state stores resurfaced. This was unexpected, because I had supported Dick Thornburgh on the assumption that he would support the union in any policy proposals to cut the system. Hardly a month after he took office, Governor Thornburgh went back on his promise. In February 1979, a Pennsylvania state senate committee, headed by Westmoreland County senator James R. Kelley, a Democrat who chaired the Law and Justice Committee, recommended privatization of the liquor trade, seeking to phase it out over a three-year period. Thornburgh went along with this plan and would back it through his terms in office. I knew I needed to fight this and put $250,000 toward a campaign, hiring two permanent lobbyists in Harrisburg and launching an advertising blitz on radio and television.

Many of the store clerks testified at public hearings on the privatization issue at the state capitol. Liquor store clerks played a vital role in the community, as they were the front lines of ensuring better safety and compliance of age rules. Compared to surrounding states, Pennsylvania had the lowest rate of highway fatalities from drunk driving, in large part because of how clerks are trained to enforce strict underage drinking laws through carding enforcement. This was important, because reports showed that a large percentage of drunk driving accidents were the result of teenaged drivers who were under the influence. State ownership of the stores provided a financial windfall for the commonwealth, and eliminating this function would wind up costing more money than it saved. In 1980, Pennsylvania made 169 million dollars from wine and spirit sales, and if the system was abolished, this gap would have to be made up by raising taxes, as well as possible cuts to state police funding, courts, and health services. Since these jobs were unionized, the liquor clerks had stable benefits for themselves and their families, and gutting the PLCB would lead to more low-end retail establishments with meager wages and high turnover. I also believed privatization was a racial issue, since so many of the workers in the stores are minorities and needed these jobs in areas where few other decent jobs were available.

With the shutdown of Food Fair and the looming privatization of the liquor stores, I knew that stronger political responses were needed. I felt this was true for all working people across the entire nation. Over ten thousand Philadelphians had lost their jobs in 1978–1979 alone, and conditions looked worse in the days to come. On February 10, 1979, six hundred workers and community activists met at the Amalgamated Clothing and Textile Workers Hall on South Street for an event sponsored by the Retail Clerks and the Philadelphia Unemployment Project. Local lawmakers including Congressmen William H. Gray and Peter H. Kostmayer met with us to discuss a proposed bill, the Employee Protection and Community Stabilization Act, which would address what was happening to workers and their families when factories and stores shutdown. When Food Fair closed earlier that year, they only gave us two-days' notice, shutting so quickly most had no chance to prepare and find a new job. The act stipulated that companies give one-year notice to employees if they were planning to shut down, severance pay and job training for those who lost jobs, and loans to companies on the verge of closure.

The Retail Clerks Union, as the Retail Clerks International Association (RCIA) was more commonly known, was one of the few unions in the United States that had expanded its membership since the 1950s.

Figure 12.1 Local 1357 member Thomas Gregory stocks shelves at Acme Market, 15th and Spruce Street, March 17, 1977. Supermarket clerks formed the largest section of the United Food and Commercial Workers. (Special Collections Research Center, Temple University, Philadelphia, Pa. Photograph by Michael J. Maicher.)

Many people thought that this pattern of growth would continue through the 1970s, but the kinds of shutdowns we were experiencing in the Philadelphia region were happening in other areas across the nation, and the union was losing members by the thousands. Faced with this crisis, the union's top leadership considered a range of options to deal with the changing times. In 1977, RCIA president Jim Housewright died, and was replaced by William Wynn. At that time, merger talks were under way with the five hundred thousand-member Amalgamated Meat Cutters and Butcher Workmen of North America. Since the early 1970s, the Amalgamated had been shrinking, in part because precut meat was being shipped to the stores in plastic packages, eliminating the need for butchers. Because they were so highly unionized, supermarket butchers made good wages, akin to the building trades—a bit more than your average retail clerk. They were militant, too, and retail management wanted to cut down on the kind of power they wielded in the industry. Combining forces with the butchers would strengthen our political power and make us more of a force at the national level. I thought the proposed merger was a great idea, and supported it all the way. The Meat Cutters, by and large, had always been a more socially progressive organization than the Retail Clerks, more attuned to racial equality and social justice, in part because they had absorbed the more radical CIO union, the United Packinghouse Workers of America, which going back to the 1930s had a long tradition of commitments to these goals. In August 1979, the merger was formalized, launching a new union, the UFCW. (See Figure 12.1.)

With this merger, the 1.2-million-member UFCW was now one of the largest unions in the country. The new organization was premised on organizing the expanding service sector, which was then beginning to replace manufacturing-based jobs as the primary employment category in the United States. It was predicted that these new organizing drives would happen not only in supermarkets and department stores but in health care, nursing homes, financial services, and other areas beyond retail, all of which fell under the jurisdiction of the union. The birth of the UFCW paralleled changes in the national AFL-CIO leadership. As he had promised he would, AFL-CIO president George Meany served into his eightieth year, but he stepped down in November 1979 and was replaced by his longtime adviser Lane Kirkland. Kirkland came out of the merchant marine union but most of his career had been as an AFL staffer in Washington. I didn't know Lane too well personally, but I did know he came out of the same conservative union mold as Meany. He wasn't aligned with the social justice traditions of the labor movement I believed in, and so the entire movement was still locked in old ways of thinking, at a moment when we needed fresh mind-sets. Within my own organization, UFCW president Bill Wynn supported the incoming regime, and there wasn't much I could do about that.

I N 1978, I TURNED FORTY, not old by any means, but by now no one would call me a kid anymore like they did when I first got involved in the labor movement. I was an experienced negotiator and a known figure in the labor movement and in Democratic Party politics both nationally and in Philadelphia. Even though I was more established, I still believed in change and I wasn't afraid to challenge the mainstream ways of thinking. Through the 1970s, I stood against Cold War policies and wanted dialogue across nations. I was against nuclear weapon proliferation and was a regular participant at antinuclear protests and demilitarization rallies across the region.

In 1979, I was among a group of twelve unionists from the United States and Canada invited to travel to China on a 28-day tour coordinated by the U.S. China Friendship Committee, a group of American radicals in California in the early 1970s who wanted to strengthen ties with Maoist China. The trip was possible because of the implementation of new diplomatic ties between the nations following the death of Chairman Mao in 1976. Two years later, Deng Xiaoping took over the Communist Party and initiated reforms, including reestablishment of full diplomatic relations with the United States. I suspect I was included on the list of invited guests because I had a reputation as being on the left wing of the labor movement, and because of my peace activism. Most of the other labor activists who made the journey with me were Socialists from the West Coast, primarily out of California's International Longshoremen's Association, the left-leaning union founded by Harry Bridges. I forget their names, but I know that some were veterans of the Abraham Lincoln Brigade, the American unit that fought alongside the Republicans in the Spanish Civil War against Franco's Fascist army. There was also a contingent from Canada who were real Reds, die-hard Communists.

I didn't agree with their far-left politics, but I thought it over and agreed to go along with them because I believed in dialogue between nations. I thought the AFL-CIO position against peaceful engagement with America's Communist enemies was ridiculous. I was against Communism, too, but I thought there was a better way to go about changing that system than by isolating it. I believe that dialogue with enemies is necessary; it's what I learned from the Jesuit tradition and Christian social ethics. Our enemies are human beings, too; they have children just like we do. You shouldn't villainize them. My reason for going was to learn about the socialist system firsthand. I believed we should learn from other unions all over the world. Besides, by the late 1970s, business leaders were opening up dialogue in China, so I reasoned, why shouldn't working people and their organizations?

My decision to go to China was strongly disapproved of by both the Retail Clerks international and the AFL-CIO. The union's Foreign Affairs Committee told me, in no uncertain terms that I couldn't go. If I went against this order disciplinary actions might be taken against me. I went to international president Bill Wynn, who said he couldn't authorize it because the AFL-CIO wouldn't sanction it. He let everyone know that he wasn't happy about me going, although in private, he said he wished he could go, but for me to go and find out what's happening, just not to do anything in the union's name. I got an official letter from the AFL-CIO also forbidding me to go, but I ignored it, and left in May 1979.

This group of twelve trade unionists were the first North American labor officials to visit China since President Nixon had opened up relations in 1972. We were there for six weeks, starting out from Hong Kong, and then traveling south by train to the mainland and up to Beijing. China's railway system seemed ancient, and I'm sure some of the cars I rode in dated from the early twentieth century. The coal smoke would come into the cabins, almost gagging us and covering our clothes in black soot. It was incredibly hot for most of the time we were there—no air conditioning anywhere. When we pulled into Beijing, I saw thousands of people riding bikes and hundreds of road repair workers walking with shovels and picks on their shoulders.

One of my main questions about Communist China was about religious liberty, which as a practicing Catholic was a significant issue for me. Under the communist system, religious practice was outlawed. If anything, the communist state itself was the religion, and Chairman Mao, who had died just a couple of years before, was still revered. Everywhere we went, there were huge portraits of him, and the workers I talked to always brought him up. But I made a point to bring up religion when I spoke to people, and I brought a rosary with me, and showed the people how I prayed with it. One of the AFSCME members in our delegation was a Catholic priest, Father Albert Blatz, a shop steward from St. Peter's state hospital in Minnesota. He asked some of the communist authorities if he could celebrate a mass, and they agreed, the first Catholic mass in Beijing since before the Cultural Revolution. They gave us a Catholic Church, the Immaculate Conception of the Virgin Mary, and everything was done in Latin. For the first time since I was a child, I served as an altar boy, with one of the guys from the Lincoln Brigade as the other one! It wasn't a big event, there were only a handful of Chinese in the church, but it was still an important statement.

Just by being there, by having personal interaction, I was hoping to promote dialogue. I spread information through conversations about what the American system was like. I wasn't giving speeches to thousands of people in soccer stadiums like I had in Brazil in 1967, but I believed the private conversations I had with people were a way to open up better understanding about our societies. The thing I've got to say was how impressed I was by the Chinese people; they were friendly, and curious, and always hospitable. It convinced me that people around the world want the same basic things: security and peace, a good job, and the chance to raise a family. I invited some of the Chinese trade union people I met there to visit me in Philadelphia, but they were never allowed. I always wanted to go back again but never got the chance. Writing this now in the early twenty-first century, with so many American computers and other basic goods manufactured in China, I still think that American labor leaders need to begin to understand Chinese workers, so that we can work together.

As we were walking down the street, some of the people would come up to the delegation, wanting to speak English. Many of the younger Chinese people had never seen a white person before, and we must have been real curiosities. Back then, I was a pretty avid jogger, logging about two or three miles a day. I brought my running shoes with me on the trip and went out jogging whenever I had a chance. I remember one time, I was wearing a chartreuse sweat suit, and I went running down a village street. Next thing I knew, when I turned around, it looked like hundreds of people were running behind me.

THE DAY BEFORE I LEFT for Hong Kong, Bill Green won the Democratic mayoral primary, and when I got back to Philadelphia in midsummer he was already on the trail, raising a lot of money and meeting with civic groups. The liberal coalition that had formed earlier in the decade mobilized around him, as did the Democratic organization, including ward leaders who had once supported Rizzo. In 1976, Bill lost a senatorial race to John Heinz, but took Philadelphia by over three hundred thousand votes, which demonstrated how much support he could count on in 1979. Bill was one of the most popular Philadelphia politicians of his generation, and I knew he stood a good chance of winning.

Bill's Republican challenger was David W. Marston, a former assistant federal attorney who'd gained notoriety in 1978 after President Carter ordered him fired in a political patronage purge. The race was a three-way contest when Lucien Blackwell resigned from city council to run on Max Weiner's Consumer Party ticket, which had a platform that called for increased federal assistance to the urban poor, expansion of housing aid programs, an end to gentrification of working-class neighborhoods, and job training for the unemployed. The AFL-CIO endorsed Bill Green early on and I made speeches for him in various ward meetings across the city, and at retiree club meetings of the Retail Clerks Union. Bill won a strong majority, pulling in the blue-collar row house Democrats. After the Rizzo years, and the polarization that marked them, Bill Green brought a more civil tone to City Hall, a breath of fresh air. As he knew he would, he faced a hard set of problems. City finances were in shambles, and after the lay-offs of a thousand police and firefighters early on in his term, he made a lot of political enemies. Jobs continued to leave the city. Consumer prices remained high and I thought more was possible to address the needs of working-class people.

Many of the problems that faced working people during these years were, at their root, the result of the nation's energy policies. Since the oil boycott of 1973, gas and utility prices had skyrocketed and this affected people in immediate ways, since everyone needs gas and heats their homes. A range of new coalitions formed in these years to try to protect people's interests. By 1978, there was a new response by trade unions with the formation of the Citizens Labor Energy Coalition (CLEC), a national organization that brought unions and community activists together to fight for new energy policies that put the needs of people first. I backed the idea right away, and put the UFCW behind it, and was named one of the organization's cochairs. CLEC's program backed the introduction of alternative kinds of energy, including solar and wind, while fighting en-trenched power that dictated the current policy. To do so, the oil com-pany monopoly would be curbed through legislation nationalizing the entire industry. The year that CLEC was founded, President Carter ap-pointed me to the Windfall Tax Commission, which called for legislation limiting oil profiteering. Around the country, CLEC organized rallies, sent out literature to trade union members to drum up support for this program, and put these kinds of measures at the heart of the labor move-ment's agenda.

Even with these efforts, I was frustrated about how many of the most important points about the energy crisis weren't getting out. This con-vinced me that to get these kinds of programs through, I would need to run for national office myself. I had considered running for Bill Green's old congressional seat in 1976, and again in 1978, but decided against it.

Now, by 1980, I knew stronger legislative measures to address the problems of jobs and Big Oil at the national level were essential. I lived in Pennsylvania's fourth congressional district, comprising most of Far Northeast Philadelphia, as well as sections of Port Richmond and Mount Airy, which, for years, had been represented by Congressman Josh Eilberg. He was indicted in a bribery scandal and lost to Republican Charles Dougherty in 1978. I knew Dougherty pretty well, as he had graduated from St. Joseph's College a year before me, and we shared a lot in common. He came from a union family—his father was a truck driver and a Teamsters member, and Charlie's legislative record on labor issues was good overall. Charlie was a liberal Republican, but I still thought it was important to have a Democrat representing the district and I decided to challenge him.

I felt I had a good chance of winning in 1980, especially if I had labor support. Charlie was vulnerable because he was independent and no longer had the support of Philadelphia's Republican boss William Meehan, who was slating an opposition candidate in the primaries. Besides that, incumbents were on the defensive because of the Abscam scandal that resulted from an FBI undercover operation that exposed political corruption in the region. Charlie was not involved with that in any way, but incumbents were vulnerable as it was all over the news. On February 11, 1980, I announced my candidacy at a press conference, outlining a proworker program that promised to cut down on the power of Big Oil. Right away, a bunch of other Democrats entered the race, seven in all. My most formidable challenger was Thomas J. Magrann, the former head of the sixty thousand-member Philadelphia Building and Construction Trades Council who had made his name in politics with his strong support of Mayor Rizzo. Almost every other candidate I faced that year was also from the ranks of organized labor. John R. Fitzpatrick, a teacher at Dobbins Technical High School, was very active with the PFT, and Eddie Goldstein, business agent for the Carpenters Regional Council, joined the race after I did. The only candidate not out of the labor movement was Michael Mustokoff, a former assistant district attorney who worked in the law firm of Howard Giddis. Giddis was Bill Green's lawyer and one of his chief advisers who helped run the city behind the scenes.

Most of the city's political observers said the Democratic primary race was really a contest between Tom Magrann and me. The Philadelphia Building and Construction Trades Council endorsed Tom right away, which swayed a number of ward leaders to line up behind him. With so many union guys running, it diffused the kind of sway that labor usually played. The most solid support I got was from among UFCW members in the supermarkets and their families across Northeast Philadelphia and Kensington. I asked UFCW international president William Wynn to assist with the campaign and he raised money and sent two full-time staffers to help me in the closing weeks of the race. They had me do all kinds of things to spruce up my image—had me cut my hair and changed up my wardrobe. I was way casual in the way I dressed. I hated wearing ties, but some of the political advisers from the UFCW insisted that I wear them, to make me look more serious on the campaign trail. I felt a little uncomfortable with this advice and said that I needed to be myself, but in the end I went along. I had some help with this when the leaders of Philadelphia's locals of the ILGWU took me down to one of their shops and bought me three new suits as their campaign contribution to me. When I see the photos from that year's campaign, I do look different, better dressed, and a little more mature. (See Figure 12.2.)

If you look at the policies put forward by every Democratic congressional candidate in Philadelphia that year, my platform was the most daring. The heart of my message was nationalization of the oil companies, which would take the Crude Oil Windfall Profits Tax Act, which sought to curb the price gouging practices of energy conglomerates and was passed by Congress earlier in the year, to its logical end. Utility companies were making incredible profits after the oil embargo, and even after supply had returned, prices remained exorbitantly high. The nation needed more money because of the deficit, which in 1980 was almost eighty billion dollars, seventy-seven billion more than what it had been just ten years prior. Federal control of oil was a way to work to correct that fiscal imbalance. Congress needed to regulate the price of oil, because people were always subject to prices surging. In addition, I spoke for increased funding to aid the unemployed, job retraining, support for struggling industries, increases in educational budgets, and labor law reform. My platform was well received by the union members in the stores, and from people throughout the region, although some thought my position was too radical. Even so, I had a lot of support across the city, including the editorial endorsement of the *Philadelphia Inquirer*, the *Daily News*, the *Philadelphia Tribune*, and local papers like the *Mayfair Times* and the *Northwood News Gleaner*.

Figure 12.2 From left: Philadelphia Building and Construction Trades Council president Ralph Williams, Thomas J. Magrann, Wendell W. Young III, city councilwoman Joan L. Krajewski, and John J. McCullough, president of Philadelphia Roofers Union, Local 30. October 1980. (From the collection of Wendell W. Young III.)

By April 1980, I had the strongest ground game of all the candidates, with a thousand door-knockers working to get out the vote in neighborhoods across my district. I expected to win and did my best, but on April 22, after all the votes were in, I came in third behind Magrann and Mustokoff. I got 20,308 votes, about two thousand fewer than Magrann. Tom won, in large part because a lot of building trades guys live in Northeast Philadelphia and they had a lot of people working to bring out the vote. I won the African American vote, concentrated in two sections, the 10th and 60th wards over in Ogontz and West Mount Airy, taking those precincts in a landslide. There was a larger Jewish contingent in the district, and I think I would have had many of the community's votes, but Mike Mustokoff, who is Jewish, campaigned well and got the majority. Had Mustokoff not run, I think I would have beaten Magrann. On election night, I drove over to Tom Magrann's headquarters, shook his hand, and told him I'd do anything I could to help him out. I liked Tom Magrann, personally, even though we didn't always agree on some topics.

The 1980 primary race had a larger turnout than usual largely because Pennsylvania voters would have a say over who the eventual Democratic Party candidate would be. Going into April, Jimmy Carter was low in the polls, and facing a primary challenge from Massachusetts senator Edward M. Kennedy. I considered asking the president to come to Pennsylvania to help me campaign, but I decided against it. I knew he had a lot to deal with in Washington, and besides, it was questionable if his support would have been a plus or a minus. Organized labor, which had only ever been lukewarm to Carter, had turned from him decisively when he didn't deliver on some of his promises to the unions, such as making labor law reform a legislative priority. I was one of the few Pennsylvania labor leaders who was backing him, as even my closest allies Norman H. Loudenslager and Henry Nicholas were for Kennedy. Most of the Democratic Party in Philadelphia, including Mayor Bill Green, also backed Kennedy, who won the Pennsylvania primary, scoring a landslide victory in Philadelphia's wards.

Through those months and into the fall, I campaigned for President Carter and Magrann. The fact that Ronald Reagan was the Republican nominee made this election cycle even more serious, as he represented a view that was opposed to everything I stood for. As governor of California, he was antilabor and an open critic of Cesar Chavez and student activists and had cut funding to higher education and other social programs. I could hardly believe that he was even a viable national candidate. But the economy was in shambles, and people were seeking change. Most of Philadelphia's ward leaders, it's fair to say, were halfhearted about the Carter-Mondale ticket that year, and as the polls had predicted, the Democratic Party did poorly in Pennsylvania and all over the country on Election Day. In Philadelphia, Carter won a narrow victory, but provided no coattails for Tom Magrann, who lost to Charlie Dougherty.

I was also troubled as I looked back on some things about my congressional race in the earlier part of the year. All during my campaign, I had asked Mayor Bill Green to help me out, to officially endorse me and come out and campaign with me, to introduce me at public events and ward meetings and things like that. He didn't owe me anything, but I had always been very loyal to him, and I could have used his support. I knew it would make a difference. He kept putting me off, though. I tried to come down and see him, but he wouldn't even meet with me. He always said he'd get back to me, but he was only stalling. The way he had treated me during the campaign really stewed in me, and after a while, I decided to write him a letter. In it, I explained how I was very disappointed in him; that I was always loyal to him, and I had given him no reason not to be for me. Even the major newspapers gave me their endorsement, but still, he just didn't do anything for me. Rather than mailing that letter, I decided to go down to City Hall to give it to him myself. I went into the reception room outside his office and told his secretary who I was and that I wanted to speak to the mayor. I waited there for over an hour and, finally, I went to the receptionist again and asked her to go in and give him the letter herself. I waited for her to come back, and she said she had given it to him, and that he was reading it.

I decided to leave. I'm walking out of the office, and I see Bill emerge from an outside door in the corridor. By that time, I was already on the elevator, but he yelled down to me, "Wendell, Wendell—wait. I want to talk to you." I put my hand up and said, "Forget it!" He was coming down the hall toward me, but the elevator door closed and I went down.

13

EMPLOYEE OWNERSHIP

A T THE END OF THE 1970s, Philadelphia's Retail Clerks Union Local 1357 faced a serious crisis, losing almost one-third of the membership in a two-year period as department stores and supermarket chains went out of business. With such a cut in membership, it was difficult to maintain the kinds of services I had worked to secure in my years as president. The scale of this problem intensified in 1981 when A&P Markets, which employed four thousand union members in Southeastern Pennsylvania and New Jersey, announced it would phase out all operations in the region over the coming year. Even before this shocking news, I was convinced that a more proactive response to store shutdowns was needed. If we couldn't stop the stores from closing, then the union needed to find a way to help members secure some other kind of work. In 1982, I made the boldest decision in all my years as a labor leader: initiating an employee ownership plan in which union members would buy stores and run them by themselves.

The shutdowns of factories, mills, and warehouses and the loss of thousands of manufacturing jobs that came with them was the single most important economic fact facing the Philadelphia region in the 1970s. Since the end of the Civil War, Philadelphia was known as the Workshop of the World: its incredible range of high craft, mostly small batch specialty manufactories producing everything from high-quality ironworks, lithographic prints, fashion garments, and medical textbooks to lager beer, locomotives, radio parts, and chocolate truffles. Even before the Great Depression, some of the city's main manufacturing centers were struggling to stay open but revived during World War II as production demand surged. In the postwar period, many of these industries declined, went out of business, or relocated to the South. In the most devastating example, the city's once-vibrant textile sector, which had specialties like silk hosiery, Morocco leather goods, and the iconic Stetson Hats Factory in North Philadelphia, disappeared.

Over the course of the decade, Philadelphia lost over one hundred thousand manufacturing jobs. Many of Philadelphia's best-known manufacturing firms closed down in this period, including Budd Auto Frame, Bluebird Meat Packing, Sun Shipyard, Bond Bread, Abbotts Ice Cream and Dairies, Good and Plenty Candy Manufacturing, and U.S. Steel's Fairless Hills Plant in Bucks County. The city's once-vibrant brewery sector went under, too, as Ortlieb's, the city's oldest beer-making facility, shut down in 1981, followed by Christian Schmidt and Sons a few years later. Machinists and autoworkers in tool and dye firms and electronics shops were unemployed and unions like the Bakery and Confectionary Workers, the Machinists, and those who represented the textile industry lost thousands of members. Even the *Philadelphia Bulletin*, the city's oldest newspaper, closed in 1982. The shutdown of these sites impacted local businesses, neighborhood dinettes, and hardware stores across the city.

With so much economic disruption, a range of proposals emerged on how to preserve jobs and secure resources for entrepreneurs to create new ones. Economists, legislators, and trade unionists increasingly looked to worker cooperatives, ventures where employees owned the businesses they worked for, as a possible solution. Cooperatives could be traced back to the nineteenth century, but, in the 1960s, these kinds of programs took on new relevance, as more people sought self-sufficiency against large bureaucratic organizations as a way to reshape society. In the early 1970s, the Federation for Economic Democracy, a national group of academics and students, was organized to promote worker ownership, and a small chapter was set up in Philadelphia. From this group, a young lawyer named Sherman Kreiner devised plans for introducing such ventures locally, and, in 1977, he teamed up with Andrew Lamas to found a non-profit agency, the Philadelphia Center for Cooperative Enterprise (PACE). By 1981, PACE was active in promoting these kinds of employee ownership programs, launching a small number of industrial firms and meatpacking firms in the area.

I had read about the new cooperative movement and was excited by its possibilities in the food industry. My first thoughts of such an employee ownership idea came as a response to the threat of the privatization of Pennsylvania's Wine and Spirits Shops. In 1979, after Governor Richard Thornburgh signed onto a plan to sell off the state's liquor stores, I considered the possibility of Local 1357 buying them and running them on our own. It was a bold idea, no doubt, but I knew it was the surest way to protect the jobs of union members. There were other people in the food industry who believed such an approach was viable, and I began a series of meetings to find out the feasibility of the concept.

The person I knew who was most knowledgeable about cooperative business ventures was Jay Guben, a local entrepreneur who I had gotten to know through the antiwar movement. When he was still a student at Temple University, Jay did an internship with Retail Clerks Union Local 1357, which showed him the role of trade unions in the food industry and the ways that politics often shaped these conditions. Jay was very involved with the social movements of this period and worked with the Model Cities program before opening a series of successful and innovative restaurants in Center City Philadelphia. In 1974, he opened the Restaurant School, which taught aspiring entrepreneurs how to run their own establishments. By the end of the 1970s, Philadelphia was witnessing a culinary renaissance, in large part because of Jay's vision. With such a background in the food industry and the most innovative practices in the field, Jay was the perfect man to advise me on how to move forward with cooperative ventures in the retail trade, and he stressed the importance of owning property from which to start these plans. When the union negotiated its next liquor clerks contract with the commonwealth, I got a provision that gave the union first right of refusal to bid on the state stores should they ever be put up for sale.

At the end of 1981, I attended a series of conferences with A&P executives who outlined the financial difficulties the company was facing. Over the previous five years, they had lost ten million dollars, and they felt they were confronted with some stark choices. Soon after, the chairman of the A&P board announced store closures in the New York area, along with some places in Northern New Jersey, Maryland, and across the South. I knew it was only a matter of time before they did the same in

Philadelphia. I called Jay Guben and said we needed to forget our plans with the state liquor stores and focus instead on A&P. The Retail Clerks Union in Philadelphia had about four thousand members in that chain alone, and I wasn't sure the local could survive the collapse of these stores after it had lost so many since the Lit Brothers shut down in 1977. Just as I feared, in early 1982, A&P announced they would close most of their Philadelphia-based locations, and were placing these stores up for sale.

Right away, Jay and I got our plan together to buy the stores, lining up financial and legal experts to advise us. As Jay made clear, the first step was to buy some of the A&P stores that were on the market. The union couldn't do this on its own—it would have to work with members, and I organized a series of meetings to propose the cooperative plan. Before I did that, I contacted Local 1357's credit union officers to talk about the feasibility of a plan to have five hundred of our members each take out a five-thousand-dollar loan that we could then pool to make a bid on the stores. As this process was under way, I sent a letter to A&P president James Wood on the behalf of Local 1357, announcing the proposal. A couple of days later, Wood called me up himself. I'd never talked to him before in my life. He asked me if I was serious and I told him I was and that I would send him the money to prove it. The next day, I called a press conference because I wanted to put pressure on him and to show him I meant it. He called me again the day after and told me that he'd been speaking to his associates and that they were willing to sell us the stores if the union sent a down payment that was pooled from the funds that our members agreed to provide from the credit union. Since Jay Guben and I had already been meeting with some of our most active union members to discuss this option, we had enough to send in as an initial deposit and once I did so, A&P took the stores off the market. I would still need to convince even more Local 1357 members to take out similar loans, but the process was now underway. That same day, I started getting calls from other business interests who were interested in purchasing the stores, including Shop Rite and Acme, and I knew as soon as I had those calls, I had made the right move; I would be able to do something to save my members' jobs.

The announcement that the Retail Clerks Union were buying stores and launching worker-run cooperatives was a major news story. This initial plan Jay and I had thought up was ambitious: Local 1357 would establish a new food company, collectively owned by its members without any outside management oversight. Each worker, from deli managers and cashiers and utility clerks, would have a say in how the enterprise functioned, from the produce sold to scheduling and advertising. It would be a democratic organization, everything determined by regular meetings where everyone's voice counted.

This kind of plan was essential to the history of the cooperative movement, but there was a lot of skepticism about how feasible it would be. Much of this push back came from within the labor movement itself, including my own organization. There was a more prevalent tradition in the labor movement that understood a trade union's role as grounded in the collective bargaining process, mediating wages and conditions. It drew a sharp line with not assuming managerial functions. Leo Cinaglia, who represented UFCW Meat Cutters Local 56, which had about two thousand butchers in the A&P stores, was especially cynical. He wanted nothing to do with a collective supermarket plan, he just thought it was too complicated, too big a venture. Many Local 1357 staff members were equally reluctant, but I was convinced that employee ownership was the right thing to do and took the idea to the men and women who worked in the stores to see if they'd go along.

All during these first weeks of 1982, I must have spoken to hundreds of men and women who worked in the stores across the region. Many called me on the phone or stopped by the union offices. Other times I drove out to stores and met with clerks, cashiers, meat cutters, and night crews in break rooms and in parking lots after their shifts. I'll never forget these conversations. Some of the people were in tears. They felt desperate. Some had worked for A&P for over twenty-five or thirty years and, now, here they are in their fifties with few options. They didn't think they could find jobs somewhere else, not at the wages they had been making. These men and women would do anything to save their jobs.

I told them about the cooperative venture plan, and they supported it and would be willing to raise the money from the credit union. I called a big meeting at Lincoln High School up in Northeast Philadelphia and three hundred clerks and cashiers showed up. I told them about the plan, and what they needed to do to start things, to provide some more seed money to buy the stores and launch a new venture. Five thousand dollars is a lot of money to borrow, and I couldn't sugar coat it—it was a major risk they were taking. But I told them of the history of the cooperative movement, and how worker-owned enterprises could succeed and how owning their own stores would allow them more security, more say over their work lives, and more creativity. By taking up this challenge, they could work together to make a better future. They cheered! I set up other meetings around the city, and told them of the idea, and, by the end of March, I had raised all the money needed to purchase the stores from A&P.

As these plans got under way, I met with Mayor Bill Green and other politicians in the region to get their support for the cooperative supermarket. Because there had been so many factory shutdowns across Pennsylvania, politicians were getting behind new initiatives that encouraged job creation and provided incentives and financing to do so. Jay Guben and I met with Joseph M. Egan Jr., head of the Philadelphia Industrial Development Agency, in charge of promoting business starts and planning, and he took me to Harrisburg to pay the consultants to do the work to buy the company. Gov. Richard Thornburgh helped secure some state funding. Because the plan was promoting job growth, you could get 90 percent financing. The Philadelphia Citywide Development Corporation also helped with a loan package that matched the seed money the members were contributing. In March, PACE called a conference to pool ideas about how to move ahead with the cooperative idea. Hundreds attended, and experts on employee ownership from the University of Pennsylvania's Wharton School of Business and Cornell University spoke.

With the workers agreeing to the plan, Local 1357 moved ahead in March 1982 and bought twenty-one markets. I scheduled meetings with top A&P officials to negotiate on the price of the final arrangement, and the first one was just me and James Wood, the chairman of the A&P board. I told him my plan to take over the stores and operate them as union cooperatives. He looked at me and said he couldn't sell the stores to us. He'd do anything to keep them in operation, but A&P had to control them. I told him that the company didn't know how to run the stores, that they were failing. He listened to me, but he said he couldn't go along with selling the stores to the workers outright. He said, "Wendell, I make a certain amount of dollars. I'm chairman of the board and I have all these stakeholders. If you're a success, what does that do to me? If you guys are successful, I'm getting all this money, what am I going to do? I'll look like an asshole." I continued to argue with him, to try to get him to budge. "I can't sell you the stores; get it through your head, Wendell," I remember him saying. We went back and forth some more, but I left the meeting knowing that the plan had changed.

Another set of negotiations was set up. Here, I made it clear to A&P executives that whatever the outcome, it would have to be an entirely new arrangement. Sherman Kreiner proposed a kind of hybrid cooperative model: A&P would own the stores, but they would set up a formula where each employee would get a cut of 1 percent of the yearly gross volume in the store they worked in. To qualify for this bonus, labor expenses would have to be below 10 percent of yearly costs. In addition, we worked out another innovation. To save costs for the struggling A&P, the union agreed to salary decreases, limited vacation time for employees, and a cut in holidays from ten to seven. The union accepted this but as a trade-off, workers in the new enterprise would have a Quality of Work Life Plan, guaranteeing more of a say in how the store operated, from the scheduling of hours, determining what items were sold, and all other aspects of operation. From these negotiations Super Fresh Food Markets, a new subsidiary of A&P, was formed and James Wood agreed to provide a nine-million-dollar start-up fund to get it off the ground.

On May 13, 1982, I called a press conference at the Local 1357 headquarters to announce the setup of Super Fresh Food Markets. James Wood was there, along with top UFCW officials, Governor Thornburgh, Mayor Bill Green, and Gerald Good, the newly announced president of Super Fresh. The terms of the new system were outlined, along with a proposal that I believed would guarantee employment for unionized supermarket workers across the region should their stores be slated for closure. Built into the incentive program was a stipulation that whatever bonuses were given at the end of each year, 50 percent of the payout for the first five years would go into a Save Our Stores fund to put the money down to buy the stores if they ever closed.

It would take a few months before the new Super Fresh stores would open, so it wasn't an easy time for the union members from A&P who were without work. From May 1982 on, this is when the work really began, training workers to run the new stores. I never saw enthusiasm in our stores like it was in this period. Hundreds of our A&P members came to the union hall at A and Courtland Streets every night taking classes to learn how to control inventories, buy produce, coordinate truck delivery, prepare financial statements, and do everything about running a store. Jay Guben taught weekend seminars on supermarket management at St.

Joseph's Food Marketing Institute, overseeing the program fifteen hours a week for seven months. I was so happy to see how enthusiastic everyone was. They loved this idea and couldn't wait to get started.

In July 1982, the first Super Fresh opened for business, the first of twenty-four planned across the region that would employ over two thousand workers. I have never in my life seen people more happy than in those early Super Fresh stores. The men and women—they loved their jobs, they loved going to work, they loved the fact that they could have a say over every aspect of their job. They had a taste of unemployment and really were grateful for every day they could go to work. It was a total revolution in how they understood themselves in relation to their jobs. We reconstructed how things would be done to have ideal departments, to give the lowest level of management full authority. If a produce manager got a load of poor-quality fruit because some buyer made a deal off some farmer, she or he had a right to turn it down and send it back. Stores had more touches of creativity—handmade signs, choice of music played over the intercom, seasonal decorations. They'd put the name of the produce manager up and pictures of store personnel, create suggestion centers that encouraged consumer feedback, and, in some areas, sidewalk sales were set up. Customers were flocking in, bringing higher sales than when A&P called all the shots. Super Fresh was actually competing with Acme Markets, something A&P hadn't been able to do in the previous decade.

In December 1983, workers in the stores were slated to receive their first bonus checks. The union arranged for formal ceremonies in the stores, where workers were given their payout. The individual checks they received ranged from a few hundred dollars to some that were more than two thousand dollars. When some of them saw what their check was—they had never seen so much money in one shot—some people couldn't even speak. (See Figure 13.1.)

THE LAUNCHING OF THE SUPER FRESH Food Markets coincided with my twenty-year mark as president of Local 1357. I was now forty-three, had a little gray hair showing, and was one of the best-known labor leaders in Pennsylvania. The early success of the employee ownership program with Super Fresh generated a lot of coverage in the local media and in the retail food industry, and reporters who remembered me from my

Figure 13.1 Super Fresh Food Markets workers receiving annual bonuses, December 1984. (From the collection of Wendell W. Young III.)

earlier days noted that I had aged. I never used strong language when I was younger, but, by now, I cursed more and drank more as well. Being a labor leader is difficult, and the stresses in my life took a toll. People thought that I had sunburn because my face seemed blushed all the time, but it was from high blood pressure. I was diagnosed with diabetes. At a personal level, the demands of public life had, over the years, put a strain on my marriage, and, during this time, Marilyn and I separated and would eventually divorce. So there were a lot of changes happening all through this period.

The early successes of the Super Fresh Food Markets venture garnered a lot of attention in the media and were widely covered in food industry journals and even some academic studies. Along with Super Fresh, a smaller group of former A&P union members opted to move ahead with a cooperative supermarket idea where workers owned the stores outright. From some loans from the credit union and grants from government agencies, the union bought some additional stores and launched Owned and Operated Markets (O&O), which eventually had six stores across the region. With both the Super Fresh and O&O

experiments up and running, Local 1357 was recognized as a trailblazer in trade union responses to a changing economy. In 1984, I was invited to England to attend an international symposium on New Industrial Relations at Oxford University, where I explained the model we had set up in Philadelphia. My experiences there helped me think about all that was happening through the early part of the decade. This was during the infamous British Miner's Strike, and what I saw of that and my meetings with English, Welsh, and Scottish trade unionists convinced me of the parallels between Margaret Thatcher and Ronald Reagan. Federal cutbacks to urban services were beginning to take a toll, with increases in transportation fares, a decline in mental health services, and fewer programs to help the unemployed. Reagan's firing of striking air traffic controllers in 1981 represented a frontal attack on unions and the interests of working people. He promoted a harsher worldview, one that favored the most affluent and powerful in society, a program that was the exact opposite of the values I held. I felt that most Philadelphians were more in line with the views I had and would take a stand against the direction in which he was leading the nation. This was evident in 1982 when Bob Borski, a relatively unknown candidate, beat Charles Dougherty for Pennsylvania's third congressional district's seat. I had seriously considered running for this seat, but decided before the Democratic primary that I had too much going on with the negotiations with A&P to focus on a campaign—but I realized that had I run that year, I probably would have been elected to Congress.

Philadelphia's political world had been jolted the day before Election Day when Mayor Bill Green called a press conference announcing that he would not seek a second term. Bill and his wife, Pat, had a newborn, and he explained that he wanted to spend more time with his family. Many political observers thought this was a wise move, since second terms tend to be tougher than the first years, and he needed to maintain his good standing with voters since it was believed that he wanted to run again for senate. Bill's decision not to run opened the possibility of a field of candidates. Former Mayor Rizzo made no secret that he would run again and was joined by W. Wilson Goode, Bill Green's managing director, who was a rising star in the party. Even before Bill made his announcement, there was a movement to draft Goode, led in part by Hospital Workers Union Local 1199c president Henry Nicholas, although no one really thought he would challenge an incumbent mayor. He announced his candidacy in early December, and made bringing more jobs to Philadelphia's economy his highest priority.

Goode had long been involved in the Democratic Party and was critical in helping to forge the black political power base, having worked as campaign manager for Hardy Williams's campaign, in 1971, and in the anti-Rizzo wing of the party in West Philadelphia. He was an early favorite, but, although he had backing among liberals across the city, he didn't have much connection to organized labor. As city managing director, he had served as chief labor negotiator with the public sector unions, and there had been a lot of difficult sessions, especially the fifty-day teachers strike in 1981. Still, a lot of the labor leaders, including Earl Stout and Thomas Paine Cronin, the new president of DC 47, thought he was fair and honest, someone they could work with. Goode's strongest support in organized labor came from the Hospital Workers Union Local 1199c, which represented about ten thousand men and women in thirty-two different health care facilities across the region. Local 1199c leader Henry Nicholas believed strongly that black citizens would benefit from having a black mayor, and his support for Goode was probably the most influential from within labor's ranks. I knew Wilson from the civil rights movement and various community programs he had led, and I agreed with Henry that he was a good man and capable and I backed him early on.

By early 1983, Frank Rizzo had raised a lot of money and secured the promises of dozens of ward leaders for their support in the primary. State Senator Joseph M. Smith, who replaced David Glancey as Democratic City chairman in 1981, was supporting Rizzo as well, and this was an important plus for his campaign, even though I knew from the 1967 Tate reelection campaign that the backing of the political chairman didn't guarantee a win. Unions were also a key part of his coalition, having the backing of the Building and Construction Trades Council, the FOP, and the Teamsters. The campaign was a tough one, and Goode defeated Rizzo in May. By the end of the summer, all of the AFL-CIO endorsed Goode, and, in November, he defeated Republican candidate stockbroker John J. Egan Jr. and became Philadelphia's first African American mayor.

Going back to Rizzo's run in 1971, Philadelphia's mayoral contests were blatant displays of the city's racial divisions, with predominantly African American wards going for black candidates, while white sections supported white candidates by overwhelming numbers. Goode's win in 1983 broke this pattern, as he tallied overwhelming majorities in places like Germantown and North and West Philadelphia but also a sizable victory in the city's predominantly white wards in Kensington and in the Northeast. As he began his term, he had a lot of momentum behind him to lead a revitalized city. In his first few months at City Hall, he faced the same kind of problems that Bill Green had, with federal cutbacks in funding for municipal programs making it difficult to implement progressive programs. Philadelphia faced an unprecedented homelessness crisis, as an estimated two thousand people were sleeping out on the streets every night. A lot of factors were to blame. Plant and factory shutdowns swelled the ranks of the unemployed. Northeast Philadelphia's Byberry State Mental Hospital shut down in 1981 and this contributed to the problem by releasing hundreds of severely mentally ill persons who were unable to fend for themselves onto the city's streets. Both of these causes were the result of federal policies that directed funding away from the poor toward an increased military budget and tax cuts for the affluent. The Catholic Church addressed these matters, criticizing the focus on military spending at the cost of social services. I believed broader organization was needed, based on such a moral understanding of the crisis, and wanted to build a coalition with students, peace activists, environmentalists, advocates for the poor and women's organizations. Only by bringing together our different voices could an effective challenge to Reaganism be realized.

I knew organized labor needed to take the lead in bringing together these social forces, just as they were doing around the world. But the broader regional labor movement did not place its power and resources behind these kinds of activities. It came down to leadership, to educating members and mobilizing our power on the streets, and through our votes. Without question, Philadelphia's Central Labor Union (CLU) president Ed Toohey wasn't providing this kind of direction. He never got involved in anything and didn't back the civil rights movement, and later, the women's and youth movements, which were all opportunities to revitalize the labor movement. He took no chances and would stay away from anything that seemed a little radical. Never once did he come out with a statement in favor of Cesar Chavez's grape or lettuce boycotts or join the pickets. The only things the Philadelphia AFL-CIO council did get involved with under his watch were campaigns to increase the minimum wage, making sure building construction sites in the city were union, and getting out the vote for Democratic candidates in local and national political races. At labor events, Ed would get up and drone on and on without inspiration, talking and never really say anything. I'd sit there with the other labor representatives up on the stage, embarrassed that he was representing us.

Everyone knew Toohey was weak, but within the local labor movement, he had important backers who wanted him at the helm because he was predictable and wouldn't cause them any trouble. It was clear to me by 1983 that the man who was really shaping much of the Philadelphia AFL-CIO policy behind the scenes was Patrick Gillespie, a former crane operator who came out of the city's Operating Engineers Union who had replaced Ralph Williams as head of the Building and Construction Trades Council in 1981. Pat understood the importance of politics and had even served one term in the Pennsylvania legislature beginning in 1974, but he was very conservative on most issues and we didn't usually see eye to eye. Like a lot of the building trades' guys, he thought I was too radical, but I could talk to him, and we knew where we stood. Pat didn't particularly like Ed Toohey either, but he knew that he could control him, and he continued to support him as leader of the council.

By 1983 it was getting to a point where even some people in the Building Trades wanted a change. Some of the leaders in the AFL-CIO Food Council asked me to consider running against Toohey for Philadelphia's CLU presidency myself, and I said I would. Through the summer of 1983, I lined up my supporters and let them know I was going to challenge Ed. My campaign was cut short, however, because one day, just on the eve of the election, I was driving to a meeting somewhere; I had the radio on and heard a press conference held by Ed Toohey where he announced that the Philadelphia Building and Construction Trades Council had unanimously endorsed him for another term. I immediately called everyone who had told me that they would support me and told them to forget it. I wasn't going to run if the building trades weren't behind me, I felt it was a lost cause. But sentiment against Toohey was so strong that the day after I stepped away, Danny Chmelko, the thirty-three-year-old business agent from the International Association of Machinist Local 1717, announced a challenge slate.

Danny Chmelko worked at the Eaton Forklift Manufacturing plant up in Northeast Philadelphia, and in early 1981 he was laid off along with six hundred workers of his fellow employees. This was what got him involved with the labor movement, and he gained a lot of attention by organizing demonstrations at the factory gate and leading civil disobedience actions that on one occasion blocked traffic on six lanes of Roosevelt Boulevard. In the face of Reagan's policies, Danny believed the federal government needed to step in and support the workers who faced layoffs. He joined me in pressing Philadelphia City Council to pass a law in April 1982 specifying a sixty-day notice for employees working for companies with more than fifty employees that planned to close down. This was the first law of its kind passed by a municipality, and it became a benchmark for similar legislation around the country. Years later a federal bill known as the Worker Adjustment and Retraining Notification Act was introduced by Congressman Tom Foglietta and passed in 1988. To continue to change policies, Chmelko wanted to get the unions involved in social causes and showed he could gain attention by organizing marches to City Hall, building coalitions with clergy and civic groups, and reaching out to both Republicans and Democrats. In late 1983, he was arrested with other trade union activists for blocking departing buses during a drivers strike at the Greyhound Bus Terminal at 18th and Market. It was a rare sight to see this kind of front-page media attention for labor causes, and Danny was behind it.

On December 14, 1983, delegates met to vote for the city's CLU president and the divisions in the labor movement were out on display. The teachers, city workers, and machinists, along with the UFCW, went for Chmelko. Toohey had the full backing of the Building and Construction Trades Council, and with a sizable bloc of the other unions, he won the election pretty handily. Chmelko's supporters claimed that there were voting irregularities and demanded that AFL-CIO president Lane Kirkland investigate the proceedings. Shortly after, the national body called it a fair election and approved the results. In response to the schism in our ranks, Ed Toohey promised to have more transparency and to initiate reforms that would allow more dissent in the council, but many other union officials and I simply stopped paying our dues to the CLU, since we considered it a waste of money.

The 1983 CLU election was important because even though organized labor was facing hard times, it still had a lot of power in the city. Its top leader could shape policies and set the tone with the new mayor. Wilson Goode knew Philadelphia was a staunchly union town, and he wanted labor at the table. From his first days in office, I could call him up and ask for his help and consultation, and he came to the grand openings of Super

Fresh and O&O to show his support, which I appreciated. He was committed to preserving jobs and expanding employment opportunities in the city. This was especially apparent in his focus on major Center City building projects. In 1985, he supported 3.5 billion dollars in public and private construction projects, a move that played well with the Building Trades. He backed plans to change the Philadelphia skyline by approving the construction of Liberty One, a 945-foot skyscraper at 16th and Chestnut Streets that would be the tallest, most modern tower in the city. Completed in 1987, the structure was the start of a building boom over the coming decade that provided good jobs for the construction industry. Along with that, a multiyear City Hall refurbishing was initiated, providing employment for hundreds of carpenters, ironworkers, masons, bricklayers, and roofers. Ground was also broken for a new Convention Center, which was built over a two-year period with union labor. Mayor Goode maintained his contacts with the unions, appearing at rallies and meetings, and Henry Nicholas remained one of his closest advisers.

Wilson Goode faced a major crisis in his second year in office that, for a time, caused me to question whether I could continue to support him. In May 1985, the Philadelphia Police Department confronted a radical group known as MOVE, founded by John Africa. I always found it difficult to define what MOVE was all about. In a sense, they were fundamentalist Earth people, a kind of back-to-nature group, although they lived in a West Philadelphia row house, which didn't really go together. They would leave food scraps out for rats, and use their own excrement as fertilizer in the small patch of backyard they had. In August 1978, MOVE engaged in an armed standoff with Philadelphia police in the Powelton Village neighborhood, in which an officer was killed. Sometime after, they relocated their headquarters to a row house on Osage Avenue in West Philadelphia. Here, they constructed a rooftop bunker where they had a loudspeaker and members broadcast profane messages at all hours. After putting up with this for months, neighbors complained to the mayor and asked him to intervene, essentially to go in and evict them from the house because of sanitary and noise violations.

Mayor Goode understood how volatile the situation was, and delayed action for a while, but on the morning of May 13, 1985, the police department was sent in to enforce MOVE's eviction. Shots were fired from the house and a tense standoff began. Later that afternoon, a police helicopter dropped a duffle bag filled with explosives onto the rooftop bunker and the house went up in flames, the blaze spreading to other houses. Before the night was over, the entire block of homes had burned down, spreading to other surrounding homes across the street and back driveway. Eleven MOVE members died in the carnage.

As I watched these events unfold on television, my support for Mayor Goode crumbled. Local 1357 Secretary-Treasurer Herman Wooden was head of the Active Ballot Club, the union's political fund-raising committee, and we agreed that we had better find someone else to support in the 1987 election. Herman worked as a part-time liquor store clerk in North Philadelphia in the late 1960s and got involved with the state store organizing campaign; he joined the union staff soon after and was my main political adviser for many years. It was clear that Frank Rizzo wanted to run for office again, and Herman suggested that we give him a serious look. I told Herman that would be tough for me, and he said he felt that way also, but we needed to be realistic. I called Joe Rizzo, Frank's younger brother, in to meet with us to act as a liaison. Joe had previously served as fire commissioner and I had gotten to know him through various political events in the city, and because some of his kids worked in supermarkets and were members of the union. Joe told us Frank would do whatever he could to help out the UFCW. "You don't know Frank like I do," he told us. "He's not the way you think he is. I want to tell you something, Frank's a lot of bluff." I told him about what happened at that AFL-CIO meeting years earlier, the time when he used racial epithets to describe the Black Panthers. I still remembered those words. But Joe and I used to have these long discussions, and he tried to explain how his brother had changed and how we should give him a serious look.

Right after the MOVE bombing, Mayor Goode lost a lot of political support around the city. There were calls from within the black community, from some prominent business and civic leaders for him to step away and not seek a second term. Wilson was absolutely determined to fight for reelection. Many of the unions still backed him. He still had a lot of support from the building trades, the transit workers, Teamsters, and the hospital workers. As they so often did, labor issues were a factor in how Philadelphia's political world was shaped going into the election year. Goode gained back some political capital in the summer of 1986 when he came out on top in a dispute with the city's powerful municipal workers' union. By that time, a serious opposition movement in AFSCME had emerged against Earl Stout, led by James Sutton, a leader of the sanitation division. Stout felt he needed to shore up his power with a show of force against Goode in the 1986 contracts. The mayor, however, pledged to gain more control over the union's health and welfare fund, which was completely controlled by the union, although the city made direct contributions to it. He demanded immediate raises, more money for the benefits programs, and sole control over funds. This standoff led to a two-week trash strike in the summer of 1986. Goode refused to back down and gained public support, and eventually court injunctions threatened workers with arrest. Workers started going back to work and the strike was broken, a major defeat for Earl Stout.

With his strong hand against the city workers, Goode gained a lot of respect in the city and entered the election year with better footing. As many expected, Frank Rizzo made moves to enter the race, but this time with a new strategy. In the summer of 1986, Rizzo started appearing at Republican events with party chief Billy Meehan, and, by the end of the year, formally announced he had changed his political registration. By February 1987, the majority of GOP ward leaders were behind the former mayor. Meehan believed that Rizzo's candidacy was a way to gain Republican power in the city, and he was right: by the time of the election, over fifty thousand of Rizzo's staunchest supporters—the Rizzocrats—had switched their registration to vote for him.

Through most of my life in the labor movement, Philadelphia's unions had played a big role in determining who would control City Hall. Many in the unions, especially Ed Toohey and the Building Trades, had always been the most loyal Rizzo backers, but the AFL-CIO was split and refused to endorse either candidate. Rizzo always underscored his South Philly working-class background and union support. I remember there were lawn signs and campaign posters in people's windows that had a picture of the former mayor, with the words "Another Working Family for Frank." A score of unions, led by the International Brotherhood of Electrical Workers (IBEW) Local 98, the Steamfitters, and the Fraternal Organization of Police Lodge 5 went for Rizzo, forming the United Labor for Rizzo Committee. I'd given it serious thought; Frank was very demonstrative about his feelings for unions and had a strong record to prove it. In the early part of 1987, the discussions Herman Wooden and I had initiated with Rizzo and his team fell apart. I don't know why; I just don't think we could bring ourselves to back him. Henry Nicholas was talking to Herman and me, trying to convince us to stay with Goode, and

Bob Brady the new Democratic chairman also pushed us, and eventually I too came out in support of the mayor's bid for a second term.

All through September and October, the mayoral race polled at a virtual tie, the city divided, mostly along racial lines. On November 3, 1987, Mayor Goode won close reelection, taking Frank Rizzo by just over seventeen thousand votes. That evening, after the results were in, Rizzo came on stage at his campaign headquarters, surrounded by hundreds of supporters. I watched him on television, his voice was hoarse by this point, telling his supporters, telling the whole world, that he would never concede, not to Mayor Wilson Goode.

14

FRENCH INVASION

OVER THE YEARS, I'D BEEN on many picket lines, standing with members from the supermarkets on strike at Food Fair or Acme, or in solidarity with teachers, meat cutters, coal miners, and Greyhound bus drivers. One picket line I never expected to be on was outside Philadelphia's Veteran Stadium, holding a strike sign along with the entire defensive line of the Philadelphia Eagles football team. A few weeks into the 1987 season, the NFL Players Association called a strike to change the league's free agency clause, which held players under the control of teams and limited their abilities to play on their own terms. The NFL owners vowed to continue the season and were fielding teams of scabs to try to break the union. On October 4, 1987, about four thousand union supporters showed up outside the stadium in Philadelphia, in a show of support for the players.

A court injunction forbade more than a couple picketers outside the entrance, but there were dozens confronting anyone who crossed the picket lines. Words were exchanged and a couple fistfights broke out, with police on horseback trying to keep order. Eagles' tight end John Spagnola, the team's player representative, was asking everyone to stay back and avoid arrest. Local 115 President John P. Morris mobilized the Teamsters across the region, showing up in force, dozens of trucks circling the stadium, their horns honking, tying up traffic on Broad Street. By kickoff, there were more protesters outside than there were spectators watching the game.

THE PROTEST OUTSIDE VETERAN'S STADIUM that day highlighted the power of organized labor in Philadelphia. At first, I was hesitant to support the players, since so many of them were millionaires. It's easy to look at these guys as football players, not as workers; but on average, most of them don't last too long in the league, since it's such a violent game, and many of them have health issues years later. More than anything, it was the NFL owners' determination to break this strike by fielding scab players, that deliberate attempt to bust the player's union that united Philadelphia's labor movement. Around the United States, unions were struggling against aggressive union-busting campaigns. The players' strike was one example that was in the public view, and we felt it was important to take a stand.

Since the mid-1970s, the Retail Clerks Union across the nation had been losing members as stores went out of business and as abrupt economic shifts weakened industries across a range of sectors. There were many reasons for this, but the growing impact of globalization was a main one. As manufacturing moved outside the United States, and cheaper products flooded inventories, retailers were forced into greater competition. Many companies that started out as locally owned were bought out by international firms in places like Germany, Great Britain, and the Netherlands. This globalization process was felt as a distancing between company owners and directors whose headquarters were thousands of miles away. For example, in 1979, A&P was bought out by the West German Tengelmann Group. Such changes altered companies' relationship to the workers they employed in basic ways. When I first started out as a labor official, companies like Food Fair and A&P Markets had a local identity and took an active role in the region's civic life, providing decent jobs for people who lived in the region. This underscored a kind of social contract, where companies provided a fair wage and employees remained committed to the company for the duration of their working lives. Company presidents and business owners usually lived in the same communities where their customers did. To give a sense of this, I actually used to see Food Fair's president Lou Stein or Acme Market's head Paul Cupp at the Phillies games at Connie Mack Stadium. By the 1980s, most of the top brass and shareholders of the chain stores that serviced Philadelphia lived in other parts of the country, or in other nations, with little understanding of the region.

In late 1987, Carrefour, a French company that was the largest retail outlet in the world, with stores across Europe and Brazil, announced it was opening a store in Northeast Philadelphia, its first complex in North America. This massive outlet would be the first of twenty-one stores planned for Pennsylvania, New Jersey, and Delaware. Carrefour was something known as a hypermarket, a retail center once described as a supermarket on steroids. A standard-sized supermarket in the 1980s could be anywhere from twenty thousand to sixty thousand square feet, but a hypermarket might have as many as three hundred thousand or higher. When you walked into one of these stores, they had everything from fresh produce and meats, entire areas that sold pets, an auto center, a huge music section—really multiple stores within a store. The sheer volume of goods allowed for low prices, so low that the competing stores would go out of business. The shop floors were so big that they had managers on roller skates literally racing from the front-end office over to the checkout booth to do price checks.

Plans for Carrefour's opening in Philadelphia moved quickly, as it took advantage of five-year tax rebates that were part of a program the Philadelphia Redevelopment Authority launched in the mid-1980s to lure new businesses to the city. French managers already cut a deal with the region's Building Trades Council, promising to construct the planned three hundred thousand-foot store using only union labor. However, the store's commitment to the unions only went so far. In retail trade magazines, Carrefour's president Vivian Goulond made it clear that although their French employees were unionized, their operations in the United States would be strictly nonunion. As soon as I heard these plans, I knew it would pose a major problem for the unionized retail sector in Philadelphia. Local 1357 represented workers in twenty-one stores in a ten-mile radius of this proposed site, and Carrefour threatened every one of these fifteen hundred union jobs since, by undercutting their competition with their ridiculously low prices, it would lead to the closure of unionized stores like Acme, Super Fresh, Shop n Bag, and Rite Aid. I knew I would have to fight this move. Pat Gillespie, the president of Philadelphia's Building and Construction Trades Council, promised that he would help us organize the five hundred clerks and cashiers Carrefour planned to hire, but what good would it do to bring in those new members if it meant an overall loss of one thousand union members who already worked in the other stores? Based on this fact, the core message I underscored was the need to protect American jobs. The only way I knew that could bring this pressure on was through a boycott, and building a community labor coalition.

Carrefour opened in February 2, 1988, and union volunteers were out in the parking lots and entranceways, giving out information and educating shoppers about the reasons we didn't want them patronizing the store. I knew this would be a long, protracted struggle and to help our efforts, I got a permit for a trailer to become our campaign office and positioned it right off Knight's Bridge Road, just off the store's main parking lot. Local 1357 members in the various stores we represented voted to raise their dues to help with the boycott, paying for advertisements, the renting of the trailer, and for T-shirts that said "Buy American, Save American Jobs." I must have been on every radio and television news program across the region, getting the message out, talking about what was at stake. Since so many other stores were in jeopardy, some of the companies impacted by Carrefour issued special coupons to encourage people to patronize their stores, and our volunteers went door-to-door, handing them out along with flyers explaining the boycott. The campaign also gained attention through big public rallies that we organized outside the store. The first large gathering we sponsored was on Flag Day in June 1988 when over a thousand people, comprising UFCW members and their supporters, showed up from across the East Coast to join our volunteers in a demonstration of solidarity. We hammered home the fact that Carrefour was threatening American jobs and organized similar events on Bastille Day and the Fourth of July.

From early 1988 on, we were out there every single day and were making an impact on the store's bottom line. Carrefour managers didn't let on, but they could see how effective our campaign was, and they resented our actions. They set up video cameras at the site, held mandatory in-store meetings with their employees to try to scare them, and countered our messages in the media. One day, there was a terrible smell in the trailer, and we found a load of rotten fish had been dumped on the roof. There was a lot of petty vandalism. Some of the union staff found their car doors dented and a couple times had their tires slashed. The worst instance happened the evening of December 5, 1988, when the trailer was firebombed. Luckily, no one was injured, but I demanded a more vigorous police investigation. Carrefour made a press statement where they actually claimed that the union had orchestrated the firebombing to gain publicity. I knew that the company had brought in some goons to do this work, but no arrests were ever made.

THROUGH 1988 AND 1989, THE boycott campaign against Carrefour remained the most important effort of the UFCW in Philadelphia. We committed almost a million dollars to it, and planned to outlast them. Much like the A&P closing and the response with the cooperative super-markets, I saw it as a basic struggle to keep the union in existence. We had a lot of power in the region, and I knew we could draw on the support of our members and their families to get behind the boycott. Despite the store shutdowns that began in 1977, Local 1357 took in more members through the early years of the 1980s, due to a series of aggressive organizing campaigns. The union represented a growing assortment of retail and service workers in the region, including caseworkers at the American Arbitration Association, cashiers and clerks at Rite Aid Pharmacy, maintenance workers at Pineview Village Apartments, and cleaning crews at Air Terminal Services at Allentown Airport and Philadelphia's Spectrum Sports Arena, home of the Philadelphia Flyers and 76ers. In 1981, Philadelphia's Local 9B of the Barbers, Hairdressers and Cosmetologists Union, which had a few hundred members in the region, merged with Local 1357 and expanded the range of service workers we represented. Similar mergers with UFCW locals in Reading and Allentown added four thousand new members, and, a few years later, we took in Boot and Shoe workers in Wilkes-Barre, food processing workers at Hanover Brands and Knouse Foods, and Local 49-I of the Philadelphia Insurance and Professional Workers Union. By the end of 1985, Local 1357 represented twenty-three thousand members, the most members we ever claimed. We fostered a sense of community across the various sectors we represented. In the summer of 1986, over thirty-three hundred members and their families and friends—forty-two busloads of people—gathered at Local 1357's annual picnic at Clementon Lake Amusement Park in New Jersey with Acme Markets and Super Fresh donating food and prizes.

With the merger of these existing locals across Pennsylvania, the union was no longer a separate Philadelphia or Allentown local, but one unified organization across the wider region. As a part of this new identity, the union left its Courtland Street facility in Philadelphia in 1988 and moved to a new headquarters in Montgomery County, a series of offices

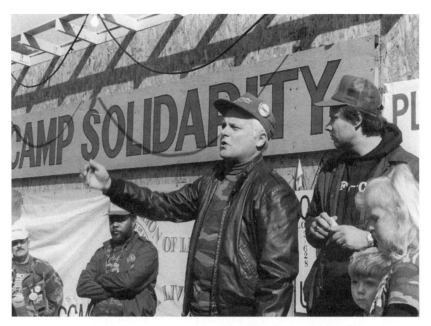

Figure 14.1 Wendell W. Young III speaking in support of striking miners, Pittston, Pennsylvania, 1989. (From the collection of Wendell W. Young III.)

at 3031 Walton Road in Plymouth Meeting. The union rebranded itself in another important way. For years, I had wanted to switch our local number from 1357 to 1776, since we represented one of the largest unions in the City of Brotherly Love. A section of the union in Jacksonville, Florida, already had it, though. When that local disbanded and the number became available, I moved to claim it, and the UFCW international chartered it to us in 1989. I felt since we had recently merged with the Boot and Shoe workers, who traced their roots back to the cordwainers—the shoemakers of the early American Republic—who organized one of the first unions in the United States, that we were part of their legacy. Local 1776's new letterhead and business cards were printed in red, white, and blue and we started using the Liberty Bell on our logo, along with the American flag. The members loved it, and they were calling up the office to get T-shirts and baseball caps with the union logo. (See Figure 14.1.)

With the union relocating its main offices outside Philadelphia, I decided to relocate as well. In 1988, I bought a house in Lafayette Hill, in Montgomery County, which marked a new beginning in my personal life. Through these years, I was still single and living alone, and, when I started dating again, a friend encouraged me to go out with someone he knew named Kathy Donovan. We went out on a date and really liked each other, and very soon, I fell in love with her. From the time we met, Kathy was the one person I could turn to in all the things that happened in my life. She was interested in my work in the labor movement. She became an integral part of my total life and the best thing that ever happened to me. In the summer of 1988, we were married in the backyard of the new house with a small gathering of close friends and family. Judge Nix officiated at the ceremony and my son Wendell was my best man. We hadn't thought to invite Mayor Goode, but he found out about it and came to the ceremony and stayed for the reception. We felt honored to have him with us.

With all of these changes happening, the Carrefour boycott remained the union's most critical campaign. While the protest had an impact, by the end of 1988, four stores in the ten-mile radius shut down just as I had predicted. Among the stores that went under were a Super Fresh and a couple O&O cooperatives, but the hardships in these two ventures were not limited to Northeast Philadelphia. Although the cooperative model had been celebrated as a success in its initial three years, there were roadblocks. Super Fresh's original chief officer Jerry Good had been committed to the power sharing experiment, but when he left in 1984 and was replaced by A&P vice president Julian DiFiore, things started to go downhill. Under the new leadership, the system where employees controlled most of the everyday decision process began to change, as more and more things reverted back to supervisors. A&P saw all the bonus money workers were getting each year and started looking for ways to get around it. Stores started bringing in items with higher profit margins, rather than cheaper items that would bring in larger volume, which was what the revenue sharing formula was based upon, therefore impacting workers' end-of-the-year bonuses. For example, they were stocking Green Giant green beans that sold for forty cents a can over a more generic brand that sold for thirty cents. Workers wanted to keep lower-priced products in stock so that people would purchase greater numbers of the lower cost item, increase the overall volume of the store, and lead to higher bonuses. With these kinds of shifts toward higher priced goods, the whole model was in jeopardy.

There was a hard core of Super Fresh workers who understood what was at stake, and who decided to fight back. In November 1989, twenty-six hundred Super Fresh workers in the forty-four stores in the region went on strike, demanding pay increases and more of a say in determining the merchandise stocked in the stores by calling for a new warehouse to be built or purchased by 1992. The call for the separate warehouse that serviced only Super Fresh Food Markets was critical, because bringing in higher quantities of cheaper items that would ultimately sell more over the course of a year was the key determinant in what kind of annual bonus was secured by the workers. As it was, Super Fresh had two warehouses in New Jersey and Baltimore that also served all the A&P stores in the area. These warehouses were small, dating from the early twentieth century, and stored a limited variety of goods. A&P insisted that merchandise be the same for both A&P and Super Fresh stores, ignoring employee suggestions from the cooperative venture about what goods to stock. A walkout began just before Thanksgiving but lasted only two days. Negotiations resumed, Super Fresh was emphatic that they would never give us the warehouse, so I pressed them for higher wages—thirty cents an hour—which they eventually conceded. A commission to investigate the possibility of a new warehouse was set up, but it never led to one, just as I feared. The Super Fresh Company stayed in business, but the power-sharing system I'd worked to design in 1982 died. A&P management essentially took over all aspects of the store's operations, doing away with the Quality of Work Life councils that encouraged workers to have a direct say in how their stores were run. The company's top brass also stopped giving out the annual bonuses that were promised in the initial plan. Not one of the stores gives the 1 percent bonus today. Super Fresh Food Markets continue to function, but they are really no different than all the other stores in the A&P chain.

All the blame for the failure of the cooperative movement with Super Fresh and O&O cannot be pinned on management alone. Another key reason for the shortcoming of these experiments was the unwillingness of the union's members to contribute adequately to the investment fund that was started in 1982 to allow for the opening of additional cooperative supermarkets in the region. When we first set up the fund, it was on the assumption that Super Fresh workers would contribute a designated portion of their annual bonus money to it, to pool their economic resources in order to keep our employee-owned markets going. It was projected that over one million dollars would be available in order to launch new stores and support existing operations, but actual investment over two years was only sixty-eight thousand dollars. By 1985, the investment fund was penniless and almost all of the O&O Stores were on the verge of collapse. Local 1357 pumped over two hundred thousand dollars to the fund to keep it afloat, but this wasn't sustainable.

The Carrefour Boycott continued through into 1990, but it was at a stalemate, tied up in legal challenges, picketing, and media war. I tried a new tactic to bring pressure on the company, reaching out to the French labor movement. I sent Local 1776 recording-secretary Peter P. Huegel and Wendell IV, who was now a business agent, to France to talk to the union leadership, to explain what we were up against, and to see what kind of pressure they could bring. They met with Force Ouvriere (FO)— or Workers Force—one of France's labor federations. FO's leader Gerard Fosse came to Philadelphia, joined us on picket line, and spoke to our members. In Paris, he organized rallies to bring attention to our struggle. This alliance with FO was an important step in bringing some stronger pressure on Carrefour. In February 1990, however, without my knowledge, the international union announced a truce at a meeting in Miami, suspending picketing and litigation.

I opened the *Philadelphia Inquirer* one day and it announced that the UFCW international had reached a deal with Carrefour, and that it is going to be union. I immediately called up Gary Duckett the international director in our region and asked what was going on. He told me that the UFCW international had made a deal with Carrefour where the store in Northeast Philly would be unionized but rather than representation by Local 1776, it would be handled by an entirely new local that would cover that one store. We'd already spent almost two million dollars on the campaign, and this was the result? The international union was looking ahead, seeing all the new stores Carrefour planned to open, and they didn't want to harass them.

The model of the hypermarket depended on high-volume sales, and this was a gamble. The economic recession of the early 1990s hit sales hard, and the drop in volume and cut in profits worked against the French giant, which was now saddled with too much stock. After struggling through this period, Carrefour announced it would close the Franklin Mills store in September 1993, and end further operations in the United States. In the end, Carrefour wound up selling the Franklin Mills property to Walmart, a company that is nothing short of the American version of the French giant. A few years later, Walmart opened its first store in the area, impacting the region's economy in similar ways to Carrefour.

THE RECESSION OF THE EARLY 1990s had a devastating impact on the region's economy. Scores of manufacturing centers, including iconic Philadelphia brands like Breyers Ice Cream and Frank's Beverages were sold to firms outside the city, and eventually their local plants closed. In 1990, the federal government announced that the Philadelphia Naval Shipyard, after nearly two hundred years of operation, would be scrapped, a loss of almost nine thousand jobs. The city continued to lose population and financial resources, with resulting cutbacks in basic services. By the end of Wilson Goode's second term in 1992, Philadelphia faced a deficit of over two hundred million dollars. Issues faced by Philadelphia and other cities were made worse by a decade of the Reagan-Bush administrations, which channeled resources and programs away from cities toward military spending and tax cuts for the affluent. Philadelphia's services were neglected, the crime rate was high, and the overall quality of life suffered.

Thousands of Philadelphians looked to Frank Rizzo as a kind of charismatic leader, the single person who could save the city from further collapse. Rizzo believed this, too, and so long as there was a possibility opening, he would run for another term as mayor. By now Frank was seventy years old, but he showed no signs of slowing down. Until 1988, he had a talk radio program called "Frank Talk with Frank Rizzo" on a local AM radio station in the afternoon, and he used it as a platform to berate the policies of Mayor Goode and to give his views on what was needed. Sometimes people would call up with problems they had, and Frank would make phone calls to city agencies to get some action. Often, the next day, people would call back up thanking him for his help. This kind of personal connection is what made Rizzo so popular to so many, and why they wanted him back at City Hall.

In 1987, he came just shy of seventeen thousand votes of winning, and many thought he could do it this time. Republican party boss Billy Meehan wasn't one of them. He believed Frank had his shot and came up short, and now he was just too old. Instead, Meehan convinced former district attorney Ronald D. Castille to take up the banner. Although he had the support of some ward leaders and the fifty thousand Rizzocrats who had changed registration for him, Frank knew he needed to rely heavily on organized labor support, reaching out especially to the Teamsters, the Building Trades, and police and fire organizations that had stood by him over the years.

This time around, Frank Rizzo, who was again running as a Republican, was hopeful that I might break with my years of bitter opposition and give him some support. In late 1990, there was a big meeting hosted by the Urban Affairs Council at LaSalle University and I was invited and onstage with Local 1776 recording-secretary Herman Wooden and a bunch of community leaders. Rizzo had just announced he was running and was appealing to everyone for his campaign, explaining about how broad his tent of supporters was. We're sitting behind him on the stage and he's telling everybody, "This time when I run, I'm almost sure I'm going to get Wendell W. Young's support." I shouted back from the stage, "You never know, Mr. Mayor!" Herman and I had actually been talking about it before we went to the meeting and planned to discuss a possible Rizzo endorsement with the union's executive board. I ran into Rizzo in the men's room after the session and I said, "You know, Frank, we are seriously thinking of backing you." He looked at me and said, "Are you bullshitting me?" I told him I wasn't, that Herman and I had been talking it over. UFCW Local 1776 would be an important endorsement for the campaign, not only because of how it would show Rizzo had broadened his support but because of the get-out-the-vote game we would bring to key areas of the city that Rizzo needed to win. When Bob Casey ran for governor in 1986, Herman Wooden was critical in mobilizing the vote for him in West Philadelphia, where we had a lot of members and pull with ward leaders.

The election set for November promised to be a real clash of positions and ideas over the city's future. Running against Rizzo was Edward G. Rendell, Philadelphia's former district attorney. Rendell won the Democratic primary against Lu Blackwell (who quit his city council position so he could run), George R. Burrell Jr., and James S. White. The three African American candidates split the vote. Rendell represented a new kind of Democrat, connected to the conservative Democratic Leadership Council, and with fewer ties to organized labor as liberals like James H. J. Tate or even Frank Rizzo. A fiscal conservative, Rendell was more allied to new technological industries and viewed Philadelphia as needing to draw venture capital into the city, loosen regulations, and develop downtown infrastructure to compete globally after the end of the Cold War. City government spending needed to be reduced, even if it meant breaking the city workers' union. These terms and proposals mobilized the public sector unions and would shape the way that the AFL-CIO responded.

Purely pragmatic reasons shaped why I was considering Rizzo in 1991. When Herman and I discussed the campaign, we knew we could get things done with him. We were interested in keeping Walmart out of Philadelphia and once Frank Rizzo made a commitment to us, we knew that would hold. He had made friends in the black community in the past few years, and many African American business leaders were open to supporting him. He had learned a lesson; he was not the same man he had been when he was mayor. There were many people I spoke to who believed Rizzo had the leadership to change the city and to address the crumbling city services, the drug epidemic, and, especially, the rampant crime problem. The Republican primary was very mean-spirited. Frank mocked Castille's character, claiming that he was a drunk and that there were reports that he brandished a pistol. These kinds of tactics seemed desperate, and most experts thought Rizzo was a long shot, but on May 21, he secured the nomination, beating Castille by just over a thousand votes.

Herman Wooden and I were in informal discussions with Frank's team into that summer, and we were seriously considering endorsing him. There was a lot of hope that Frank would win the general election that November, and I thought he had a real shot at it. On July 16, 1991, Frank Rizzo returned from a campaign event and died from a massive heart attack. News of his death shocked the city, and people were dumbfounded. Thousands of people stood outside his funeral mass outside the Cathedral Basilica of Saints Peter and Paul, the lines forming for blocks. I'd never seen anything like it.

Rizzo's death pushed the city into political chaos. Most of the Rizzocrats—the thousands who changed their party affiliation to Republican to vote for the former mayor—were more committed to him personally than they were to the party at any kind of ideological level. There was talk about Frank's brother, former fire commissioner Joe Rizzo, running in his place, while others thought Sam Katz, who had shown well in the primary, should head the GOP ticket. Within a week, Billy Meehan picked Joseph M. Egan Jr., an urban finance expert and former director of the Philadelphia Industrial Development Agency, a decision quickly sanctioned by the city's Republican ward leaders. Herman Wooden and I talked it over, but we just didn't think Egan had any chance of winning, and UFCW Local 1776 wound up not endorsing either candidate that year. In November, Rendell won in a landslide.

THROUGH THE 1990S, GAY RIGHTS ACTIVISM was a growing movement around the nation, and it was impossible not to take note of the direct actions that were taken, and the kinds of new coalitions that were forming. Philadelphia had long been a national center for gay rights and in the 1970s the Gay Liberation Front (GLF) organized a number of protests that gained media attention and called for changes in the treatment of gays and lesbians. Mark Segal, one of the young GLF activists, established the *Philadelphia Gay News* in 1976, and became a forceful advocate for change. In the 1980s and early 1990s, a small but militant section of ACT-UP organized sit-ins and actions in the city, gaining a lot of attention for sex education reform and federal funding to address the AIDS epidemic. Mayor Rendell was one of the first politicians in the city to see the LGBTQ community as a support base, and this reflected changing attitudes. Through the 1970s and 1980s, gay rights was not a cause I aligned myself with or supported in any way, in large part due to my Catholic background, which defines homosexuality as a sin. In those days, I was totally against homosexuality and had no sympathy for its cause.

Within the labor movement, I wasn't alone in this position, as there was virtually no support for LGBTQ rights, it wasn't even on the radar. I started to rethink my position on this by the early 1990s and took up the issue of sexual minorities, rights at the bargaining table. This shift in views stemmed from a personal transformation that challenged my earlier views. My brother Joe Young, who is just a couple years younger than me, is a homosexual, and he struggled with this for years. For about four years, he trained to be an Oblate priest, but three months before his ordination, he left and joined the Peace Corps. After two years' service, he went to work for the United Nations helping refugees fleeing Vietnam to get passage to the United States. During that time, he got married and had a son, but, soon after, he met a man and left his wife. When that happened, no one in the family would deal with him. I remember one time he made some plans to bring his boyfriend home to introduce him to my father and mother, and he asked if he could stay with me and my family.

I told him no way. I said it would be a bad influence on my sons, that I wouldn't know how to explain it to them. I told him I wasn't cutting him out of my life, that I'd still talk to him, but I didn't want him hanging around my house. I don't know where he stayed that time, because my father wouldn't let him in his house either.

Some years later, Joe called me up and said he wanted to have dinner with me. I agreed to meet him in New York City at some fancy restaurant. He started to tell me all about what happened to him when he was growing up. He told me all about his life, and how he had to hide who he really was, even from the people he loved the most. I really listened to him that night. By the time I left that dinner I was in tears. Joe completely changed my opinion about homosexuality. I didn't comprehend the great struggle that he had been facing all those years, all through his life. Being openly gay was the only time he had been truly honest about who he was, and it was the happiest time of his life.

If my brother faced such difficulties, I started thinking about all the people I represented in the stores. There was no coalition group then, but I knew there were gays who worked in the stores, and I wondered how they were impacted day to day, and if the union might help. I met with some of the members who were gay and lesbian, and they told me about what they faced on the job. So many of them were afraid to be open about who they were. There were things that could happen on the job: bullying, verbal intimidation, and, if a manager found out, they could be fired. There were no laws on the books that protected LGBTQ workers; they were vulnerable.

The American labor movement did not have much of a record in placing the needs of LGBTQ members at the front. The AFT issued resolutions in support of gay rights, and AFSCME's 1983 convention had done the same thing. There were pioneers who were open about their sexuality and demanded protection and rights on the job. One of the most outspoken on the matter was Bill Olwell, an international UFCW leader out of Seattle, who ran for union office as an openly gay man back in the late 1960s, which took guts to do. For the most part, organized labor had not been vocal on this issue; to make gay rights an issue would cause problems in labor circles, I was warned. Many in the labor movement were hard enough on the retail clerks because we represented so many women; it was a macho thing. I became very aware of the issue, and I was determined to do something about it with the union to give people like my brother some security. I decided to make it an issue as I opened contract negotiations with A&P. I picked them because I knew they would be the toughest since their top leadership were mostly Irish Catholics, and very socially conservative. I'm up in the middle of the night, negotiating, and my fight is to put in a clause of no discrimination for sexual persuasion. Marty Quinn, A&P's lead negotiator says, "No way am I putting anything in there to protect queers."

I said, "You have men and women working for you who are gay whether you acknowledge it or not. Would you fire them because they're queer?"

He said, "No, I don't want to fire them. Not if they're doing their job."

"Good, that's what I want," I said. "I want to protect them so they don't get fired because they're queers, because not everybody in the company thinks like you. A lot of people don't like gays and lesbians and they find reasons to fire them."

We stayed up all night arguing about it, but, finally, I could see I was starting to make some headway with Marty. I got the protection clause in, and I'll never forget the night of the contract ratification meeting. When I announced it, about fifty members yelled out, "Yeah!" jumping out of their seats and clapping. After it was over, a crowd came up to me and said how good the protection clause was, and how much it meant to them. It didn't stop at A&P. All of a sudden I got it in all of the contracts. I used to argue, "There's nobody more conservative than the Catholics at A&P; they put it in their contract, why can't you?" We were the first local in the UFCW to have that kind of protection in the contract language, and it remains one of my proudest achievements. When I retired as union president in 2005, I got letters from some of the members about this saying how important it was, and how much it meant to them.

15

THE NEW VOICE

I N 1992, I was elected to another three-year term as president of the twenty-three thousand-member UFCW Local 1776, marking thirty years since I'd first taken that office. Over those years, I'd seen a lot of changes and waged many campaigns. At the start of this new decade, I felt like a kind of resurgence was happening in the labor movement across the nation and the world. The 1980s had been difficult, but it seemed like new kinds of coalitions were coming about with the end of the Cold War, and with this I felt that an understanding and support of social justice unionism was growing stronger.

All through the 1980s, there was growing dissatisfaction with the way CLU president Edward F. Toohey was leading the Philadelphia labor movement. In 1983 and again in 1986, challenge slates came close to removing him from office, but he managed to stay in. By the turn of the new decade, Ed was close to ninety years old and no longer able to do the job, although he still refused to step down. In 1992, all of the leadership of the city's AFL-CIO unions were finally on the same page.

I've mentioned earlier how I didn't think Ed Toohey had much of a vision for labor's role in society. He didn't support social causes, didn't take risks, and seemed only interested in securing political power. Toohey used to boast of his close relationship with important political leaders like Hubert H. Humphrey, who would consult with Ed in the 1960s. But by the beginning of the 1990s, he just didn't have these kinds of connections or clout.

In early 1992, I was supporting Iowa senator Tom Harkin in the Democratic presidential primary, a very strong liberal who had a lot of labor support around the country. By the early primaries, Arkansas governor Bill Clinton was in the lead, benefiting from the backing he had from AFSCME, whose international president Gerald W. McEntee believed he could win. By the April Pennsylvania primary, Clinton was close to clinching the nomination but still faced opposition from former California governor Jerry Brown. Despite McEntee's backing, many Pennsylvania labor leaders were cool to Clinton, since, like Carter before him, he was governor of a so-called right-to-work state. On April 8, 1992, Bill Clinton made a campaign stop in Philadelphia, accompanied by Tom Harkin, to try to drum up some support by addressing the city's AFL-CIO monthly delegates meeting at the Wyndham Franklin Plaza Hotel.

Clinton had just won the New York primary and had a lot of momentum, but the event that night was pure chaos. I remember I met Senator Harkin outside, escorted him into the hall, and sat next to him on the stage. Right from the start, the meeting was loud and disorderly. The key reason for these antics was John P. Morris, president of Teamsters Local 115. His men were out in force, standing on the sides and making it hard to hear anything. Morris was nursing a big grudge against Pennsylvania state senator Vince Fumo over something Vince did in the state legislature that Morris didn't like, I forget what it was, really. Morris had a practice where he would surround himself with members in their blue jackets and T-shirts, some of them dressed like Green Berets, but instead they wore blue berets and Local 115 arm badges like they were military commandos. They're all in the first couple of rows and lined against the walls of the perimeter. The ruckus they were causing got ridiculous. Some of them had handmade signs that said things like "Fumo Sucks," and "Fumo's an Asshole," the most ridiculous kinds of statements. Even worse, they started chanting "Fuck Fumo!" over and over. When all this was happening, Senator Harkin leans over to me and says, "It'll be a long time before I come back to Philly. This place is ridiculous. I heard about the crazy sports fans here, but I didn't know the union guys were the same." I tried to explain things to him, pointing over to Johnny Morris and his men, saying, "Well, it's just him, it's just one union really."

In the midst of all this chaos, Ed Toohey was up at the podium trying to keep things under control. He was talking right through it, talking on without getting to the point. No one was listening to him, and, in a mock gesture to try to get him to sit down, some of the delegates actually stood up and started to applaud. I felt sorry for Tom Harkin because he had to follow Toohey to introduce Bill Clinton. When it was finally his turn, he knew just how to handle the crowd. "That's a tough act to follow," he said, referring to Toohey, which caused many of the assembled delegates to break into laughter. Clinton's turn at the podium wasn't as good. I could tell he was uncomfortable, not used to being before such a tough crowd, and he had a difficult time. At one point, when discussing the right to strike, he made the mistake of using the term "permanent replacement workers," instead of "scab." The place erupted with loud cries of "Scab!" Clinton was ruffled, and, when someone interrupted him again, yelling out, "Say it!" a testy exchange followed.

The scene at Philadelphia's AFL-CIO delegates meeting that April was an indication of how bad things had gotten under Toohey. He had lost the backing of nearly every union leader in the city, except Johnny Morris, but he still refused to step down. I encouraged Harry Lombardo, the young leader of the Transit Workers Union Local 234 to run. When Harry was still at Cardinal Dougherty High School in the late 1960s, he got involved in the antiwar movement and developed media and organizing skills. He dropped out of community college to take a job as a bus cleaner in the early 1970s, and he got involved with the union. After he took over as president of the five thousand-member local in 1989, Harry proved a very dynamic leader. He knew how to give a good speech, understood the importance of media relations, and articulated the needs of SEPTA's riders, along with his members. He held rallies at City Hall to protest fare hikes and brought commuters to testify at city council hearings. Lombardo was willing to take on Toohey but didn't have enough support from across the labor movement. He just couldn't get past the Building Trades. I spoke to the influential president of the Philadelphia Building and Construction Trades Council, Pat Gillespie, myself to try to get him to change his mind, but he wouldn't budge. He thought Harry was too controversial. In my opinion, Pat wouldn't go along because he thought Harry he was too strong, too opinionated, and too aggressive. He'd rather have someone in there who was less dynamic, someone whom he could control.

Even though he refused to get behind the proposed Harry Lombardo ticket, Gillespie knew that Toohey couldn't continue on as AFL-CIO head. I went through more names of potential candidates with him, and Joe Raucher, the president from the Bakery, Confectionary and Tobacco Workers Local 6, came up. Raucher called me up to say that he would be interested in challenging Toohey if we couldn't decide on anybody else. I liked Joe, because he understood the economic issues facing workers in the region, as many of his own members had faced layoffs in the 1980s. He understood the need to build alliances, to engage with the media, and to mend fences across the labor movement, too. Pat Gillespie was more agreeable to him. Joe put together a slate called Labor 2000, which underscored a progressive vision for the new challenges of the coming century. Linda Butler of the Operating Engineers, joined the slate as recording-secretary, an indication of the growing influence women were bringing to the labor council. Toohey dismissed Raucher as "the Cake Man," and swore he'd beat him back, just as he had all his previous challengers. But when he realized that even the Building Trades weren't backing him, he counted the noses and decided he'd better step down. Joe Raucher was voted in as Philadelphia's CLU president without opposition in December 1992.

THE ELECTION OF JOE RAUCHER came at a time when many in the labor movement felt they were on the cusp of a historic turning point. Bill Clinton was elected to the White House the previous month with support from unions across the country, and it was hoped that more progressive programs were on the horizon. Clinton headed the Democratic Leadership Conference, a conservative section of the party that steered it away from the liberal positions I had fought for from 1968 on, but he had some good tendencies, and, now that he was president, he promised to work with organized labor. In a positive immediate step, he appointed a progressive economist Robert Reich as his labor secretary and moved forward on national health care legislation.

Not much came from these stances, though. By the end of 1993, the proposed National Health Care Bill had failed, and the North American Free Trade Agreement, which the AFL-CIO denounced as a job killer, was passed with the full support of the Clinton administration. The following year, a radical right-wing Republican Congress was elected, with House

Speaker Newt Gingrich overseeing a major upheaval that strengthened corporate interests over those of working families. Organized labor seemed to have no sway over a president it had supported from enacting laws it didn't want, or the ability to mobilize its members to stand up against its political foes at the polls. Many of us felt that this was a reflection of stale leadership. Since 1979, the AFL-CIO had been headed by Lane Kirkland, a conservative who had been strong on issues like backing the Polish Solidarity movement but who lacked any bold ideas for moving organized labor in a new direction. A section of powerful national leaders, especially those in the service and governmental sectors, believed that fundamental change was needed.

Going back through the twentieth century, AFL-CIO presidential elections were rarely contested, but AFSCME international president Gerald W. McEntee put together a coalition that would become a challenge slate. When Lane Kirkland announced he would stand for reelection in 1995, a reform movement was ready. Jerry didn't want to leave the AFSCME presidency to run the AFL-CIO himself, and he convinced John Sweeney, the international president of the SEIU, to take it on instead. Sweeney came out of New York City's SEIU Local 32BJ, had a reputation going back to the 1960s for militancy, and was to the left of the labor mainstream. As far as I was concerned, Sweeney had been right on so many issues: on civil rights and aggressive organizing, for instance, and he had been against the war in Vietnam, which was unusual in labor's ranks. He wasn't afraid to go on strikes or to use civil disobedience. He brought this kind of attitude to the international in 1980, when he was elected president and oversaw an organizing blitz that brought thousands of new members in, in nursing homes and health care and with bold drives such as the Justice for Janitors campaign that brought in thousands of mostly Latina building cleaners in Los Angeles in the 1980s. By 1995, the SEIU had over a million members.

With Sweeney leading the challenge, the reform movement, called "A New Voice for American Workers" slate, was gaining support. Ron Carey, president of the Teamsters Union who had led a reform coalition in his own organization was an early supporter, as were major unions from the building trades such as the Operating Engineers and Carpenters, and the newly formed UNITE-HERE, which brought together the needle trade unions and the Hotel and Restaurant Employees. When Lane saw the campaign against him gaining speed, he decided to step down and was replaced by his secretary-treasurer Thomas Donahue, who agreed to run. I was behind the New Voice reform program from the start. I had been pushing for similar kinds of new initiatives toward social justice unionism all of my years with the Retail Clerks Union. My position put me at odds against the top leadership of the UFCW, most of whom thought Sweeney was too radical. Douglas H. Dorrity, who succeeded Bill Wynn as UFCW president in 1994, and the other top leadership of the UFCW were backing Donahue. Jay Foreman, who'd been executive assistant to Bill Wynn was Donohue's campaign manager, so my refusal to back the incumbent ticket really did set me apart from many of my peers in my own organization.

When John Sweeney's reform slate was elected, there was a lot of national media coverage on what the change in AFL-CIO leadership meant for the possibility of a resurgence of the American labor movement. One-third of the federation's budget was channeled into new organizing campaigns, especially in the service sector, in retail, and in other low-wage areas. Greater emphasis was given to building community-labor coalitions that could address issues such as immigration rights and equality for sexual minorities. Important structural reforms, including the placing of state labor federations on the AFL-CIO general board, efforts to give underrepresented unions more of a voice in how the federation operated, and a move to jump-start central labor councils to coordinate organizing drives and political campaigns across regions were all implemented. A Working Women's Department was initiated to develop more female leaders and place women's concerns at the heart of the labor movement. The most important of all these reforms, though, was the new administration's promise to fund aggressive organizing campaigns, to sign up thousands of new union members in retail and service industries, and to rejuvenate the role that the labor movement played in shaping the American economy.

There were a lot of obstacles to reaching people because unions are so often painted in a negative light in mass media. I had an idea about how to bring a different message to more people. Since the mid-1960s, I'd always wanted to have a radio program that addressed issues of working people. Joe DeSilva, the innovative leader of the Retail Clerks Union in Los Angeles, had a weekly radio and later television program in those years, and he was my model. Joe explained union positions on legislation, highlighted organizing campaigns, and interviewed leaders and workers he represented in the stores. I knew how influential a talk radio program could be, since Frank Rizzo's show had thousands of listeners and was an important part of how he relaunched his political career in the 1980s. I had an opportunity to start my own show on WHAT AM when station executive Cody Anderson invited me to fill in occasionally for Mary Mason, the lead personality in the daily lineup. When I did my shows, I talked about the concerns of working people, and I always had a lot of callers. In 1995, Cody asked me if I wanted to have my own regular program, and suggested Friday mornings at 9:00 A.M. WHAT was Philadelphia's premier African American station, and I'd be the only white guy on the station. I was a little skeptical about this, but I asked Herman Wooden what he thought, and he urged me to do it, joking that they had to have one token white person in the lineup.

My show was called "Talking Unions," and focused primarily on labor issues and the concerns of working people in the Delaware Valley. For the program's theme music, I picked Peter Tosh's version of Bob Marley's "Get Up Stand Up!" an old popular reggae song that I felt epitomized the kind of fighting spirit of the labor movement. The very first show was autobiographical, where I talked about how I had gotten involved with the union as a teenager at Acme Markets, and the various campaigns I had been involved with over the years. The lines lit up. As calls came in, time flew by, and, before I knew it, the three hours were up.

I started to get some advertising, and I became a regular WHAT broadcaster. I usually had in local activists who would come on and talk about their causes, and I'd have conversations with them and take questions from callers. I had the building trades on to provide information about their apprenticeship programs, covered negotiations between the Transit Workers Union and SEPTA, and had young retail workers who were trying to organize Borders Bookstores in the region on to talk about their campaign. I interviewed some all-star figures like President Bill Clinton and Pennsylvania governor Bob Casey, and various progressive figures such as filmmaker Michael Moore, labor historians Dorothy Sue Cobble and Alice Hoffman, and Catholic social justice activists Philip and Daniel Berrigan. Cheri Honkala of the Kensington Welfare Rights Union was a guest, as was Anne O'Callaghan, founder of the Welcoming Center for New Pennsylvanians, an organization that provided resources for immigrants who had recently settled in the region. I broadcast taped interviews I did with workers and labor leaders I met on travels

Figure 15.1 "Talking Unions" radio broadcast, early 2003. Wendell W. Young III on left with Patrick J. Coughlin, president of UNITE-HERE Local 274, and Minister Rodney Muhammad of the Philadelphia branch of the NAACP. (From the collection of Wendell W. Young III.)

to Zimbabwe, Cuba, and South Africa. Sometimes I would air live from the grand openings of Acme Markets or from the conventions of national unions, and even from the floor of the Democratic National Convention in 1996. My listeners called in with their own news and comments on the stories we presented. "Talking Unions" was successful in bringing working-class people's voices into the public forum, and other labor activists from all over the country wanted to start up similar programs. (See Figure 15.1.)

The 1990s are usually remembered as an era of economic prosperity, but not everyone in the community was thriving in this period. Unemployment remained a critical fact for thousands. Cuts to welfare and the excesses of the crime bill, both of which were supported by President Clinton, were points of discussion. Some callers questioned whether they could continue to support the Democratic Party. Along these lines was the emergence of a Labor Party, which was primarily the idea of Tony Mazzocchi, the progressive leader of the Oil, Chemical and Atomic Workers International Union. In June 1996, fourteen hundred delegates met in Cleveland in a founding convention of the Labor Party, adopting a platform that called for universal health care, free college tuition, an end to war, commitment to green energy, and a massive organizing of working people. The week before, I had Tony on my show to discuss the new party and its programs. Despite the fact that he had been engaged with Democratic Party politics since the 1940s, he saw its leaders moving away from their traditional commitments of support for working-class issues. Through his legislative activities, he understood political force as based on the mobilization of working people rather than complete loyalty to the Democratic Party.

On most points, I couldn't disagree with Tony. I joined the Labor Party, but I didn't give up my affiliation with the Democratic Party and continued to vote for Democratic candidates. Over the next few years, the Labor Party had a lot of devoted activists at the local level, and they launched some good campaigns, but it didn't gain momentum. Despite his flaws, I supported President Clinton again in 1996, because with him in the White House, at least workers' safety laws and appointments to the National Labor Relations Board (NLRB) would be sound. What else could I do—vote for Bob Dole?

IN THE SAME YEARS THAT I WAS HOSTING my radio show, I worked to improve educational opportunities for union members. Many of the contracts I negotiated for UFCW Local 1776 since the late 1980s had an innovative education benefit that provided funds for members to help pay for tuition. A lot of the members in the supermarkets were young college students, and this was a tremendous aid for them. I wanted the members to have an opportunity to take some advanced classes and continue on to complete their degrees. Education had always been important to me, and after I finished at St. Joseph's College in 1960, I started taking night classes at Temple University to get a master's degree. Once I was elected to union office, however, I dropped out as I was too busy. In 1989, I enrolled at Rutgers University's School of Management and Labor Relations and completed the master's degree three years later. After my time there, I made it a priority to open up more opportunities for worker education in the immediate Philadelphia region. Hundreds of trade unionists had received training through the program Father Dennis J. Comey, SJ, set up during World War II, but, by the 1980s, the Comey Institute of Industrial Relations had declined, dwindling to about fifteen students. I believed that the program needed rejuvenation and had a series of meetings with St. Joseph's University president Rev. Nicholas S. Ashford, SJ, who agreed to support it. Teamsters Local 115 president John P. Morris believed in the importance of worker education and he collaborated with Johnny Butler, Pennsylvania secretary of industry and labor, to get funding from the state to help pay for expenses and subsidize tuition. I asked John Lavin, communications director for Local 1776, to oversee the program, and he developed a curriculum, organized a planning committee, and reached out to the local labor movement to publicize the venture.

In September 1997, the new Comey Institute of Industrial Relations was up and running with classes offered at St. Joseph's campus two nights a week. With funding from Harrisburg, a single course cost only forty dollars, a nominal sum that made it affordable for everyone. Almost all of the students were working adults and union members who took classes that met for three hours a night in five-week modules. Course offerings ranged from grievance resolution, U.S. labor history, and occupational safety and health to environmental justice and international politics. Many of the students wanted to learn basics to be better advocates on the job, but courses could count as credits toward getting an undergraduate degree in labor studies, or a certificate in industrial relations after sixteen classes were completed. Some of the region's most respected arbitrators and employment lawyers, including Joseph Lurie, senior partner at Galfand, Berger, Ltd., were on the faculty, and gave students opportunities through mock trial classes and with trips to the offices of the region's NLRB. Wendell IV taught a class on economics and collective bargaining, and my son Eric, who had joined Local 1776's staff as a legal counsel, participated in many of the programs as well.

One of the most important things that the revitalization of the Comey Institute brought about was a kind of meeting place where new ideas could be discussed, and new forms of connections developed between activists. This was a very hopeful time. Now that the Cold War was over, money could be channeled away from military spending and directed toward programs that addressed social problems and promoted economic prosperity. There was shared belief that change was possible. Events around the world indicated this. Workers were organizing in India, China, and Africa, and there was a growing awareness of the right of workers on an international scale. One of the highlights of this period came in December 1999, when thousands gathered in Seattle to protest the meeting of the World Trade Organization (WTO). The WTO sought to coordinate global economic policies that for years had depleted local communities and deprived workers of fundamental safety rights and living wages. No one expected the kind of impact this protest had. The protests brought the WTO meetings to a halt, with streets barricaded and no traffic in the central district. In what came to be known as the Battle of Seattle, activists confronted police in riot gear leading the mayor to declared a state of emergency. My son Brian was there as an independent journalist, and he called in to my radio program with live reports of what he saw.

The protests brought the issue of antiglobalization into the news, and sparked an interest in challenging what had become economic norms. One of the local manifestations of this was the emergence of United Students against Sweatshops (USAS), a student-run organization that mobilized to demand fair pay and decent working conditions for apparel workers across the globe. In February 2000, a dozen USAS students staged a sit-in in the University of Pennsylvania's president's office for nine days during which they held a forty-eight-hour hunger strike. I was impressed by this because the actions had the support of a coalition of local religious leaders, environmental activists, students, faculty, and unions from across the city. Students at Bryn Mawr and Haverford College started their own campaigns and joined in organizing fasts to show their support, which inspired students elsewhere around the country to issue calls of solidarity. As a result of the actions, USAS got Penn to agree to stronger monitoring of the conditions of university apparel and to withdraw from the Fair Labor Association to join the Worker Rights Consortium, which had a more strident record of standing up for textile workers around the world. I hadn't seen this kind of coalition building since the early 1970s with the grape and lettuce boycotts, the growing antiwar movement, and organizing drives in retail and hospitals.

By the late 1990s, the internet was changing how social movement organizing was happening, and new kinds of independent media shaped the spirit of the times. By the 2000 election year, I was hopeful that Al Gore could continue to build on this spirit that I was feeling. The 2000 election showed how divided the nation had become. The election was a farce. George W. Bush wasn't the choice of most American voters, and his political agenda was devastating to working people. The kinds of political divisions that year were made even worse by the partisan news—or the pure propaganda posing as news that came from Fox News. I knew, just as I knew in 1968 when Nixon came to office, that it would make the hopes of realizing social justice even more difficult. In the face of this, I felt that the most important task ahead for those committed to social justice unionism and progressive politics was to find a way to keep this emerging, dynamic coalition together.

In early September 2001, I was in France with my wife, Kathy, meeting with officials from the Carrefour Company. Ten years after the union's battle with their operations in Northeast Philly, they contacted me and said they wanted to come to the United States again and that they would sit down and work with me on it—and that they would be union. Kathy had gone back a week earlier as she was teaching at the time, and I planned to return at the end of negotiations one-week later. After one of the Carrefour meetings, I was walking back to the hotel and I collapsed. I was in really bad shape. Sweat was pouring all over me.

I was there in bed when the terrorist attacks happened in New York City, Pennsylvania, and Washington, DC. On TV, I saw the World Trade Center buildings coming down in New York City. As sick as I was, I pulled myself out of bed the next morning and went down and waited in line to get to the airport. My son Brendan was getting married that Saturday, and there was no way I would miss it. All air traffic in and out of the United States was suspended indefinitely, but, with some persistence, I was able to get a flight to Toronto, Canada. When I got there, the flight ban into the United States had been lifted, and my son Wendell worked it out that someone would fly a private plane from Northeast Philadelphia Airport to Canada to get me home. I got back in time for the wedding, but I was sick as a dog. The following Tuesday, I had a stroke. I was rushed to the hospital and pulled through this initial attack, but before me was a long journey of recovery.

Because I was able to get immediate medical attention, my physicians had hoped that I could regain my abilities to talk and walk on my own, but to do so required months of rehabilitation. I had to learn how to do the most basic things, how to train myself to make out the sound of words instead of mumbling. With Kathy by my side, I was absolutely determined to do so. The first thing I worked on in rehab was learning how to talk again. I wanted to come back to lead the union and to keep my radio show going. I worked with a speech therapist pronouncing words, starting over again, day by day. I'll never forget, about eight weeks later, I returned to do a broadcast on WHAT 1390 AM. With some help from John Lavin, I managed it. I didn't do great; I just did decent. When I got back to the Bryn Mawr rehab center late that afternoon, my therapists gave me a standing ovation. Of course, I wasn't 100 percent: it was hard doing little things, my left side was affected, and I had to slow everything down. I had excellent health care and could take the time I needed, and this reinforced my commitment to address the disparities in health care that faced so many people across the country and the world.

While I was still recuperating from my illness, some important developments in Philadelphia's labor movement occurred. By 2000, there was some disagreement over the direction the trade unions were taking, and much of this focused on Joe Raucher's leadership of Philadelphia's AFL-CIO CLU. Since 1992, when he took over from Ed Toohey, I felt there had been some important steps in the right direction, but I felt we needed some more forceful leadership. I think if you're AFL-CIO president in a place like Philadelphia you've got to sit down with stakeholders and talk to the editorial pages of the papers, show we're a factor in the community. Joe decided that he wouldn't seek reelection, opening up an opportunity for someone else. Before I got sick, I was among a group of local labor leaders who met to consider who might replace him. One person a lot of us felt was up to the challenge of representing the region's 115,000 union workers was Patrick J. Eiding, the business agent of Insulators and Asbestos Workers Local 14. This was a small union, but Pat was very well respected in the labor community, never backed away from hard decisions, and had led his members on a strike in 1983. Along with John Dougherty of the IBEW Local 98, Building and Construction Trades Council president Pat Gillespie and Tom Kelly of Sheet Metal Workers, I urged him to run for the seat and got behind his campaign. Pat ran unopposed and took over from Joe Raucher in January 2002.

Pat faced a lot of challenges. There was still a lot of division within the labor movement, and he did a good job at bringing opponents together. He started his own radio program, was effective with the media, and built strong ties with Mayor John Street. Some of the issues I thought Pat handled well were on an international scale. One of the biggest problems facing working people was the Bush administration's push to invade Iraq in 2003. During the Vietnam era, I was among a handful of labor leaders around the nation, and virtually alone in Philadelphia, in my opposition to the war. Now, however, I felt that I was part of the mainstream of the labor movement against the Bush program. On January 8, 2003, the Philadelphia AFL-CIO issued a resolution against the planned invasion. Pat Gillespie supported this measure and stated that we were being manipulated—lied to—and that he wasn't going to make the same mistakes again that he did in Vietnam. Pat Eiding pushed for this resolution, and our council was the first AFL-CIO section in the country to issue such a statement denouncing the war. This was the right thing to do. Labor has a role to play in ending wars. To me that's what unions are all about, the social agenda. A month later, Kathy and I and the rest of our family joined thousands of others in a protest march in Philadelphia to send a message that the war was wrong. I was pleased to see that organized labor was taking this stand and that for the first time in history the national AFL-CIO was against militarized U.S. foreign policy.

By this time, I had recovered enough from my stroke to return to my duties as UFCW Local 1776 president. In the months following my illness, I wasn't able to do any work, and my son Wendell took over as the union's chief officer: overseeing contracts, organizing drives, and managing media relations. Wendell had so much experience with the union, having joined the staff full-time as a representative in 1983, and was respected by the staff and well known to the membership in the stores across Pennsylvania. When I returned, I felt that I could continue in office for another term, but my health continued to decline after I was diagnosed with Parkinson's disease. I announced in 2004 that I would not seek a new term, and would retire at the end of the year. Wendell IV ran for the office and took over as president in January 2005.

Even though I was now retired, I stayed involved with labor affairs in the city and attended the meetings of the AFL-CIO executive committee as an emeritus member. I stayed active as I had been all my life. It was important to do so, because I felt that George W. Bush's foreign policy was destructive and immoral and the emphasis on constant warfare deflected from investments in domestic programs, ones that would support jobs in infrastructure and training. The Bush administration weakened workplace safety regulations, and packed the NLRB with antiunion types that refused to look into wage theft violations and made it more difficult for unions to organize. Everything was geared toward big business and supporting the very rich. For the majority of American workers, wages continued to stagnate and conditions got worse. Organized labor's membership was withering and the AFL-CIO did not put forward much of a response to the problems facing the country. Despite the AFL-CIO's emphasis on politics, progressive Democrats had not taken back Congress, and millions of workers remained unorganized. From within the ranks of labor, criticism of John Sweeney's administration was growing, with the harshest coming from within his own organization, the SEIU. Andy Stern, international SEIU president, oversaw some of the boldest organizing campaigns of the past generation, and he made it clear that he would not back Sweeney for another term.

To generate a new direction in the labor movement, Andy Stern formed the New Unity Partnership, a dissident group within the AFL-CIO that included the Teamsters, UNITE HERE, the Carpenters, the International Laborers Union, and the UFCW. Some of the demands they brought to the table were the merging of smaller unions with larger ones and the streamlining of departments within the AFL-CIO—all geared toward maximizing organizing drives. In June 2005, Stern led this faction out of the AFL-CIO into an alternative coalition known as Change to Win. Stern's plan was modeled after the 1936 historic break between the more conservative AFL unions and the new industrial organizations of the CIO. By doing so, John L. Lewis, the powerful leader of the United Mine Workers and the pivotal figure in this split, was able to unite the nation's progressive labor organizations to concentrate on organizing, a move that led to the greatest membership boost in the history of the labor movement. I felt it was a serious misreading of history to assume that conditions in 2005 were identical to the way things were back then. Breaking up the national labor federation would weaken organized labor at a time when the radical right wing was moving ahead. I was absolutely against this split and spoke out against it at the UFCW convention that year and again, in a more dramatic speech at the AFL-CIO convention. After I gave that speech, I got a standing ovation and was mobbed by delegates who came up, hugging me and lifting me up on their shoulders.

I still think that the UFCW and the other unions splitting from the AFL-CIO in the summer of 2005 was a mistake, but I am still hopeful that unions will continue to make progress in the United States and across the world. To do this, there has to be a real commitment to the ideals of social justice unionism and a movement that works to lift everyone up to achieve full citizenship and economic security. This is what I dedicated my whole life to. As I look back over more than half a century of struggle, certain themes have been constant. I believe political engagement is critical in the work to gain better conditions for working people. This is a fundamental way that people have a voice in any democracy. We need to shape the agenda, run for office ourselves if we need to, and mobilize the voters. For there to be success at the ballot box, sometimes there also needs to be dissent. Protesting is not bad. It's supposed to be done in America. There were many times over the years that I was arrested, and many times I led members on strike. This kind of militancy is needed. Sometimes civil disobedience is necessary in a democracy. I don't mean violent action. I mean breaking no-strike laws, taking the consequences, and being tough. You've got to break the law sometimes.

All Cesar Chavez and I did was break the law. When he was leading strikes fighting for decent conditions for the farm workers on the West Coast, Cesar took the heat and often faced arrest for breaking court orders against picketing. When the grape strike and lettuce boycotts were happening in the late 1960s and early 1970s, the Retail Clerks Union in Philadelphia refused to put nonunion produce on the shelves. I'll never forget that. Just by that act alone, we helped the UFW and put real pressure on the supermarket owners in a major city to change their practices. Our refusing to take the nonunion grapes and lettuce off the trucks was against the law, against the clause of the Taft-Hartley Act that forbade secondary boycotts, but we did it anyway. I remember that meeting I had in 1969 with a couple dozen or so union stewards and produce managers in a back break room of one of the Acme Markets, all of them gathering there to meet with me after their shifts were over. We talked over what we needed to do to help out the grape pickers out in California, and we just decided we had some power over what was put out on the shelves to buy, and we were going to exercise that power. Philadelphia was thousands of miles away from those fields, and these guys knew they would never meet any of the men and women on strike, but they decided they had to stand with them because they knew their cause was right. Those guys didn't flinch. That's what social justice unionism is all about. It's more than just our own conditions we need to be concerned with. We're not just isolated individuals. We have to work together with others and build a labor movement that can take on the big challenges in society.

The results of this kind of collective action make a real difference in people's lives. Recently, I attended a reopening of an Acme Market in Flourtown, Pennsylvania, a big celebration with a luncheon, and some of the people who worked there for over twenty years were recognized. There's not many retail places where you still see that kind of longevity, where people can make a whole life out of it, raise a family, and be able to retire. In places like that, customers get to know the men and women who work there behind the deli, in the produce section, and at the checkout lines, and it feels like a community. It's one of the reasons they come back and shop there. Our union members have decent wages and good health care, and when they retire they have a pension. That is dignified work. Our union has worked with stores like Acme Markets to provide that kind of workplace. These benefits weren't just given to us, they were things we bargained and fought for, over a long period of time. We've got to remember the struggles it took to secure these gains. There are well-organized and well-financed political forces around the world that want to take this away, to make people work for less and have no kinds of benefits. It's bad for America and the world. But working people are organizing around the globe in the early twenty-first century and I have hope for the future.

I stopped driving a few years back, but I have lots of friends who help me get around. Sometimes, when I go to North Catholic High School alumni events, we go down Roosevelt Boulevard through the old Northwood neighborhood where I lived as a boy. I remember how I would walk to Acme Markets at Adams Avenue, passing the Sears building with its ornate clock tower. Years later, Sears's regional headquarters relocated and the store shut down its operations at the site. Finally in October 1994, the entire structure was demolished. On the day of the implosion, the boulevard's twelve lanes were blocked from traffic and about a thousand people showed up to watch the building come down. I wouldn't have been there to see that, not for a million dollars. For me, it was a sad day, the end of an era and a way of life that provided jobs for thousands of people in these neighborhoods. That old building on Roosevelt Boulevard was beautiful. At night, when its clock tower lit up, it gave off a kind of golden glow, the clock's hands positioned against big Roman numerals. All those years when I lived in Northeast Philadelphia, when I saw that clock tower light as I drove past, I knew I was almost home.

INDEX

Fluehr, Marilyn, 28, 37, 228
Food City, 72–73
Food Fair Markets, 9; and African American
employees, 54–55; and arbitrary transfer of
union business agents, 61–64; closure, 202,
206–208; and expansion in the 1950s, 18;
and Lou Stein, 239; and 1962 contract
negotiations, 56, 58; and 1964 strike, 72–77;
and 1973 strike, 184; Noah White, 78; and
UFW grape and lettuce boycott, 143–147;
unionization, 45–46
Foglietta, Thomas, 187–189, 233
Force Ouvriere (FO), 246
Ford, Gerald R., 198
Fosse, Gerard, 246
400 Ministers, 66–68, 119
Frankford-Unity Stores, 18
Fraternal Order of Police, FOP Lodge 5,
173–174, 230, 236, 248
Fumo, Vince, 254

Gay Liberation Front, 250
German-Americans, 12, 96
Gibbons, Harold J., 109–110
Gillespie, Patrick, 232, 240, 255–256, 265
Gimbels Department Store, 160, 200
Ginsberg, Allen, 170
Glancey, David, 230
Gola, Tom, 186
Good, Gerald, 226, 244
Goode, W. Wilson B., 229–237, 244, 247
Gore, Al, 263
Gorman, Patrick, 109
Gouland, Vivian, 240
Goulard, Joao, 102
Great Atlantic and Pacific Tea Company. *See*
A&P Markets
Green, William J., Jr., 4, 33, 42, 86, 92
Green, William J., III: challenges as mayor,
231; courted for 1975 mayoral primary, 186;
decides against second term as mayor, 229;
election and service as U.S. Representative,
86–88; and 1971 Philadelphia mayoral
primary, 155–157; and 1979 mayoral
campaign, 213–214; Philadelphia
Democratic Chairman, 99, 152; and St.
Joseph's College, 33; support for Edward
Kennedy in 1980 primary, 218; support for
peace plank at 1968 convention, 115;
support for Robert F. Kennedy in 1968
primary, 113; support for protesting
department store workers, 160; support for
supermarket cooperatives, 225–226

Grey, William H., 208
Guben, Jay, 222–223, 225–226
Gudenkunst, Frieda, 77

Haletsky, John T., 56, 72, 122–123, 126,
129–131, 133
Halferty, Joseph F., 151
Halpin, Pat, 6, 183
Hansen, J. P., 163, 200–201
Harkin, Tom, 254–255
Haverford College, 35, 108, 263
Hellmack, Jack, 62–63
Hemmert, Ray, 71
Hemphill, Alexander, 92–95, 98
Herman, Martin J., 1
Highland, Henry, 24, 47–50, 54–56, 58–59, 61,
71, 118–119, 123, 131
Hill, Louis G., 186–187
Hispanics, 130, 165, 257
Hoffman, Abbie, 170
Hoffman, Alice, 6, 259
Honkala, Cheri, 259
Hoover, Judy, 6
Housewright, James T., 56–57, 121–122, 124,
126, 128, 131–133, 209
Huber, Carl, 127
Huegel, Peter, P., 246
Huerta, Delores, 142
Hughes, Monsignor Edward, 37, 91
Humphrey, Hubert H., 38, 97, 113–116, 152,
166, 168, 170–171, 196, 253

Icaza, Rick, 130
Independence Hall, 144, 152, 175–178
Insurance and Professional Workers Union,
242
Insulators and Asbestos Workers, Local 14,
265
International Association of Firefighters
(IAFF), Local 22, 71, 173, 248
International Association of Machinists
(Machinists Union), 6, 192, 203, 221, 233
International Association of Sheet Metal
Workers, Local 19, 69, 265
International Brotherhood of Electrical
Workers (IBEW), Local 98, 236, 265
International Brotherhood of Teamsters
(Teamsters Union): dissidents, 126; and
drivers' salesmen dispute with retail clerks,
51–52, 55; Frank Keane, 147; Howard J.
Gibbons, 109–110; John P. Morris, 162;
membership in AFL-CIO, 117; and New
Unity Partnership, 267; and 1978 charter

Wendell W. Young III (1938–2013) led Philadelphia's Retail Clerks Union (United Food and Commercial Workers, Local 1776) for over forty years. Beginning in the early 1960s, he was active in the city's Democratic Party and was elected as a Northeast Philadelphia ward leader, serving as a delegate to five national conventions and as Philadelphia manager for George McGovern's 1972 presidential campaign. In the 1970s and '80s, he played a pivotal role in forging a broad, city-wide coalition of progressive trade unionists, liberals, and African American voters to challenge the urban populism of Mayor Frank L. Rizzo and the administrations of Presidents Richard M. Nixon and Ronald Reagan.

Francis Ryan is director of the Masters of Labor and Employment Relations program at Rutgers University in New Brunswick, New Jersey. He is the author of *AFSCME's Philadelphia Story: Municipal Workers and Urban Power in the Twentieth Century* (Temple).